THE STORY OF MAN'S MIND

THE
STORY OF MAN'S MIND

REVISED AND ENLARGED EDITION

BY

GEORGE HUMPHREY

Queens University
Kingston, Canada

THE NEW HOME LIBRARY
New York

THE NEW HOME LIBRARY EDITION PUBLISHED SEPTEMBER, 1942
BY ARRANGEMENT WITH DODD, MEAD AND COMPANY, INC.
REPRINTED OCTOBER, 1942
REPRINTED JANUARY, 1943

COPYRIGHT, 1923, 1932, BY DODD, MEAD AND COMPANY, INC.

THE NEW HOME LIBRARY, 14 West Forty-ninth Street
New York, N. Y.

CL

PRINTED IN THE UNITED STATES OF AMERICA

THERE is a machine which can take pictures with such incredible speed that by its aid the projectile may be seen gently worming its way into a plate of hardened steel, and an exploded charge of dynamite little by little raising a ton of rock into the air a hundred yards high, slowly to drift back again to earth.

Seen through such a swift working lens, the movements of a man would seem slow, as the movements of the plants seem to us. And were there a being who looked at our world through such an eye, he might well gaze on the sons of men and say:

"Here, among these beings, is surely no consciousness and no intelligence; for see, the fastest of their motions is too feeble to be observed with the naked eye, nor can I hear the slightest sound that they produce. The creatures must live by instinct or by chemistry, slowly and blindly bending to the brute forces of nature. Of a certainty, only by a stretch of the imagination can they be said to have a mind!"

Mind and consciousness are but relative. To the eye of a different order of life, the mind and ways of the fragment we call man may well seem simple and slow, and pathetically easy to unravel; our most delicately executed work like the slow groping of a tree towards the sun, our swiftest flash of insight like the ordered unfolding of a bud.

TABLE OF CONTENTS

		Page
CHAPTER I.	In Which is Explained the Purpose of the Book	1
CHAPTER II.	Before Mankind	6
	Does a Jellyfish Think?	
	The Mind of an Ant.	
	Does a Dog Think?	
	Money and Life.	
CHAPTER III.	Babies	22
	How a Baby Begins to Make His World.	
	The Baby Makes Space and Time.	
	An Incidental Account of Mouthwatering.	
	Learning to Talk.	
	Peopling the World.	
CHAPTER IV.	Man, Marionet of His Surroundings . . Mind, the Senses, and the World About	44
	How the Nerves Help Us Think.	
	How the Brain Works.	
	The City That is the Body.	
	How We See.	
	How We Hear.	
	Taste and Smell.	
	Why We Shiver in a Hot Bath.	
	The Compass of the Body.	
	Is There a Sixth Sense?	
	Why We Cannot See the Stars by Day.	
CHAPTER V.	What Pulls the Strings? . . . . . . Attention	83
	The Streets That are in One Street.	
	How the Advertiser Gets His Message Read.	
	What it Means to go to College.	
	Odds and Ends about Attention.	
CHAPTER VI.	How the Past is Born Again in the Present	102
	Seeing and Perceiving.	
	How We Read.	
	Habit, Everybody's Private Secretary.	
	How We Remember.	
	Memory Systems.	
	Remembering School Lessons.	
	"The First Three Lessons Sent Free."	
	Testing the Imagination.	

CONTENTS

          The Gift of Forgetting. *Page*
          The Feeling of Having Been There Before.
          Is Telepathy Possible?

Chapter VII.   Man the Master 152
          Why No One Has ever Drawn a Circle.
          The Romance of the Concept.
          How We Reason.

Chapter VIII.   The Birth-Gifts of Nature 166
          Victor, the Boy who Lived Among the Animals.
          The Instincts of Man.
          Is There an Instinct of Acquisition?
          Why People Get Married.
          Falling in Love.
          Is Fighting Inevitable?
          Important to Know Which Things are Instincts.
          Why a Child Fears the Dark.

Chapter IX.   Protection in Routine and in Emergency . 195
          Likes and Dislikes. Their Importance in Business.
          How Pain May Become Pleasant.
          What is an Emotion?
          The Two Ways in Which our Body Mobilizes.

Chapter X.   Measuring the Mind 223
          The Story of the Army Mental Tests.
          Mental Tests and the Child.

Chapter XI.   Unbending the Bow 241
          How Most of Us Waste Ourselves.
          Relieving Sleeplessness by Relaxation.
          The Man who Feared a Tree.
          Relaxation as a Love Charm.

Chapter XII.   Sick Minds and What We Learn from Them 263
          Autosuggestion.
          What is Hypnotism?
          Two Persons in One Body.
          Have Dreams a Meaning?
          What is Psychoanalysis?
          Cowards of us All.
          The Feeling of Inferiority.

Chapter XIII.   Conclusion 300

Appendix.   Fifty-Four Interesting Books on Psychology 303

Index. 307

LIST OF ILLUSTRATIONS

	Facing Page
Disappointed of a Meal	8
Jesperson's Diagram Showing How Sounds are Produced	34
Illustrating the Presence of the Blind Spot	46
How We See	54
Showing How, Although We Have a Blind Spot in the Retina of Each Eye, We May Fill in the Space	58
How We Hear	62
This Diagram Explains Why We Shiver in a Hot Bath	68
The Compass of the Body	70
The Drawing Can Be Seen as a Flight of Stairs or as a Cornice	102
The Famous Müller-Lyer Illusion	106
Victor, the Boy Who Lived Among the Animals	166

THE STORY OF MAN'S MIND

THE STORY OF MAN'S MIND

Chapter I

IN WHICH IS EXPLAINED THE PURPOSE OF THE BOOK

TWENTY-FIVE HUNDRED YEARS ago the rebel thinker Protagoras proclaimed that man is the measure of all things. Since then the tide of knowledge has slowly but irresistibly risen, bringing a fulness of thought and a delicacy of experiment which has left many astonishing achievements of the Greeks behind like children's toys abandoned on the seashore. Yet the saying of Protagoras has not been submerged. It stands as a great channel along which all scientific advance must flow. Although the fashion of today would express the saying rather differently.

Dwarfs as we are, peering into the infinite from a giant's shoulders, let us see what Protagoras meant.

A great novelist has described how a rough and strong man came to a desolate country, where nothing but wild animals and wild trees and plants dwelt, a land where everything was useless, rough, and formless for human purposes. The story tells how the man set out to impose order on the wilderness, how he cut down trees and fenced off fields and made the streams work for him and give him food and drink and whatever he wanted. Then he fetched a woman, and they had children, who helped him still more to turn barren nature to his own uses. Little by little they worked upon the countryside, until, by the labour of their hand and brain, they had made nature their servant instead of their master. The book is called "Growth of the Soil," and he who runs should read it, for it describes how the mind of man in this country has made itself master.

The author might have taken for his motto the saying of Protagoras.

In the last century a French priest was interested in the way plants grew, and why the leaves and stalks of certain plants of the same kind were short, while others had long leaves. He found that it depended on the parent plant whether the stalk of the leaf of any particular plant was short or long. This work was extended to include an investigation of the "grandchild" and "greatgrandchild" plant and so on. Working on these results, he found that he could make a rule by which to prophesy how many of each kind would be born from the parents in the fourth or fifth or twentieth generation. As a result of his labours, we now have what is called the law of Mendelian inheritance, which scientists are now applying to find what will be the colour of the eyes and hair of human beings.

The human mind has made a law for hair and eye colour.

We can begin to see what Protagoras meant when he said that man is the measure of all things.

Now the farmer who goes into desolate land and transforms it into a smiling landscape *does* something to the trees and the rocks and the rest of the countryside. He ploughs the land and plants the seed which will enable him to live over the coming winter. If the ground were not there, he could not do this, and if the farmer were not there the land would remain rough and untilled as from the beginning of time. What he does is called his behaviour.

But this is only one half of the story.

If the situation in which the farmer finds himself changes, the farmer's behaviour will have to be different. He will not do the same thing when it rains as when it is fine, when a sheep is sick as when his eldest son is married or his mill dam bursts. What he does is in a sense forced on him. He does not make his surroundings. He adapts himself to them, and to a certain extent they are his master. No farmer, if he wishes to avoid starvation, can lie in bed all day.

What the farmer does to the land, he is forced to do by the land.

So that the saying of Protagoras expresses only half the truth. Man is the measure of all things, and all things are the measure or master of man. If man by his experience makes himself master of the world, still he has to be guided in what he does by the nature of the world. It is because the tree stump is hard that he has to use dynamite.

Now there are many who would be helpless in the farmer's situation. The clerk who spends all day adding up figures in a bank could not do what the farmer has done. He has been brought up in a different kind of life, one which has not called for tilling and ploughing and shearing of sheep. He can balance a ledger, but he cannot blast out a rock. If he tried, the rock would probably fall down and crush him. When the farmer wants someone to help him, he asks for somebody with the right kind of experience, because he knows that, however adept a person may be, without experience he is helpless in that situation. It is the experience of the farmer that enables him to work on the ground. He has to learn to be a farmer, and he has learnt by growing up on a farm and watching. And the clerk in turn has had to have his own experience to do his own work.

In order, then, to understand how a man works on his surroundings and makes himself master of them, it is necessary to find out what he has lived through or experienced, for that will tell us what work he is best fitted to do.

Fully to understand behaviour, we have to take experience into account.

But more. It is possible to imagine a farmer who had all the necessary experience, but could not meet the situation that the barren countryside offered. Perhaps he might be impatient, and not willing to wait for years until his labours bear fruit. Perhaps he would not be hardy enough to endure the long winters or the rainy times that come to every worker of the soil. Perhaps he would not wish to cut himself off from other men. He might be too lazy or too cowardly. In all of these cases, what is called his personality would not be suitable for the particular situation in which he found himself. The author of "Growth of the Soil" describes one such man who had all the advantages of the other, but yet could not make his farm successful.

The other thing, then, that must be taken into account before we can fully understand a man's behaviour, is his Personality.

There are then three main things that this book will deal with, and they are Behaviour, Experience and Personality. The Behaviour of a man is what he does to impose his will on his surroundings. His Experience is what he has been through and learnt, which helps to give him the power of appropriate action. His Personality, as we have here used the word, is all the rest that goes to make up a man who can respond fittingly to his surroundings.

These three things mainly concern one man's actions as seen by another man. We shall also try to understand how life appears from the point of view of the man who is acting. For this is also important and of interest, although some would neglect it.

Chapter II

BEFORE MANKIND

(a) DOES A JELLYFISH THINK?

LET the reader try to imagine, for a moment, what it would feel like to be one of the small jellylike animals that live in stagnant water. One of these has been named amœba, from a Greek word meaning to change, because it can change itself into all kinds of shapes. In order to put ourselves into the position of an amœba, we must think what life would be like without eyes or ears, or senses of touch and smell and taste, for amœba is simply a small piece of jelly without any organ at all. Cut out all sensations from inside the body as from the stomach, the lungs, the heart and the pulse, and those which go with the emotions we have when we are angry or excited. Leave a dim, vague sense of touch, which does not act as when you or I touch a book and know that it is a book, but acts in something the same way as when we touch anything when half asleep, and pull away the hand with a vague feeling of discomfort. As an amœba, we are now living in water, and if the current carries us where the liquid is little different in temperature or otherwise, we shall act as a human being sometimes does, by drawing away.

But there is one thing that an amœba can do that we cannot. If light falls on it, although it has no eyes it somehow knows and moves away. For it does not like light. It is as if the animal were able to touch the brightness. Sometimes, however, it seems to meet with things that are pleasant, and stretches out a feeler towards them. Thus when food floats into its ken, or it comes across a piece of hard substance that would be good to crawl upon, it is able in this way to keep its contact.

It is when the amœba meets with food that the most interesting thing happens. The method of taking food through a special opening for the purpose—the mouth—is impossible, for the amœba has no specialized parts. Consequently some other device must be adopted.

As a matter of fact, it gets the food inside by getting outside of the food. It stretches out arms all around the morsel, and closes these up. It makes no difference what part of the animal first happens to touch the food. In any case, whether it be back or front, the little bit of living matter closes over the food and digests it.

These then are the three things amœba can do to its world. It can move away from things it does not like and towards things it likes, and it closes round food. But it is not always moving for any particular reason we can see. Sometimes it aimlessly crawls about over the solid surface on which it lives. This it does by sending out a piece of its jelly, fastening this to the surface and pulling the rest of its body after, like a sailor climbing up a rope hand-over-hand, or a man swimming with the hand-over-hand stroke. Only of course, in the case of the amœba a fresh hand is stretched out at each motion, and is taken up again into the body at the end of the motion. If it gets lost in the water away from any solid to crawl on, the amœba stretches out arms aimlessly until it touches something, and then pulls itself up to whatever it has felt.

Thus the Behaviour of this small animal is vastly simpler than the Behaviour of a human being. Instead of the innumerable things that the more familiar animals can do, it is capable of only a very few actions, and the world, as it presents itself to the small creature, is correspondingly simple. Just as its actions are few, so the world comes to be simply a great Something containing things to crawl away from or towards, or to eat, and things which give a firm hold.

The world as it appears to the amœba holds only about six different kinds of things.

Now some have denied that the amœba has any thoughts or consciousness like ours. They say that all its actions are done automatically, something like an unconscious blink of the eyelids. But it is impossible to prove this. In fact, it has been said that the amœba has as good a right to doubt the existence of consciousness in human beings as we have to doubt it in the amœba. It certainly seems reasonable to suppose that, just as these simple forms of life have simple forms of Behaviour, so they have a simple form of consciousness, or in ordinary language, simple thoughts.

But from what has been said, it may be seen that the thoughts of such a small animal are infinitely less complicated than our own. The difference is far greater than that between any two things that man has manufactured, such as a toy spade and a battleship. Man cannot match the diversity of natural things.

The difference between the possible mind of an amœba and the mind of a man may best be imagined by thinking of the distance between their bodies. The one is wonderfully complex, with countless parts all working together for the good of the whole; with organs to take in food and change it to the right material for the nourishment of the body; with muscles specially adapted to carry the whole about; with sense organs of great variety to receive messages from the

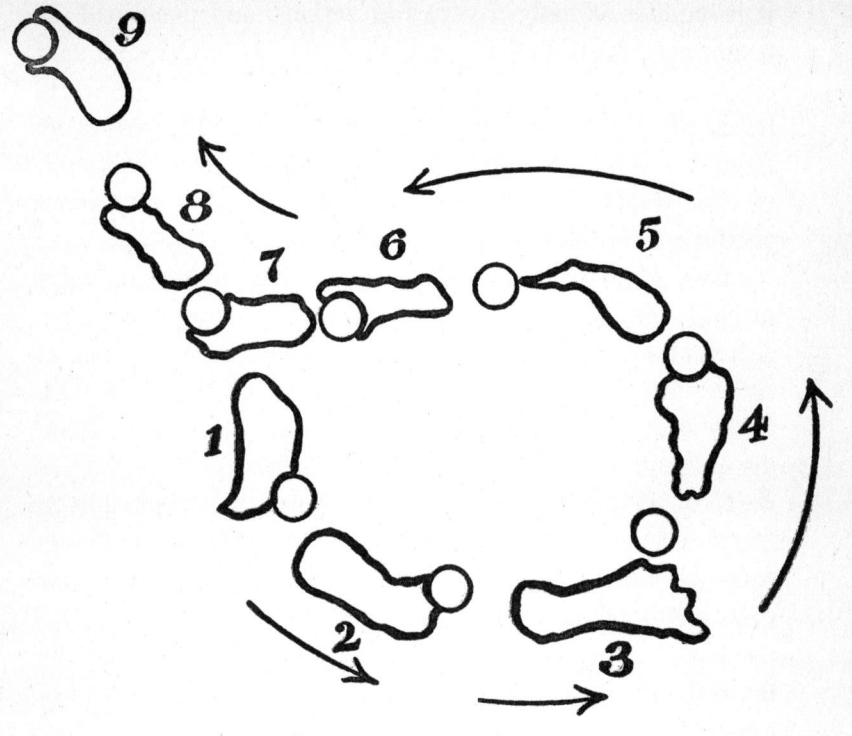

DISAPPOINTED OF A MEAL

The picture shows a tiny animal in search of a meal. The Amœba is a small organism, consisting of a single small piece of jelly too small to be seen with the naked eye. It lives in lukewarm water, such as is to be found in stagnant ponds and the like. This Amœba chased the small ball of food, which was hard to eat because it rolled away every time it was touched. Thereupon the tiny animal, under the watchful eye of Professor Jennings, pursued the food by stretching out tentacles and rolling its body after them. On two or three occasions (see positions 4, 6, and 9) the Amœba nearly captured its meal by wrapping its body round it. Each time the food slipped away. Finally another small creature disturbed the water and whisked the food forever out of reach. Then the Amœba, after fifteen minutes hard work, gave up the chase. Positions three and five well show how the tentacles are formed. The picture is taken from one drawn by Professor Jennings, who witnessed the chase.

outside world and from within the body, and a delicate system of nerves to make communication between the parts; the other a shapeless and changing mass of jelly, too small to be seen by the naked eye, simple, with no part differing from any other part, and with a sum total of not more than five or six actions that it can perform.

Existence in such a shape must be a very drab affair. There are probably stirrings of consciousness connected with the few different things recognized in the outside world, and coming up weakly and indistinctly at intervals. There is also perhaps a faint feeling approaching pleasantness and unpleasantness, which comes into play when the animal moves towards or away from a thing. But of thought consisting of memory of the past, or of conscious profiting by experience, there is nothing—only a vague and indolent living in the warm water, with sometimes dim snatches, where the dull light of consciousness glows for a moment a little brighter. Such, as far as we can tell, is the dream that makes up the life of the amœba.

This is, of course, not the jellyfish that we all know and of which the reader will have been thinking. The common jellyfish of the seashore is of a much more complicated nature. It has hardly, indeed, nerves, in our sense of the term, but it possesses the beginnings of bodily organs and more complex behaviour. And so its consciousness will be of a somewhat higher order than that of the simple amœba, but still infinitely poor compared with anything that we know. Probably, could it do so, the jellyfish, or Medusa, as it is called, would look down upon the amœba as a lower form of life. But the distance of both from us is so great that we are hardly able to imagine the difference between any states of consciousness that the two creatures may possess. To a Shakespeare, there is not very much difference between Tweedle-Medusa and Tweedle-Amoeba.

It is easier to see now the answer to the question "Does a jellyfish think?" If by thinking is meant sizing up situations and deciding upon the correct manner of action, a jellyfish or an amoeba certainly cannot think. It can only do a very few things, and it does them when it comes across the proper trigger, so to speak, to set the action off.

If by thinking is meant remembering or imagining, again the jellyfish cannot think.

If, however, you will give the name of thinking to an infinitely simple knowledge of what is in the world about, and to a vague feeling of pleasure at some things and displeasure at others, then the jellyfish does probably think in a very elementary and single-tracked manner.

And this, though it would perhaps be given a different name by the learned, is about all the thinking we can believe a jellyfish does.

(b) THE MIND OF AN ANT

When we come to an insect like an ant, we are dealing with an animal of an immensely higher and more complicated nature. This animal can run about after its food, instead of waiting for chance to float it up next to something edible. It can store up against the cold weather, defend other ants of the same nest, and fight against strangers. It can show anger and fear, build up the most complicated city for itself, even, at times, grow its own food, keep its own insects to serve as cows, and own its own slaves.

The astonishing performances of various kinds of ants have been described by many writers. We shall not attempt to repeat what has already been done so well, but will only ask, "Is there a mind behind it all?" And if so, how does it work?

First of all, there are many who say, as they do of the amœba, that the ant is entirely unconscious. They claim that it is like a machine that is wound up at birth, and continues to run until it dies. But if we believe that such a bit of living matter as the amœba has a simple kind of mind, we are bound to think that there is some kind of consciousness in the ant, with its almost human powers. And yet it would not be right to think that, because in many ways the ants behave almost like human beings, they do these things in the same way that human beings do them.

For instance, because an ant takes to its home food for the winter, it does not follow that the animal has any thought of the cold to come. A French poet has described how the grasshopper who sang all the summer came to the busy ant when the north wind had come, and begged for a little something to eat.

"No," replied the ant, "you used to sing. Now dance."

This is, of course, the way in which the world treats the artist. But I am glad to be able to acquit the ant of the charge of any such self-righteousness. It is quite certain that, because the ant worked industriously, he was not therefore industrious. He can receive no credit for his days of strenuous toil, any more than can you or I receive credit for the industrious work of our stomachs in digestion or of our finger nails in growing. No one ever heard of a school boy reproached for idleness replying, "But see how industriously my hair is growing," and if he made such a reply it would not be taken very seriously.

But this would be just as reasonable as to say that the ant is industrious, or that the bee is busy.

So one can hardly say that the ant has the virtue of industry, although this may be rather disappointing to those who deliver talks to small boys. If anyone who reads this book is told, "Go to the ant thou sluggard," he may very properly reply that the ant's industry is a reflex phenomenon, and leave it at that.

In fact, most of the work of the ant is done without his knowing the purpose of the work, just as when one falls into the water, one does not deliberately think, "I must struggle to get out of this." The struggle comes first. The thought, if any, comes after. In the same way, when a man eats his food or dresses himself in the morning, he does not have to reason out everything he does. The ant, with all other insects, performs a very large proportion of the daily work by habit, the difference being that the habit with which a man dresses himself has to be learned, while the habit by which the ant performs its toilet has come from its ancestors.

Such an inherited habit is known as an instinct, and if anyone wishes to be told just how it comes about that one ant may be born so that it does a thing, and that its descendants will be saved the trouble of learning the same thing for themselves, he will have to ask someone wiser than I. But the fact remains.

This touches the great difference between the insect and a human being. By far the largest part of the behaviour of the insect is done by means of habits which that particular insect has had no part in forming. Many of our own actions, as we shall see in a later chapter, are also performed by means of habits, but we ourselves have made by far the larger part of these. It is the pride of a man that he is constantly seeking to climb out of the rut which habit forms. While most of the insect's actions are done in the same way as our own hearts beat or as we digest our food, because we have inherited the machinery to do these actions automatically. This is not to say that insects never acquire habits for themselves. The humble cockroach ordinarily prefers darkness to light, as every housewife knows. But these insects have been trained, by giving them electric shocks, to turn back *before* they reached the dark part of a box. They had acquired a new habit. Habits thus acquired by an individual can, of course, not be handed down to the next generation.

Another curious thing about the mental life of an ant, such as it is, is that to a very large extent, smell takes the place of human sight. If a child wanders from home, it remembers the way back by looking at the landscape. If an ant wanders from home, it remembers the way back by smelling things that it has passed, very much as a dog does.

But its sense of smell works differently from that of a human being or an animal. It seems to have two noses, one on the end of each of its feelers. Now suppose that it is lost and comes across the path which has been taken by some of its nest-mates out on an expedition. It knows immediately which way the others were going, by what has been called the "smell form" of the tracks, which will point in different ways according to the direction taken. In this way, just as you or I can tell by looking at the marks on the snow which way a person has passed, so the ant smells the direction of those who came before.

So that it might be said that the mind of an ant is a "smell mind," what there is of it, as ours is mainly a "sight" mind. If there is any one of us whose mind is keener, and, as we say, can see better into the future, such a person is said to have "vision." An ant that was rather better equipped than his fellows to deal with the world around him might well be said by the other ants to have "smell."

Now in the case of both the ant and the amœba, we have used action to guess at mind. In the case of the ant, there are more fully developed sense organs through which the animal acts upon the outside world. But the two creatures are just the same, as living in the world and being able to do certain things when they find themselves in certain situations. This is true of every living thing. It can act in response to certain things in the world outside. And the higher the form of life, that is to say the nearer it is to man, the more difficult, complicated, and varied things it can do. And the mind of a person or creature is measured by the situations with which it is capable of coping.

For instance, a great many people could be found in the war who were capable of defending a small part of the line, and some who could take over a larger number of men and assume the responsibility for their actions. The situation faced by one who controlled a number of men was more complicated than that of the individuals he controlled. And the situation faced by the man in supreme command was the most difficult and complex of all.

It does not require a very high degree of mind to play one's part as a private soldier. But there are few men whose minds are capable of achieving victory as commander-in-chief.

Mind then is often said to *be* power of action to meet a situation. The more numerous and complex are the situations which can be met by any living thing, the higher the mind. Now the ant, as we have seen, in common with all insects, does most of what it can do by habit inherited from its ancestors. The number of things it does is very limited, for it cannot easily change habit to meet a change in circumstances as we can do. Remarkable though the doings of some of the ants may seem, yet we cannot on that account attribute to them any very high degree of mind. Nature has put them into a rut and they have paid the inevitable penalty of a too well ordered existence.

Before leaving the ant it is worth while to think how differently the world appears to a being whose main connection with things outside him is made by smell. The world is an entirely different place to such a creature. In fact, if the same world were inhabited by twenty different creatures who relied on different sense organs, it would be impossible to tell from their descriptions that they were all talking about the same universe. So dependent are we on our organs of sense.

Thus, the "smell-world" of an ant makes her an uncanny creature. But other things make her still more mysterious. She lives in her teeming city, with its intricate organization, but in the silence of the tomb. Not the slightest sound breaks on her ceaseless labours, from her birth to her death. But in compensation, she can, the scientists tell us, probably detect light that we find invisible! And as for what she does, almost everything is performed in ignorance of any purpose, as though by some blind, impelling force working through her.

Truly is this strange, automatic-seeming creature, this mistress of red tape, deserving of a respectful awe!

(c) DOES A DOG THINK?

A dog who shakes himself and looks round the room probably sees things very much as if they had been photographed in black and white. The trees and the sky and the sunset are like black and white drawings to him. The yellow light of the moon is the same in colour as the white light of the sun. A crowd of people is like a movie picture, a rainbow is like a black and white cloud.

The way in which the dog's colour blindness was discovered is interesting. It has been found that a dog which is fed at the same time that a green light is shown soon comes to know the light and to regard it as a signal for food. If now a red light, equally strong, is shown to him, he will behave exactly as though it were the green light, jumping up and expecting to be fed. No amount of training can make the dog distinguish between red and green of equal brightness, although it is easy to make him see the difference between a bright light and a dim light of any colour. And the same is true of blue and green lights, or any other two colours.

So we believe that the dog *cannot* see the difference!

And exactly the same is true of the cat, which has to tell the difference between things she sees by their brightness and darkness, as we do at the movies.

The world of the cat and the dog is a movie world, as regards colour.

The next thing is that the world of the dog and cat is, like that of the ant, very largely a "smell world." Things are recognized by their smells and remembered by their smells. When you or I come to a crossroads, we stop, look and listen. The dog and the cat stop, smell and listen. When we come into a room, we look around to see whether anything has been moved.

The dog and the cat smell round to see whether anything has been moved. A human being can probably never obtain an idea of the way in which the "smell world" appears to a dog. If we try to teach a puppy his letters, as most of us have done when we were children, the dog seems unaccountably slow and stupid. But if any street whelp were to teach us to cross the road, the creature would be scandalized that his master could not smell things that were so obvious. So far above ours is the dog's power of scent that it has been said that we cannot even devise a test for it, any more than could a blind man devise a reading test. This is the one thing in which the dog could instruct us.

One of the uses of thought is to help us escape from difficulties. Let us see what a dog or cat does when he is faced with a simple problem. Doctor Thorndike, the famous Columbia professor, once arranged a number of boxes so that they could be opened by certain simple movements from the inside. A cat was put into one of these and watched to see what she would do to escape. Food was placed near, and the experiment was made at hungry times, so that there was no laziness.

Tabby is very uncomfortable. She tries vaguely to get out. Openings are examined to see if they are big enough to squeeze through. She claws at the bars, bites the sides, and when she strikes anything "loose and shaky," she continues her efforts. This is kept up for ten minutes or so. All this time she is feverishly and unintelligently, according to our ideas, trying to get out. And she tries to escape by simply doing everything she can think of to anything that is in sight. She is regardless of the fact that, for all she knows, her struggles may be shutting her up faster.

After all the undirected, random movements, she finally escapes and is properly rewarded with the tasty fish. But her trials are not over. Some time later she is again put into the box and has to repeat the performance to get her fish.

On the first occasion she escaped by pulling down a wire loop which was fastened to a weight that drew up the bolt. This took her perhaps a hundred and sixty seconds, or nearly two minutes and a half. The next time she did not go at once to the loop and pull it down as a human child would do. She had to claw and scratch and squeeze half a minute before she found the loop again. The third time she took a minute and a half. At the end of twenty-four trials, she could get out in seven seconds. Then we say that she has "learned the trick."

If any one were to come into the laboratory and see the cat pulling down the loop to get free, he would say, "What an intelligent cat." And yet she has really been very stupid about it all.

Even now she does not know what she has done. She does not understand anything about the law of gravity or the working of pulleys. All she has done is to form a connection in her elegant and furry, but rather slow-working head, between clawing the loop and going free. And it has taken her over ten minutes of hard, gruelling work to do this. The sight and smell of the box now serve as a sort of sign or signal to make her put her paw through the loop. If something entirely irrational is made the signal for release, then she cheerfully performs the irrational. Sometimes the cats were freed when they licked themselves. Without any more ado, and without asking "why," they promptly learned to lick themselves as soon as they were put into the box.

The dogs were a contrast to the cats. They showed nothing like the same energy in trying to escape. Their efforts seemed "tame" and they soon gave up the struggle. But they went through the same task in the same kind of way by trying out everything they knew, so that in the end the box was simply a signal for a movement of a certain kind.

"But," you answer. "A boy who has learned to open the door does not understand the law of gravity or the working of the lever. And yet he *understands* in an elementary way how to get out of the room. Give a dog a simple problem within his own powers, and he will grasp it as well as the boy grasps the more complex one".

This plea for the dog puts the reader in good company. Headed by Köhler of Berlin and Koffka of Northampton a group of German psychologists are claiming that all learning is performed by obtaining Insight into the situation. Köhler tells of a chimpanzee in a compound with a banana placed too high to reach with either of two bamboos. By accident the ape fitted these together, when he at once obtained the fruit with the double pole. "Here" says Köhler "is understanding that comes, as it does so often, through a chance occurrence". Was it not by chance that Newton's apple fell?

Köhler's group claims that to see and solve such a problem is to bring the parts of the situation into relation with each other, thus making a new thought-shape, in German a "Gestalt", out of what was before shapeless or chaotic. Thus to bring Form out of chaos is to have Insight. We are told not to buy a dog and do our own barking. According to the Gestalt psychologists, to call an animal stupid because of what it does in a puzzle box is to buy a dog and wonder why it cannot sing. As a matter of fact later experiments do seem to show that the cat in the box is not nearly as irrational as we had thought!

(d) MONEY AND LIFE

Life, in its many forms, holds a parallel to money. The more money a man has, which can be realized, which is fluid, which can be at once put to any purpose of the moment, the better, other things being equal, can he make himself felt in business. And it is the same thing with life, which exists in so many diverse shapes about us. Experience is the capital of life. An amœba has no stored up experience on which it can draw. It can learn nothing, or only an infinitesimal little. It cannot change its behaviour to suit a changing environment. It would as lief eat poison as meat, the first time, the second time, and the tenth time, if it survived. It cannot save experience for future use. It might be called a psychological spendthrift.

And if the amœba cannot save, the ant and the insects cannot spend because they cannot realise on their securities. The ant is like the owner of a trust fund, saved by a long line of ancestors, each generation of which has decreed exactly how the money is to be used. The ant's experience is there, stored up for her by her forbears, but it is not realisable. She can do few things with it. She is like the British House of Lords, who "did nothing in particular, but did it very well"; for complicated and wonderful as are the ant's activities, they are all machine made, engine turned off the pattern cut out by the great-great-grandmother a thousand times removed. Her stores of experience are like a perpetual fund, devised for the purpose of feeding a family of parrots or of cleaning a monument. The ant does a few things well, but she cannot adapt to change, cannot realise on the vast experience bequeathed by the creators of the trust fund that is her fortune. She is the psychological ward of the court.

Such an animal as the dog has, indeed, power to use his past experience to some extent. He can learn in an elementary, tedious way, which means that he can adapt his actions to conditions around him. Indeed, as will be seen later, the most precise, the most exact, and probably the most fundamental experiments ever made on learning were made with dogs as subjects. But the dog's learning is very slight. His power of change of action to suit external conditions is almost nothing compared with the enormous learning power of a human being. His accumulated hoard of experience is ridiculously little, like the coins in a child's bank. Cent by cent, he has to save, with struggles that seem pathetic to the more gifted. The dog stores experience in a psychological money box.

Only with man do we come to a creature that can by his own past experience instantly transform his behaviour to suit the changes round him, can at once realise on his stored experience, can intelligently use his psychological capital. Just why he is able to do this, we shall try to show in the following pages.

Ring up the curtain for the Baby!

Chapter III

BABIES

(a) HOW THE BABY BEGINS TO MAKE HIS WORLD

The world is a strange place to a new baby.

Take the feeling produced by turning round and round so fast that it is impossible to distinguish anything at all. In addition imagine what it sounds like suddenly to step out of a cathedral into a noisy street. Think of the curious feeling, for example, when a tooth has been extracted, and imagine what it would be if a similar new sensation was spread over the whole body. Think of the pain that comes from a bruise at the end of an elbow and add the feeling of strangeness in the muscles and limbs on getting up for the first time after a three weeks' illness. Roll all these into one, overwhelming, meaningless chaos, spread over several months. This will begin to give an idea of the enormous, "booming confusion" that made up the world of each of us during the early cradle months.

A baby does not know that a certain sensation means a "pain in the hand." It realises that something is wrong with the world but cannot locate the trouble, so it responds by doing everything it can do in the hope that it may somehow meet the situation. It goes red in the face, takes deep breaths, throws out its arms and its legs, and if it's a lucky baby and has the right kind of mother, the discomfort disappears and all is well with the world again.

It has made an adjustment to its environment.

But there are certain adjustments in a new-born child that do not have to be made in this needle-in-a-haystack manner. These are what are called the reflexes. For instance, if the hand is touched on the inside by a pencil, even at a very early age, the baby clasps the pencil. If the white of the eye is touched, the eyelid is closed to remove the obstruction, only of course, when it is a finger that is in the way, the adjustment is not successful. In that case, the baby cries and moves its head and arms and limbs until the disturbing sensation is gone. But the eye, as an organ of sight, cannot as yet tell that an approaching finger is likely to be followed by the stimulus which compels closing the eyelids. This has to be learned.

The sight of the finger moving towards the eye has no meaning until the meaning is learned.

In the same way there is a reflex of swallowing when food of the proper kind is put into the mouth. But the sight of the food has originally no meaning. There is a reflex for breathing, reflexes for digestion and for the general work of the body such as the heart-beat. When these are absent or fail, the child dies. Thus you may see an occasional lamb in which the reflex of taking its mother's milk is absent. The mother sheep is quite unable to teach the little one to suck, and left alone, the unfortunate animal will starve.

We take for granted these complicated processes and movements which are essential to the working of our body and which we could not acquire for ourselves. It is only when one of them, for some reason or other, does not work, that we find how dependent we are upon them. Sometimes, indeed, we have perforce to be taught some of those things which ought to come to us without instruction. A good many of the people who read this book were taught to breathe by being slapped on the back the first few minutes after they were born. But none can teach us how to digest our food, how to make a plate of bacon and eggs and a glass of milk into a poet or a Buddha. That can only be taught us by the greatest of all teachers, which is Nature.

The reflexes, then, are the stock-in-trade that nature has given us to start on our journey of life. Only the things that call out reflexes have meaning to the child. Everything else is bewildering confusion. This, indeed, is what the author of the book of Genesis meant when he said, "And the Earth was without form and void. And darkness was upon the face of the deep."

Every baby has to create the world for itself out of confusion. How does it make its world?

At first it is hearing all kinds of sounds and seeing all kinds of lights and masses of various colours that come and go apparently without any connection between themselves or with anything that happens. Little by little, however, it begins to notice that certain experiences, making what we should call the "feeling" of warm arms are generally followed by something pleasant. This may be either food or relief from something uncomfortable. Remember, though, that the child does not know anything about an arm of warmth. It merely finds that certain things it feels are followed by certain other things. But the world has begun to have a meaning. The child has begun his own act of creation.

After a time he notices that certain things he hears are followed by the experiences that mean food, and the nurse says, "See how he recognizes my step." One more piece of the great confusion around him has been given its part in the world he is creating.

Next he begins to add certain experiences that come through his eyes. Then it is that the mother is delighted and says, "Baby knows me now!" But she would be very surprised if she could see how she really appears to him.

Can we get an idea of how a baby's mother looks to the child? No, for as we have grown up we have created our own world and we cannot destroy the world we have made. This is one of the cases where it is easier to make something than to pull it to pieces again.

Yet it is not until the baby begins to play that his real education begins.

One day he is moving his hand about for no particular reason. Suddenly he finds that there are two experiences instead of one. He has seen his own hand waving in the air, and two other things have become connected in his world, the "feeling" of moving his hand, and certain lights and shadows which the baby comes to know later as the sight of his own hand in motion. Soon he finds that on certain occasions there are two sensations of touch instead of one. This is when he first makes the acquaintance of his own face. This discovery of the parts of his own body marks an epoch in the life of the child. It means that the young human being now begins to recognize himself as different from the things about him. Before that it is probable that he could hardly tell the difference. From this time forward he can really be said to begin to be a "self," as the term is, the beginning of an individual.

When he begins to play with things, still more experiences have to be connected. He has to learn that a certain experience from his eyes means that, if he moves his hands in a certain way, what we call the pressure feeling will follow. This is the same as learning that he cannot put his hand through a book, which is so obvious to us that it seems impossible that we should ever not have known it. But anyone who watches a baby trying to catch hold of the smoke from a cigar will see that the connection between the sight of a thing and the way it feels is by no means clear until it has been learned.

Just which of the infant's experiences come to him ready combined, as the colour and shape of a brick are to us, and which he has to combine for himself, like Köhler's ape who suddenly sees the long pole as a tool-in-connection-with-the-banana, it is hard to say. The German group of whom we have spoken claim that many experiences, once thought to be separate at first, are ready combined from the beginning. It is a question of deciding where the dividing line lies!

(*b*)   THE BABY MAKES SPACE AND TIME

Now as the baby grows older, he finds that when he has a certain feeling in what we call his hands, sometimes other things happen. If his eyes are turned in a certain direction he sees something vaguely white and shining. And while he is doing this, if he happens to get excited and waves his arms up and down, he hears something which does not usually result when he is waving his hands about. This new noise is pleasing to most babies, and they are apt to make it too long for the patience of those near them, and the mother will say, "I wish baby would stop hitting his chair with that spoon." But perhaps she ought to be proud, for the child may have made his first recognition of an object in the world.

He has come to know a spoon, not, of course, as you or I know it, or as a jeweler knows it, but as the meeting place of several experiences and of something that he does. A spoon is for him something that, looked at, seems white and shiny, and from which follows a certain pleasant noise when the hands are moved. I have said "thing," but whether indeed there is a thing until the child *makes* it is much disputed. Originally there were a number of separate experiences and actions connected with the spoon. Until the child joined these all up there was no "spoon" for him. The important thing in this creation of an object is the action of the baby. It is only when he begins to do something for himself that things begin to have a meaning for him. All the experiences from the eye, the ear, the mouth, the hands and the muscles combine into the thing we call a spoon, the use of which is to make a noise, and use means doing something.

It begins to appear now how the eyes and ears and other sense organs of the child help it to do something to the world. In the case of the amœba we saw that certain objects produced certain reactions. And as in the case of the ant and other animals more complex in nature, sense organs are developed which make possible responses to more difficult situations; so the eyes and the ears of the human being simply help him react or do something to the outside world. The separate ways in which the object affects the child are, in the main, there from the beginning; it is the child, his mind, that joins them into a "spoon."

In truth, man is the measure of all things.

After a time the baby has created a large number of objects, food, toys, its bed and other things with which it begins to come in contact. Then it begins to notice that when one of two things is put in a certain position nothing is seen of the other. That is the beginning of what we call space.*

*The Gestalt psychologists believe that we have direct perception of objects in space.

Later the child may go to high school. It probably will never occur to him, then, that he took simple lessons in geometry somewhere round the age of ten months. But it seems to be at about this age that a baby learns the simplest things about the way objects can be arranged in space, and it is on these simple arrangements that geometry is based. Some people have said that we do not need to learn all this, that we have what is called intuition of them. If you believe this, borrow a six months old baby and watch it reach for things that are at the other side of the room. You will find it has no idea that some things are nearer or more distant than others. Its first lesson in the "space-relation" has yet to be learned.

In a similar way the child begins to understand that things *happen* before and after each other. This takes quite a long time. It is probably not much before eighteen months that a baby really knows what is meant when its mother says such a thing as, "You must have your coat on before you go out." The reader's mother and the mother of all intelligent babies will say at once with a fine scorn, "But my baby knew at six weeks old that food was coming after she had had her bath." Now one has to be very careful when one talks to mothers about the intelligence of their children. But it is easy to see that the child may expect food after bathing and yet not realise that the one thing comes after the other. The bathing serves merely as a signal for the food or, as we put it before, bathing means food to the baby.

Somewhere round eighteen months then, a sense of time begins to come. Sleep seems to be a landmark. Thus a child at twenty months said, "Baby went in car yesterday," when she had really been in the car before her midday sleep. Several months later she no longer spoke of things that happened before a sleep on the same day as happening yesterday. She appeared to have joined everything that took place between the morning of one day and the night of the same day. After she has slept on all the events between morning and night this becomes yesterday, and all the yesterdays fuse into one big time before today. About this time all her past history is spoken of as yesterday. Her mother is waiting now for her to combine the yesterdays into weeks.

This slow building up of time from "before" and "after" to "time between sleeps," and to days and weeks, shows the slow growth of our experience. Just as a crystal begins from a speck of solid substance, slowly covering it up fold by fold, and yet when the crystal is formed out of many layers, you may still see within the tiny speck that started the whole growth, so our experience takes its beginning from some one small happening, folding it round and round until a large and perfect structure is grown.

About the infant's play with a pair of blocks crystallizes all the science of geometry. Around the first childish notions of "before" and "after" grows all the lore of the nautical almanac.

(c) AN INCIDENTAL ACCOUNT OF MOUTHWATERING

One day a man saw his stop-watch start when he entered the room. Out of order? But it began to start also just before the race began, and when he spoke to it! Absurd? But something very like this happened to the earlier workers on the secretion of saliva in the dog. They had shown how a train of nerves from the mouth to the salivary glands caused secretion. But many things *not touching the mouth* had the same effect—a voice, the sight of food, the sounds of food preparing! This they called the "psychic secretion."

It was really quite simple. *They did not know!*

This was the problem that Pavlov, eminent Russian scientist, set out to solve some thirty years ago. And his solution of the problem has added enormously to our knowledge and has resulted in his remarkable discovery of what he calls the "Conditioned Reflex."

Two chapters ago we spoke of reflexes. If food is put into the mouth, saliva begins to flow, however young the baby may be. A child does not have to be taught to make saliva for food. There is a reflex that attends to this for him. In fact, if a child could not make saliva it would not be possible to teach it to him. These ordinary reflexes Pavlov called unconditioned reflexes, because they do not depend on anything else to set them off.

But, suppose, now, that when food is put into my mouth a bell is always rung, and that this is done on a large number of occasions. In time, the bell will be enough to start a flow of saliva. No food will be necessary. We have now set off a reflex by a stimulus which is not the original or natural stimulus, but one associated with it. This new stimulus, which has gained a fresh power from the one that nature gave, is called the conditioned stimulus, because it is dependent for its action upon another. The reaction is known as a conditioned reflex, or conditioned reaction.

Pavlov found that he could form these conditioned reflexes in almost infinite variety. For instance, if a dog had been fed at the same time that a bright light was flashed, whenever the light was shown, even without food, saliva flowed. Of course, this doesn't last forever, but the reaction has to be helped out from time to time by showing light with food, just as we may have to be reminded of anything else.

If a dim light was now shown, the same reaction followed and saliva was produced. But if, whenever a bright light was shown, food was given, and whenever a dim light was shown food was withheld, then the dog learned to distinguish the two; bright meant food, dim meant no food.

Some of the dogs had conditioned reflexes established to white triangles and other geometrical shapes; some to the sound of a pitch pipe; and so delicately are the animal's ears attuned that if the sound were one-eighth of a tone above or below what was proper, they could be trained to take no notice of it. A degree of accuracy that many humans might envy! Some of the dogs secreted when a certain part of their body was scratched. Others when the light in the room was heightened or lowered, others when they smelt objects which had nothing to do with their food until they had been shown at meal times.

In fact, Pavlov says that almost any stimulus may be made to set off this reflex, if it be repeated sufficiently often with the natural stimulus and at the right time.

Did your mouth ever water when you passed a pastry cook's shop and you were hungry? Mine has and Pavlov's has. Everyone's has. And these were conditioned reflexes. A student in a fraternity house near my home has learnt to play the saxophone, but he does not play it very often now. The other students have summoned the conditioned reflex to their aid. They suck a lemon when he begins, and his mouth waters so much that he cannot go on. Science has many uses!

Exactly the same kind of experiment as Pavlov's has been performed with children and grown-up human beings. A scientist called Krasnogorski worked with little babies and found that he could cause saliva to flow when bells were rung and lights were shown, just as with the dogs at Petrograd and Moscow.

This scientist formed conditioned reflexes at three months and onwards, and it appears probable that they could be made from birth and some say even before birth. It must however be remembered that a young baby's brain is not so well developed as when it has grown older, so that only very simple things can be acquired.

Now these conditioned reflexes are nothing but a simple kind of learning.

When the dog's saliva flows at the sound of a bell the animal has learned that the bell means food. The same is true of the baby, whether the sound be made artificially in the laboratory by means of a bell or in the nursery by striking a spoon on a cup. In both cases baby has "learned" to associate a sound with food and react accordingly. Of course there are other things necessary for learning. The muscles have to be trained to act together before a more difficult action can be performed, and this often depends on the physical growth of muscles and nervous connections. It would be impossible for a year-old child to learn to play a difficult piece on the piano, however long the sight of marks on paper, which we call written music, had been associated with certain movements. This is because neither the nervous connections nor the muscles of a child are as yet properly formed, so that the baby is as yet quite unable to meet or react to so difficult a situation.

But in the conditioned reflex we may see, writ small, many of the characteristics of what we call learning. Learning saves effort. So does the conditioned reflex. Pavlov calls it the *signal* reflex since it brings power to "anticipate", and thus economy of effort. Moreover in Pavlov's laboratory the dogs learned not to secrete saliva at the wrong stimulus, or when food was no longer presented, thus again saving unnecessary effort. Learning often requires repetition. So does the conditioned reflex. Learning connects events in the world without—the red sky with good weather, the appearance of a man with his name. It unifies the past with the present and the events of the present with each other. So does the conditioned reflex, for it is by connecting past presentations of light and food with what happens today that the conditioned reflex is acquired.

The conditioned reflex is the epitome of learning.

In fact, it was once my belief, as it is still the belief of many able psychologists, that the world can be split up into conditioned and unconditioned stimuli; that all the multitudinous learned activities of every day life, learning to read and write, to stop at the right building, to enter the right room, to sit at the right desk, and so on are built up of conditioned reflexes.

However, I do not now believe that this is a true description of the facts. It does not seem that we can split up the world into conditioned and unconditioned stimuli.

When we learn to read we may "learn our letters"; capital A appears on the card, and the teacher makes the sound a, and so on. Is this not a conditioned reflex? Many would call it so. Yet as every teacher knows it is of no use for learning to read! In fact, it is a positive hindrance. The same letter has to do different duty when it appears in the words ale, senate, ask, sofa, as you may see at the foot of the page in Webster's dictionary. In fact, science has amply shown that we do not read by letters at all. The word cannot be split up into letters that are conditioned stimuli; our reactions to the world cannot be split up into conditioned and unconditioned reflexes!

At least that is my belief. But many would disagree!

(d) LEARNING TO TALK

If anyone will take the trouble to sit for an hour and listen to the sounds produced by a baby just before the child learns to talk, he will be astonished at their variety. Every conceivable noise that can be produced out of the human throat seems to come up out of the cot. Sounds belonging to all languages and to no language at all may be heard, many of which are very hard for an adult to imitate. Indeed, the linguist is often surprised at the correctness with which a ten months old baby makes sounds which are usually regarded as difficult to acquire. The German "oe," which is found so difficult by English-speaking people, is often produced exactly as a German would say it by a baby, who perhaps will have great trouble in re-learning it when he comes to learn German at school.

A child's first language, or rather pre-language, is international. The Tower of Babel is built in every baby's cradle. The child is making the elementary sounds on which all language is based. Quite as a matter of accident, he will be speaking simple English or French or Chinese or Hottentot in a year's time.

How do we come to pick out the language which is spoken around us?

Herodotus, the historian, tells of a certain king in ancient times who wished to find out which was the oldest language. So he took two children and placed them soon after birth on a mountain, where they were fed by a she goat, and looked after by slaves, who came when they were asleep, and later brought them food without being observed.

When they grew old enough to talk like ordinary children, the king had them brought before him, and all they said was "Bekos." The king was surprised and sent his

UPPER LIP UPPER TEETH ROOF OF MOUTH SOFT PALATE

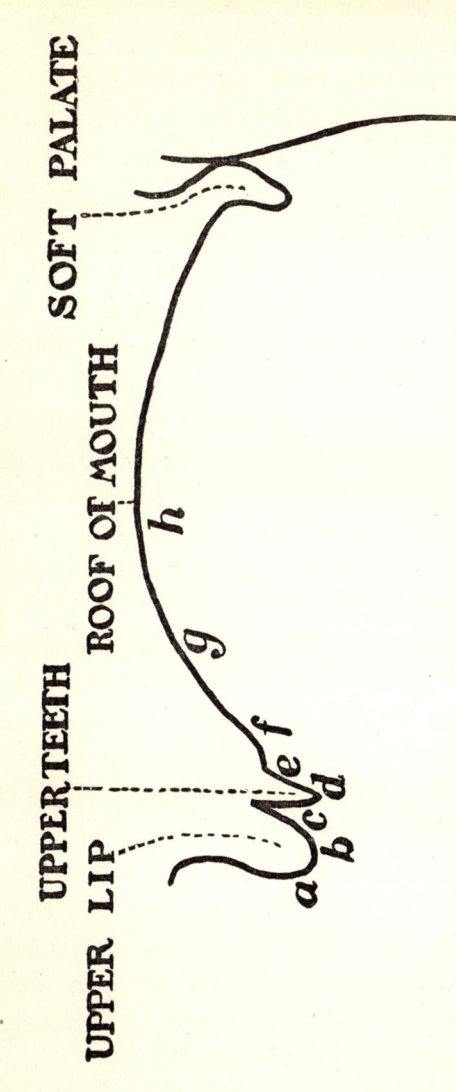

(diagram of mouth profile with points a, b, c, d, e, f, g, h marked along the tongue/palate)

This diagram shows the parts of the mouth against which the upper surface of the tongue is placed to produce certain sounds. The reader can trace these parts in his own mouth, from *a* to *h*, and farther with his tongue. If one places the tongue tip at *b*, and makes a sound by stopping the breath with it, something between *p* and *t*, or between *b* and *d*, or between *m* and *n* is produced. This position and its possibilities are generally discovered by children and used in play, but as the sound produced is not found in English, it is dropped as the child grows older. It is, however, found in the German or Danish expression of disgust, ("ptui"). By bringing the tongue in, up to the position *d*, it is possible to make the sound *t*, *d* and *n*. Different varieties of these sounds are produced by resting the end or upper surface of the tongue at the different positions up to *g* or even *h*. At first the child will place his tongue or make the necessary stopping of the breath by pure accident. Afterwards, he repeats certain sounds which he hears from others. The diagram is drawn from one made by Jesperson, a master of the science of speech.

wise men through the world to find out if there was any language in which bek had a meaning. After a time they reported that bekos was the Phrygian for bread, and the king concluded that he had solved the problem. Clearly, Phrygian was the oldest language, and they were asking for bread.

Whether this story be true or false, it shows what might very well have happened. A child may lose a good many of the sounds which it has made in babyhood if these are not encouraged and fixed by hearing other people make them. The principle on which certain sounds are dropped and others kept is that of utility. Useless noises are allowed to disappear and the useful ones retained, and this indeed is only a particular instance of what always takes place when the response to a complex situation is being learned.

The way in which the principle of utility is applied in learning to speak is very neat, and nobody but Mother Nature would have thought of it. When a child, by some accidental circumstance, places its tongue and lips or other speech parts in a certain position and breathes in a certain way, a certain sound is produced. Exactly what was the stimulus for the shaping of the mouth and placing of the tongue and so on is difficult to say, but probably in most cases it comes from within the body. At any rate we now have a sound produced by the child. This sound, once made, becomes in itself a stimulus for the ears. If it is repeated several times, this new stimulus can now of itself cause the reaction or the motions making the sound, as explained in the last chapter. Consequently, if someone else makes this same sound, the reaction is set off. The same movements are made and the sound "repeated." The presence of the other person "fixates" the sound.

To take an example. For some reason or other the ten months old baby places its mouth in a certain way, does certain things with its tongue and so on, and the sound "oh!" results.

That is, certain things that the child does, once caused by possibly a chance stimulus, are accompanied by the sound "oh!" Now as explained in the last chapter, a stimulus occurring at the same time as an action may come to start similar action. When the baby has done certain things with his mouth, etc., he has heard the sound "oh!"; subsequently the sound "oh!" makes him go through the movements producing "oh!".

Mother comes in the room and cries "Oh, baby." Baby says "Oh! Oh! Oh!". Every time he says it he *hears* himself say it, and that sets off again the actions producing the same sound.

One baby of my acquaintance would say "O dea O dea O dea" (oh, dear) until she was stopped! All that was necessary was to say "oh, dear" in her hearing.

All the various sounds that the child does not hear around him, such as the wonderful clickings and gruntings that no one but a baby can make properly, these are all lost. The movements producing them have not the necessary stimulus from other people, and the particular internal causes that first produced them are not likely to occur again.

Thus a child tends to repeat what he hears from others, and to drop the sounds which he makes but does not hear. In the same way the simpler noises are combined, and we have easy words such as "doll," etc.

This is all very much after the pattern of the conditioned reflex. Learning to speak is a special kind of learning, which seems to be imitation of others, but is really of the same general nature as any other kind of learning.

At first "talking" is like anything else the baby does, such as clasping the hands or kicking. It consists simply of reactions, without any thought of communication. This can be seen for a number of months after the baby has learned quite long words. Often he will talk to himself, as his mother says, saying "flower," "pretty" or "horse," when he has no idea that there is anybody listening. These words are not as yet for the purpose of telling someone else about a flower or a horse. Just as the sight of the horse will perhaps cause the child to run away, so it causes another set of muscular changes that result in the sound "horse." Language is Behaviour, and in its early stages exactly on a par with other forms of Behaviour.

Another interesting thing is the way in which the child will practice making the sounds. My own baby would lie for hours in the early morning, and sometimes in the middle of the night, saying over and over again the words she knew. Of course this was not conscious practice; any other activity would have served as well, such as shaking a rattle or ringing a bell. But it served the end of practice. There are certain educators who claim that deliberate practice or drill should not be used in education, but the natural method should be used, by which the individual "picks up" a thing as he goes along. But it seems almost certain that the natural method is the method of practice. All small children love to do things over and over again and you may see even the birds practicing flying, not flying somewhere, but simply flying.

We may generally be suspicious of people who advise us to go back to nature to make things easy. Nature is a hard and not an easy task master.

Besides the sound of the words there is also the tone of voice. This the baby has to learn as well. It may be seen how different the two are by taking such sentences as "Oh! what a beautiful day," and "Don't let the dog in the house." Try to say the second phrase with the same expression as the first. Or try these two, "Get off the grass there, you boys," and, "Mary's father died last night." It is very difficult for little children to learn the tone which is natural. Quite rarely is a child found, under ten years old, speaking with the expression normal to adults, and when this happens it seems a little unnatural and precocious. An adult, speaking like a child, also sounds ridiculous. Very often a grown-up person will begin to use an entirely different intonation or expression when there are children round, and particularly to babies. Women, and men also, have different intonations not entirely due to the difference in voice. Part of the difficulty of learning a foreign language comes from a difference in the tone of speech.

Thus it is only half true that a child learns a language by imitation, because the sounds have been made already before they can be repeated from others. Talking is a form of Behaviour and is first learned in much the same way as Pavlov's dog learned to produce saliva by the conditioned reflex. So that in teaching a baby to talk, only those sounds should be uttered near, which the child should keep. The baby talk, which aunts and other relatives think necessary to show their affection, is probably a hindrance.

And if a child is never allowed to hear an angry or a coarse tone of voice, he will not use such tones himself. Thus the language of a child reflects the home.

By their children we shall know them.

(e) PEOPLING THE WORLD

To a baby there is at first one person in the world, and that is the baby. He has to learn that in the world about him there are other persons, as well as things. He has created the world. He has yet to people it.

The world is peopled by all of us in something the same way as we make things. A spoon is a thing for the purpose of making a pleasing noise, and which looks so and so and feels so and so. "Mother" is at first a wonderful thing, that has a multitude of purposes and is somewhat larger and more various than a spoon, but is yet on more or less equal terms with it.

To the baby, the world is a matter of Tweedledum, and Tweedledee; persons and things are much the same. Both are there for convenience and comfort. Soon a great difference shapes itself between things and people. People have something in common with the child. A baby has learned that a point put into the flesh brings pain. He winces, whether the pin be pressed into his own or someone else's hand. He has learned to make a certain sound. Someone else can make the same sound. When he is in trouble, he cries. Other babies make the same sound. In fact the cry of another baby will often set him off crying.

Not only can he see his own limbs, as well as feel them, not only can he hear his own voice, he can see other people's limbs and parts of their bodies. And what he has learned of his own body applied to their bodies and their voices too. A distinguished Frenchman tells of a child who burst into tears at seeing an adult in a cold douche. Cold water falling on skin is disagreeable. This had been learned by the child of his own body, and the sight produced tears, although it was another person who was the sufferer!

Another is really the beginning of another self. As we watch another human being, much of our own experience, learned of our own selves and bodies, applies equally well to him. We wince when a blow is struck on him, for a blow on the flesh, we have learned, is painful. We grow faint when his blood flows, for flowing blood means pain. Whatever be his situation we are affected because of his likeness to us.

But only the beginning of another self is thus formed. A pin stuck into someone else does not as a matter of experience actually cause me pain. A stone hitting another person on the head does not cause me actually to lose consciousness. So that in this respect, the other people in the world are like the things. To a baby, human beings are halfway between him and his surroundings; like him, because they move and do things as he does, and because their situations affect him; unlike him, because he has no such control over them as over himself, and because his sensations are not theirs.

In the Book of Genesis, it is related that first the world was created, and last man. In the world that the baby makes first come things, and then people, whom the baby fashions because they are after his own image.

Right on into adult life we allow the situations of others to affect us. Our habits are made, for our convenience or otherwise. To break them is unpleasant. If others break them, this is also annoying. One who rises early every morning has great scorn for the late riser. The sight of someone else breaking the habit is unpleasant. The sight of good food being wasted fills with pain the careful mother of a family, even though the food be not hers. A good football player will almost weep to see chances thrown away, although he has no interest in either team. But his habits and his own experience have put him into the situation of the players. A man with the habit of self-reliance will view with disgust the weakling and the weak man often finds the strongest man unpleasant. Each breaks the fixed habits of the other. And this is one reason why birds of a feather flock together.

In the same way, it makes us feel uncomfortable to contemplate anyone whose whole habit of life is different from our own, and especially one who has succeeded in accomplishing what he would like to do while we have ourselves failed to overcome the necessary discomfort. Many boys at school would really like a reputation which comes from hard work at school subjects, but yet they dislike the boy who has won this reputation. The "grind" is rarely popular, for he brings up the thought not of the credit he does the school, but of the unpleasantness which would have to be endured to achieve his results.

When I was at school, one of the older boys had just passed through the University, and had taken an examination which had qualified him for a most desirable position. All of us other boys envied the position. But when I said to a friend how much I would like to be that boy, my friend answered with a gesture of disgust, "Think of all those years' hard work!"

This is why we do not like to think of anybody as being too perfect, and try to find a weakness in the hero which, as we say, makes him human. "No man is a hero to his valet," and nowadays we all want to be valets. Of course there is also usually present some jealousy or unwillingness to admit that anyone else is superior.

The farther an individual advances above the average

in things that seem to cost effort to achieve, the more unpopular he becomes. The "highbrow" represents so much concentrated essence of poring over books, and owes part of his unpopularity to this. It is not his cleverness that is disliked, for a man who can achieve the same results without apparent effort is very rarely unpopular either among adults or school children. A person who seems to be morally flawless is quite unendurable to most of those who profess the same virtues. We read in the Gospels that Christ was a friend of the publicans and sinners, and we know He was crucified by the Pharisees.

On the other hand we must take into account the pleasure that others often give us. For example, if a person has just completed something which I would like to have done myself, he may serve to arouse in me the pleasure of something achieved. Whether this or the opposite will happen in a particular case depends on the personality of the individual, and to some extent on his education, as well as on the particular circumstances. A person who is pleased at the success of others we call generous and sympathetic. One who is displeased we call unsympathetic and uncharitable. Sometimes the pleasantness or unpleasantness that others arouse in us in this way develops into an emotion, such as hatred or fear.

This is a far cry from the baby in the cradle. But the child fathers the man. All these feelings and emotions arise because we recognise that other people are in some way similar to ourselves and because, when we see them in certain situations, it affects us as though it were ourselves we were looking at. It is difficult for an adult to be angry with a brick or sympathetic with a stone. Sometimes, indeed, one may see a child or a dog furious with something that has caused pain; when this happens one laughs, because this kind of emotion should be directed only against persons. People who make a habit of this kind of thing are usually considered childish or barbarous. The king of the Persians, the Greeks maliciously said, lashed the waters of the sea because a storm had interfered with his plan. And this was a subtle way of calling him a savage.

Most of us, however, are sometimes guilty. I have seen a student pitch a text book on the floor after an unpleasant morning's work with it, and an automobile driver kick a tire which had taken some trouble to remove!

Thus from the cradle up we make our world and all the people and things in it. The people we fashion because they are of our own image, and because they are of our own image, they move us in a way that nature inanimate cannot.

The position of others is then halfway between ourselves and the rest of the world. Animals are generally on a lower plane than other people and plants still lower. Most people do not regard a tree exactly as they do a piece of granite. On the other hand, there are some who never seem to people their world. Such are the "supermen," who think they are above right and wrong, Napoleon and Alexander, and persons like these. For them there is one person in the world, and everything else is environment: Like the water where the amoeba lives, it is there for their pleasure and use. On the other hand, there are persons to whom the happiness and unhappiness of others is more than their own. These are the saints, who have a thousand selves.

Upon the way we people the world depends our own happiness or unhappiness. For it is *we* who are annoyed or pleased, joyous or sorrowful, furious or elated at others, which most men forget.

Chapter IV

MAN, MARIONET OF HIS SURROUNDINGS. MIND, THE SENSES AND THE WORLD ABOUT

(a) How the Nerves Help Us Think

A THOUGHT cannot start itself. Those physical events in the brain which seem to take place when we think must be started off by something, whether this be the fact that the body is in a situation that calls for something special to be done, or whether inside the body something is happening that calls for action. The brain is made up of nerves.

Just what these events are in the brain that seem to go with thought, or what is their relation to thought, we do not know. But without certain physical events in the body science believes that we cannot think. I may be set thinking by the sight of a leaking roof, by the sound of a phonograph playing, or by the feeling of hunger. When this happens there are occurring in my body certain events which have been started by a physical change that disturbs the sense organ in question. The physical events which occur in my brain when I am thinking are not self starting, any more than an automobile or a sewing machine is self starting.

This bodily action may be compared with the way an electric bell works. First the button is pushed. This corresponds to the ray of light falling on the eye. An electric current is started in the wire. This is the nervous impulse. Finally the bell rings. The nervous impulse results in the movement of a group of muscles.

Perhaps the reader will be inclined to disagree, and to claim, as many do, that a thought may spring out of nothing, like Venus rising from the sea-foam. But one who examines any thought of his own will find that it had its starting-point in some perfectly definite stimulus, generally coming from outside himself. Even the longest train of thought is anchored to reality. Like Venus, it has its history and its ancestry. A cloud crossing the sun may remind one of a day at home when the same thing happened. The thought will perhaps pass to "mother's home," and then to "mother," and there is surprise because a letter has not come from her. All the chain hangs from the one external happening, the cloud crossing the sun. And it was the nerve of the eye that brought the message to which was fastened the end of it.

If the human nerves are damaged in any way, by disease or accident or overwork, then the action and thought of the person who owns them is affected. For example, a person who has received a severe blow on the head cannot do anything, and, as we say, is unconscious. However powerful a stimulus comes to him, he makes no response, just as, when the electric bell is damaged, however hard the button is pressed no sound results.

One great difference, however, between the bell and the human body is that, in a great many cases, the body can repair itself, which the bell of course cannot do. A stunned man left to himself generally recovers, unless there has been very severe injury done to the complicated structure inside the skull. But no one ever heard of even a slight break in contact or defect of insulation being repaired by the bell itself!

If the nerves supplying the eye or the ear do not work, this makes a great difference to the person concerned. His thought can never be the same if he has never had this means of getting into contact with the world. Such a person has to think in terms of the senses that he does possess. He will imagine the colour red as the sound of a trumpet, or the sound of a trumpet like the colour red, as the case may be.

Nerves may be damaged less seriously by disease or drugs. When a person is very sick, as in some cases of pneumonia, stimuli are sometimes wrongly interpreted, and the patient, seeing a pattern on the wall paper, mistakes it for an old gentleman stepping out of the wall.

Thus a temporary derangement of the nerves will put a man's thinking and his actions hopelessly wrong. The same effect is produced by some drugs, such as opium and repeated large doses of alcohol. A person's thinking and his ability to deal with the situations he meets may seem for a time to be improved by these. But the fine adjustments of the nerves are ultimately spoiled. Nerves help our thinking by taking messages from the world outside.

Another way in which the nerves help our thinking is by storing up past experience. The pages before have shown how a child will behave in a different way at the sound of the tinkle of a teaspoon if the sound has occurred at the same time with feeding. Past experience has changed the child's behaviour. Now it is in the nerves that the change takes place which enables us to make use of past experience. Sometimes we speak of this summoning up of the past to help the present as memory. It is the nerves that make memory possible!

In general this storing up of experience is called learning. Without it, a human being would be reduced to the position of the lowest animal, and indeed would probably be worse off than any animal, although this is not certain.

The   eye

Illustrating the presence of the blind spot, which is the place where the optic nerve or tract enters the retina, and where the retina is consequently insensible to light. Close the left eye. Hold the "The" on the book close up to the right eye, and gradually move the book away. At a certain point, "eye" will disappear.

Thought would be impossible, for, except by instinct, no one can meet a situation where he has absolutely nothing to start off with; that is to say, where he has no stored up experience to help him. And without the nerves *we* could neither perceive a situation nor perform the actions necessary to meet it any more than could the electric bell ring without the wire.

Thinking, as we know it, could not go on without a nervous system.

Honour then to the indispensable nerve! It tells us of what happens outside, it carries the message that causes us to act, it is the safety vault in which we bank our past experience. When it is out of order we cannot meet the simplest of situations.

It is as versatile as it is indispensable! And yet it is a specialist!

(*b*) THE CITY THAT IS THE BODY

There is a remarkable thing about the body which we have not yet mentioned. Instead of being just one body with one life, it is really made up of millions of smaller bodies or lives. These lives are in cells, as they are called, which make up the parts of the body.

There are cells forming the muscles, the organs, such as the heart and lungs, cells from which the hair grows, in fact, every living part of the body is made up of cells. These all have their own life, separate from the others, but somehow helping in the larger life that forms you or me. If one is killed the rest of the body goes on living just as the other people in a city go on living when one of the inhabitants dies. If the hair cells die a man will be bald on that particular spot, however many advertised preparations he rubs in, for nothing can bring back to life a cell that is really dead. On the other hand, the rest of the body may die and leave the hair cells alive. A dead man's beard will often go on growing for some time as though a few of the inhabitants of a city were to go on ingratefully living after an earthquake had destroyed everyone else.

We may think of the body, then, as a great colony of these tiny cells, each with its own life, and each working and living for the common good, which is the life of a man or a woman or a child.

Just as in the city each man has his own work, so in the city which is the body, each cell has its own job. It is found that in civilized life it does not pay every man to make his own clothes and grind his own corn. One man will naturally be a better hunter, and he finds that it pays to hunt all the time and let someone else bake his bread for him. A jack-of-all-trades is master of none, and it is better for every one and the whole city to let each citizen keep to one kind of work. It pays to specialize.

Now if a man lives by himself, he cannot specialize. He has to clean his windows, grow his wheat, make his clothes. And his life is by so much less rich, for he is kept busy doing things that a more practiced man could do in half the time.

The amœba lives by itself and is its own butcher and baker and candlestick maker. It is a single cell and has to do its own digesting and hunting and feeding.

By living together in the human body the cells are able to specialize for the common good. There is one great army that attends to various phases of the work of digestion, another army that moves the city about like the engine on a battleship and attends to transportation and motion in general, another that is tailor's shop for the scalp, growing hair, and so on.

Now in the case of the city, the larger it is the more is the need of some method of communication between the citizens. A village of twenty does not require this, nor does a town of two thousand. But a city of a hundred thousand cannot get along without some kind of communication, and a country the size of the United States would be helpless. If there were a great fire that devastated the whole of San Francisco, and there were no means of letting anyone know, the stricken people would starve. Or if a foreign army were invading Montreal, and the rest of the country could be told nothing of it, the enemy might be in possession of half the land before proper steps were taken to repel him.

In the same way the cell citizens of the body must have means of communication in order best to transact the business of the body. And just as in civilized States there are men who do nothing but look after communications, the telegraph and telephone men and those who control the newspapers and printing generally, so are there human cells that do nothing but carry messages.

The nerves are cells in the human body that have specialized in communication.

There are estimated to be eleven thousand million of these specialized cells, about a hundred times as many as there are persons in the United States. Like the long distance telephones and telegraphs, they work by relay. Thus one cell in the receptor or sense organ will perhaps receive the stimulus of warmth or dangerous heat. The sense organ in the hand will start an impulse in the nerve that is placed there permanently for the purpose. The impulse will be carried by the nerve cell or neurone, which is the name given to the nerve unit, and thence is carried to a second neurone that is waiting to receive it. This second neurone is in touch with a large number of others, and, if the message is not repeated or urgent, will probably hand it on simply to the nerve controlling a muscle that moves the hand; so that in the very simplest movement that can be made there are at least three nerve cells or neurones at work, although this picture is really much too simple, since there are always a good many more.

Such a simple movement is what we have already learned to call a reflex. It is so named because the older experimenters thought of the nerve-message as being simply reflected back from the spinal cord.

Honour yet more the indispensable nerve, carrier of messages, specialist, swift and sure in its work, self-repairing. It attends to its own work with an efficiency that no machine can approach.

(c) HOW THE BRAIN WORKS

Suppose now, that the situation is more difficult than can be controlled by a simple reflex movement such as we have described. Perhaps, instead of feeling a pin actually stuck into the skin, something which will cause pain is seen approaching the hand. We saw in an earlier chapter that the human being has to *learn* to deal with such a situation. The unlearned or reflex action will not help. In this case, a whole series of nerves is used, each handing on the impulse to the other, and some of which are situated in the outermost part of the brain, where most of our experience is stored. If the message is not somehow or other passed through this part of the brain, the cortex, as it is named, it is doubtful whether very much of our own previous experience can be used to help us.

The whole thing is much like the working of a large store; for example, one doing a big business in dairy produce. A customer who wishes to buy a pint of milk is immediately served by the clerk behind the counter. The money is paid and the milk is taken away without further ado or consultation. Or suppose that the customer wishes to order a pint of milk a day to be sent to his house. This is a rather more complicated operation, but still it can probably be handled by the clerk in charge.

But suppose now that a customer comes and orders a hundred quarts of milk a day. This will be a transaction too big and too important for the clerk in charge. He will probably say, "I shall have to ask the manager." Now the manager is a man who knows the dairy business better than the clerk in charge, and who can appeal to and use his *business experience* to settle any particular question. That is why he is manager and the other man the clerk. In the case, then, of a moderately important order, the manager will perhaps tell the clerk that everything is all right and the clerk will go ahead and fill the order.

Perhaps a yet more important opportunity comes in, presenting a more difficult business situation. It may be that a hotel is to be started in the neighbourhood and the hotel-keeper wishes to buy all the milk, cream, eggs and butter that the dairy can supply. This will cause the manager very serious thought. It may not pay him to bind himself down to one customer, and on the other hand, he may be glad of the certainty afforded by such a permanent arrangement. In any case the mere clerk is quite inadequate to meet the situation, which has to be settled by all the experience that the manager can possibly bring to bear on it.

A very similar thing happens in the body. A slight pain

or irritation in the hand can be dealt with by going no farther than the spinal cord and by an ordinary reflex action. No experience is required. This corresponds to the occasion when the clerk served the pint of milk in the ordinary routine of business. In the situations that require some experience, but which can still, in the main, be dealt with by ordinary routine, we have a higher level of activity in which the cortex, or outer part of the brain, is to some extent involved. An example would be pulling the hand away when a pin is seen to approach. This corresponds to the order for the hundred quarts, and the cortex takes the place of the manager who has business experience at his command.

If now, something turns up which will affect every action of the body and perhaps its life or death, then the cortex has to work overtime. Suppose, for example, that I fall down a well. In this case the messages of pain will be taken to the spinal cord, which will be quite inadequate to cope with the situation. It is a case with which only the cortex with its accumulation of past experience can deal. I will know, perhaps, that no one ever goes past the well for most of the day. Consequently, to shout will be worse than useless. By hard "thinking," I remember that the well lies on the path that must be taken by a boy who goes to school, so I keep my shouting until the time I know he must pass, and if I have luck, he hears me and I get out of the well. It is certain that if I had not the cortex with its stores of experience to fall back upon, I should have a very much smaller chance of surviving.

The cortex, then, acts as a vastly complex clearing house for the nervous impulses that come from without and within the body. In the cortex the inward impulses are combined, sorted out, sifted and added to, out of past experience, and probably, as a result, a nervous impulse or series of impulses is despatched.

The activity of this part of the nervous system is inconceivably intricate, even on such a simple occasion, and decides on a course of action. There are impulses that have originated in the eyes, the ears and the body. These have already been combined by the great trunk lines, and further worked up by the astonishingly involved structures in what is called the mid-brain, below the brain proper. All this is done before the impulses reach the "brain" proper. The cortex takes these worked-over impulses, as an executive might take the reports of his subordinate, and adds, cancels, combines, checks, connects out of the accumulated stores of the past.

Mr. Jones says to Mrs. Jones:

"I think I ought to go back for an umbrella. It feels like rain!"

There is a special part of the cortex for many of the different activities of the human body. That part which has to do with the sense of vision is at the back of the brain, just above the large bump which may be felt at the top of the spine. There are areas for the senses of smell, touch and hearing and what is called the motor area. This last is to be found about the middle of the top of the head extending down on each side about halfway, and turning inwards a little at the top, where the cortex folds in under the "parting" of those who part their hair in the middle.

The lower part of this motor area controls the movements of the head and neck; part controls the arms and trunk; the leg is controlled by the upper end and the part in the fold.

But this does not mean that, when we move our leg because we hear a mosquito and have learned that a mosquito stings, the only part of the cortex that is put into operation is this small place at the top of the head. First of all, the visual centre and the centre for hearing probably have to come into play, and then communication has to be made to the motor area controlling the leg. Even when the leg is actually being moved the cortex is working as a whole. Only the part called the "motor area for the leg" is the most active.

The greatest part of what is usually called the brain is made up of an elaborate system of communication between the various departments, with cross neurones, running in great masses from end to end and from part to part, making a very much more complicated affair than the largest telephone exchange, with which the brain is sometimes compared. So numerous are these connections, that this part of the brain, including the outer covering, the cortex, contains more than one-half of all the nerves in the body.

The nerves, then, help us think and act, and without them what we call "mind" would seem to be impossible. The greater part of the nerves are to be found within the skull, and these nerves are also, for other reasons, the most important, so that popular opinion is in a way correct when it considers the brain to be somehow the organ of thought.

And yet the popular idea is only partly true. While most of what we call thinking is done through the nervous structures in the "brain," yet without the services of the nerves that bring in the messages from the rest of the body the "brain" would be powerless.

In the next few chapters we shall try to see whence comes this raw material of mind, which the brain works up by the stores of past experience. The first and most obvious source is the complicated registering structure we call the eye.

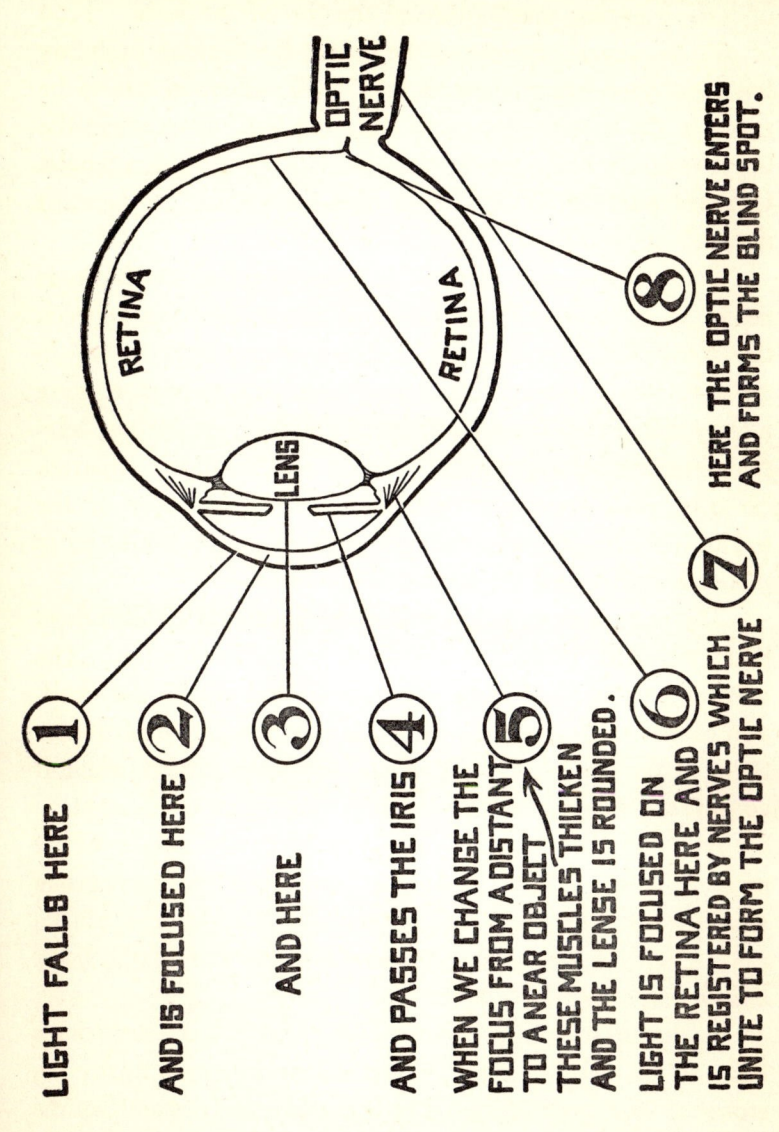

How We See

1. LIGHT FALLS HERE
2. AND IS FOCUSED HERE
3. AND HERE
4. AND PASSES THE IRIS
5. WHEN WE CHANGE THE FOCUS FROM A DISTANT TO A NEAR OBJECT THESE MUSCLES THICKEN AND THE LENSE IS ROUNDED.
6. LIGHT IS FOCUSED ON THE RETINA HERE AND IS REGISTERED BY NERVES WHICH UNITE TO FORM THE OPTIC NERVE
7. HERE THE OPTIC NERVE ENTERS AND FORMS THE BLIND SPOT.
8. (OPTIC NERVE)

(d) HOW WE SEE

The eye is very much like a camera. A camera has three main parts, a lens, by which the light is brought to a focus, a box to keep out disturbing light, and a sensitive plate. In the same way, the eye has a lens, of a kind which would be called a compound lens in photography, to focus the light on the sensitive plate, called in the eye, the retina. Both lens and retina are contained in what is usually known as the eyeball, which corresponds to the box in the camera.

The sequence of the events that go on in the eye during the process of seeing the external world may be seen in the diagram.

In a camera, different focuses are made, at least in the more elaborate kinds, by moving the sensitive plate towards or away from the lens. This is impossible in the eye, as we cannot move the back of our eyeball backwards or forwards. Accordingly, focus is made by changing the shape of the lens, which is easily done, as this is composed of a soft and yielding clear substance. There are special little muscles whose purpose it is to make this change in the lens. The tiny fastenings to which the lens is attached are joined to the middle of these muscles. When the muscles thicken, the fastenings slacken. It is as though one glued a piece of string to the middle of the muscle of one's upper arm and kept the string tight by fastening the other end to something else. On contracting the arm muscle by bending the arm, the muscle would thicken and the string would slacken. (The string is fastened to the muscle as with a piece of sticking plaster, not fastened around the arm.)

On relaxation of the muscle by straightening the arm, the string would tighten again. In the same way, when the small focussing muscles of the eye are contracted, the strings attached to the lens are slackened and the lens takes its proper shape, which is somewhat round, and the eye is then focussed for a near object. When the muscle relaxes the strings are tightened and the lens is pulled into a flatter shape suitable for seeing a more distant object.

So that this muscle works in the opposite way to that which would be expected. When the muscle is contracted, and the strain is on, then the connecting strings are slack, and vice versa.

This explains why it is more tiring to read and to keep the eyes focussed on near objects than to be out of doors, where the eyes are generally resting on more distant scenes. When one is reading, the muscle in the eye is contracted and under strain. When one is looking at a distant object the muscle is relaxed and the strain is eased. Some oculists give the advice never to read for more than an hour without resting the eyes by letting them fall on some distant object. Those whose eyes have become strained by too much reading are often sent to live in the country, where the strain on the focussing muscle of the eye is likely to be very much less. One who wishes to see for himself how the lens thickens and becomes more rounded when a near object is being looked at should watch the eye of some one who is reading a book, and then notice what happens when the other man raises his head to look at something in the distance. It is best to observe the eye from the side.

When the light is focussed on the retina, as on the sensitive plate of a camera, it has to go a short distance into the retina before it reaches the nerves which can register it. Exactly how the different colours and shapes of things can be registered and taken as a nerve message to the proper part of the brain has not yet been decided with certainty.

We know that a nerve message is started, as the electric current is started in the wire that rings the bell. But light falling on the push buttons would of course not ring a bell, and the difficulty is to see how the ray of light falling on the retina nerves can start a nerve current.

Many people believe that there are three substances present in the retina in the part that receives the light. When the light falls on these substances it either builds them up or breaks them down. One of them, which produces the sensations of white and black, is present over most of the retina. When this substance is being split up, which happens when white light falls on it, we "see" white. When the substance split up by the white light builds itself up again, we "see" black. When the eyes are closed the substance is being built up, or one might say is recovering, and consequently we see black.

In a circle, smaller and more towards the middle of the retina, "blue-yellow" substance is found. This acts in much the same way as the black-white substance. When blue light falls upon it, this substance is built up. Yellow light breaks it down, so that the retina may be considered as originally like a blank circle on which a target is to be made. In the middle of this circle paste a slightly smaller one containing the black-white substance. The ring between the two circles, the outer ring of the target, will contain no sensitive substance, and consequently we cannot see with that part of the eye. Now on the "black-white" circle place another smaller one containing the "blue-yellow" substance. The corresponding part of the retina will be able to register both black and white, and blue and yellow. Lastly, on the "blue-yellow" ring paste a smaller circle containing "red-green" substance. This part of the retina will register red and green, blue and yellow, black and white. It is just as though one took four different sized plates, registering no colour, black and white, blue and yellow, red and green respectively, and laid them on each other to form a small pyramid.

It is possible to test this last fact by a small experiment. If any green object such as a leaf is taken and held as far away as possible with the hand to the side, it will not be seen as green, but as grey. Now gradually swing the arm round in front of the eyes. Unless the colour chosen is a pure green, which it is not likely to be, the leaf will be seen first bluish or yellowish, and when the hand is moved round, the leaf will flash out green. We are all colour blind in the outer rings of the retina.

Some people, of course, are entirely colour blind to certain colours. The commonest form of this defect is inability to distinguish red and green, and is due to the absence of the red-green substance that is found in the centre of a normal person's retina. A student told me of a boy that had been asked by his father to take a pot of green paint from the storehouse and do over the verandah and chairs with it. The result must have been surprising to the father when, after some hours' hard work, he saw that his son had made the verandah a very fine pink! If this story is true, and one does not believe everything students may say in class to help things along, that boy lacked the red-green substance! Possibly his father called the trouble by a different name.

Consider now what happens when one looks at a thing of a pure green colour such as is found in the rainbow. The lens of the eye focuses the object by stretching or contracting the ciliary muscle, and a small green image is formed on the retina.

SHOWING HOW, ALTHOUGH WE HAVE A BLIND SPOT IN THE RETINA OF EACH EYE, WE MAY FILL IN THE SPACE

Close the left eye. Bring the left V close up to the right eye, and gradually move the book away, keeping the gaze fixed on the *top of the left V.* At a certain point, the right V will disappear, because it falls on the blind spot. Now, still keeping the gaze fixed on the top of the left V, examine the rest of the line to the right. Do you see it continuous to the end, or **is there a gap?** If the first, you are filling out a part of **the line** for which there is no image on the retina.

The red-green substance undergoes a change and is built up, and this building-up acts upon the nerve of the eye, causing an impulse to be started in the nerve, just as pushing the bell button starts a current in the wire. One "sees" the object as green, or "reacts to the colour green." If, now, the green object is taken away, the red-green substance has to recover by breaking down again, and this recovery produces the sensation of red. One may convince himself of this by holding a green leaf up against a grey surface such as a neutral wall paper and watching it carefully for about half a minute. After a time red will begin to creep over the edges of the leaf. If, then, the leaf is taken away, a distinctly reddish pattern will be observed.

There are a number of interesting things connected with the eye and how we see, but we have not time for all of them. One of the most surprising is what is known as the blind spot. Where the nerve of the eye, the optic nerve, enters the retina, one's eye is not sensitive to light. Any ray of light falling on this spot is not seen at all, but generally the rest of the retina fills in the space. If Lord Kitchener, who had one glass eye, was addressing an audience, those of the faces whose image fell on the blind spot of his good eye would be missing. At about six feet the head of a man would be invisible. But the rest of the eye would fill in faces, and he would not notice the empty place unless it was pointed out to him. In England, cricketers sometimes say that they use the blind spot of the left eye by making the ball bounce on the proper place on the turf, thus confusing the batsman.

This is a brief account of how we see, or how the disturbance outside of us known as light causes a message to be taken in the nervous system. If that particular message has been accompanied in the past by any action, the message may now cause the same action. If I see a mosquito on my hand, I will automatically bring the other hand down upon it, but if what I see has never been connected very definitely with any particular action, no definite effect is produced and the message passes unheeded.

One thing more. Those who do not know very much about it are apt to tell us with great emphasis and excellent intentions, what a wonderful and perfect instrument the eye is, and how it would be impossible to make so good an instrument artificially. As a matter of fact, from a scientific point of view the eye is very imperfect. Of two lights, a red and a green one, placed at equal distances, the red one appears to be nearer, owing to a defect in the eye. Further, the retina is not straight but curved, causing all kinds of mistakes which we have to correct. The blind spot is in itself a serious fault. Indeed, a great investigator once went so far as to say that if any scientific firm sent him an instrument so faulty as the human eye he would send it back!

Which cripples another well intentioned fiction!

(e) HOW WE HEAR

If the damper is taken off the piano by pressing the "loud pedal," and some one sings a loud, deep note, the instrument takes up the tone, and may be heard to sing in answer to the voice. It is in much the same way that our ear works.

A sound is first taken through the outer ear, which is the part we see, and which acts, if it has any use, at all, like a trumpet. At the small opening of the trumpet there is a thin skin, the drum, which beats rapidly backwards and forwards, or vibrates to the sound. One can feel a similar vibration in a piano string which is sounding, or in a violin string.

The drum carries the movement or vibration to the middle ear, which consists of three tiny bones. The first one is shaped something like a hammer, with the head resting on what looks to be a small anvil, and one leg of the anvil is fastened to the third little bone, which is called from its shape the stirrup. When the drum vibrates, the motion is at the same time damped by the hammer and passed by this small bone to the anvil and the stirrup. The broad part of the stirrup, between the prongs, rests on another skin, which is like an oval window opening into the inner ear.

Now the inner ear is full of liquid in which small waves are caused by the vibrations of the oval window. The hearing part of the inner ear is shaped like a snail shell, through the middle of which runs a bone with fibres or strings of many different lengths upon it. If a musical note of medium pitch falls on the outer ear, the vibration of motion is carried through, by the bones and the liquid, and one of the strings in the snail shell is set in motion, just as in the piano with the damper off.

Here again is what corresponds to the push button in the electric bell. The auditory nerve, which is the nerve of hearing, receives an impulse from the particular string that is moved, and the impulse is carried to the brain. It might be thought that there could not possibly be as many strings in this tiny snail shell to register all the sounds which we can hear. If the reader were to see this part of his own ear, which is about the same size as a largish pea, it would certainly seem incredible that such a tiny thing could ever hold so many strings. But those who have examined it through the microscope and reckoned up the number of the fibres, say that there are between eighteen and twenty thousand of them, while we cannot hear more than about eleven thousand tones, so that there are really about seven thousand strings to spare.

People are found who cannot distinguish tones around a certain pitch. If the fingers were run up from the bottom to the top of a piano, glissando, as the pianists call it, such a person might hear a break in the sounds which to most of us would be continuous. This is called tone-deafness, and when the ear is examined after death, it is found that, for some reason or other, disease or what not, those particular strings are not in working order. But there are many tones that no one can hear, just as there are kinds of light that no one can see.

We are all of us, to some extent, tone deaf, just as we are colour blind. Some tones are so high that there are no fibres small enough to take them. At the other end of the scale some are too low. And as we grow older, the smaller strings begin to fail. These are the ones that register the higher tones and pass on the impulse through the neurones to the brain. The boy of fifteen cannot hear quite so well as his little brother who is five, nor he, in turn, so well as a baby in the cradle.

Your grandmother, if you are lucky enough to have one, even though her hearing is perfectly good for ordinary occasions, cannot hear such high tones as either you or I, and this is because the smaller fibres on the basilar membrane of her ear cannot vibrate.

Most of the sounds which we hear are noises and not tones. When a noise strikes the ear drum, a movement is set up in just the same way in the small bones of the middle ear, and is taken thence to the liquid of the inner ear and

AUDITORY NERVE

CAUSING THE FIBRES OF THE BASILAR MEMBRANE TO VIBRATE. THESE CAUSE AN IMPULSE IN THE NERVE WHICH TAKES IT TO THE BRAIN.

⑥

WHICH STARTS VIBRATING THE LIQUID OF THE INNER EAR

⑤

THESE SET IN MOTION THE OVAL WINDOW

④

③

② TO THE DRUM

WHICH SETS MOVING THE BONES OF THE MIDDLE EAR

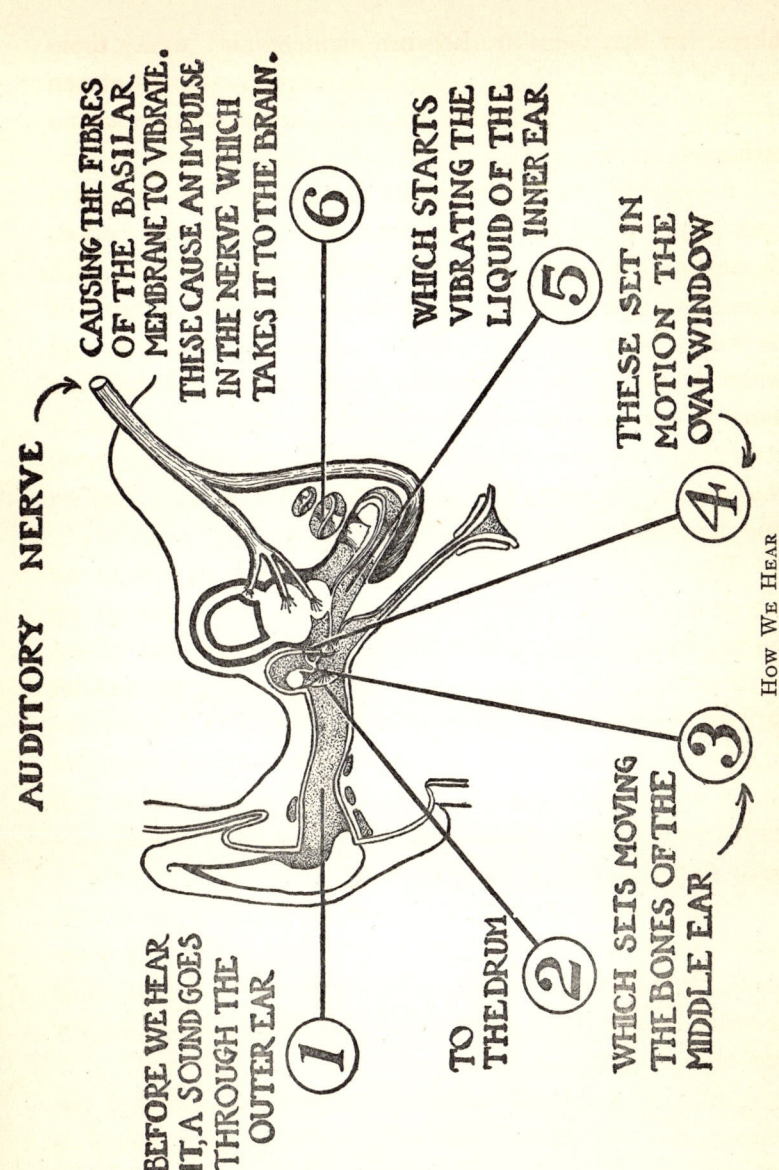

① BEFORE WE HEAR IT, A SOUND GOES THROUGH THE OUTER EAR

How We Hear

The drawing of the ear is by Professor Calkins.

the strings. But a large number of strings are jangled up together, and there is no order or connections between the different movements. You can hear something like the effect of a noise on the fibres of the ear by pressing down the right pedal of a piano, and having someone slam the door. All the strings seem to jangle at once, as indeed they do, like skittles falling at a good strike.

Of course, tones may be sounded together without producing a noise as in a musical chord. In fact, it is very difficult to produce a pure tone, and most of those which we hear are really chords, just as most of the colours we see are really mixtures, so that it is very rare, indeed, that just one fibre of the ear is set in motion, and unless anyone has heard it in a laboratory this has perhaps never happened to him. It is difficult to cause the small waves in the air, which start the vibrations, to move in such a simple way. The bells and springs and other things which set the air in action really move in a very complicated manner, not simply, as one might think; just as a man who is walking moves his arms and legs and head, as well as his whole body.

Animals have sometimes better powers of hearing than we have; that is to say, they can react to sounds that would pass us by. It may be that their ears are tuned to catch fainter movements in the air, as seems to be the case with the dog, or that their ear is so constructed that they hear pitches too high for our range. Some people cannot hear the squeak of the bat, which is, of course, a perfectly audible sound for most of us.

(f) TASTE AND SMELL

Like touch, taste and smell are found to depend on special sense organs in the tongue and nose respectively, and again there is an unexpected fact lurking round the corner. Although there seem to be hundreds of different tastes and smells, yet these can all be produced by combining a very few simple sensations.

The special organs for tasting are found mainly over the tip, side and edges of the tongue. In the middle part of the tongue adults cannot taste at all, nor in the lips or gums. Four different organs are found. One registers sweet, such as honey or sugar. One responds to bitter, the taste of acorns. Two others are set in action by salt and acid respectively.

All tastes can be produced by combining these four, much as all colours can be produced by combining red and green, blue and yellow. The sense of taste is helped out by the varying temperatures and the roughness or smoothness of the food. "Astringent and oily tastes" are really sensations of touch.

Sweet is not, then, the opposite of bitter, as is often thought; the taste of lemonade is produced by a mixture of sweet, acid and sometimes bitter. Sweet and salt generally produces an unpalatable compound, as you may tell by putting salt into half-sweetened water. If other things are present, however, a not unpleasant effect is sometimes produced, as when we eat sweet apple sauce with pork.

But by far the greatest addition to the sense of taste comes through smell. If it were not for the organs in the nose, it is certain that we should not be able to distinguish nearly such a large variety of tastes.

Everybody has noticed during a cold how hard it is to distinguish between tea and coffee, and the "taste" of cinnamon cannot be distinguished from that of flour, nor that of apples from onions when the nose is held.

One of the strange things about the sense of smell is that certain odours seem to work in opposite ways, and cancel each other out. This was of very great importance during the war, when the officers of each side tried to find out how the smell of poisonous gases could be disguised so that the enemy could be disabled before he realized that there was poisonous gas about. Sometimes, indeed, we are apt to assume that because a thing has a pleasant odour there is nothing present that might give the opposite smell. A good many men have made fortunes by selling strong-smelling disinfectants that cover up, but do not really destroy, unpleasant smelling substances. The proprietors of a London underground railway used to advertise the fact that ozone was forced into the air in their tubeway, as if the atmosphere was really rendered more sanitary because it was impossible to smell the musty substances that must have been present.

This sort of thing makes a real danger, and one should always suspect a disinfectant with too strong an odour just as one should always suspect a person that is too highly perfumed. As Cicero long ago observed, the best personal perfume is no perfume at all.

There are other ways in which we abuse the delicate sense of smell whose purpose is in part to detect the unhealthy. Sometimes we grow so accustomed to a particular unpleasant odour, that it ceases to have any effect. A person who has lived in a stuffy house no longer notices the difference between the atmosphere of his home and the open air, except when he returns after an absence. A chemist who works in a laboratory all day long is hardly moved by an odour that would send the ordinary man rushing to the street. In these cases the sense of smell has been fatigued, but the harmful result goes on all the same. The nose is a good servant in time of danger, but like any other good servant, if overworked, it falls down on the job.

(g) WHY WE SHIVER IN A HOT BATH

The last two chapters have described how sound and light in the world outside us are received by the body and changed into nerve messages which help in the task of suiting an action to a situation. But there are other ways in which it is possible to receive impressions from the outside world. Besides the senses of smell and taste there is what is known as the sense of touch. Like a good many other things in nature, this turns out to be not nearly so simple as it appears. Indeed, there are really four senses of touch, registering heat, cold, pressure and pain.

It might at first seem strange that there should be two distinct sets of apparatus to register heat and cold, as though there were two ears, one for loud and one for soft sounds. But experiments have proved that this is so. A small point of metal is used which can be kept at a certain heat by passing a fluid through it. If the point is kept at a temperature a little above that of the body, it is found that warmth is felt only at certain places on the hand, so that it is not correct to think of the whole skin as able to feel warmth, but only certain small spots or sense organs, which average about six to the square inch. These are the "warm spots," where warmth on the skin is changed into a nervous impulse, and they are organs of sense, or receptors, in exactly the same way as are the eyes and ears.

The cold spots are much more numerous, and of these there are some fifty to the square inch. They are entirely separate from the places which register warmth, and this, as we shall see a little later, brings about some curious results. Neither the warm spots or the cold spots are affected by gradual change of temperature, but the change must be fairly sudden to have any effect. There is an old and rather cruel experiment of placing a frog in cold water, which is gradually heated up. The frog dies before it gives any sign of pain. Some parts of the body, for example, the outer surface of the eyeball, called the cornea, have no warm spots. In these parts it is impossible to feel the sensation of warmth, any more than it is possible to see out of the back of the head.

Sometimes these spots may be set in action by other means. For instance, when menthol is rubbed over the head to cure a headache, the cold spots are stimulated, and one says the menthol "feels cold." Whether it is cold water or menthol that is on the head, there is started, in the organs of warmth, a nervous impulse of exactly the same kind in either case. In the same way, when a mustard plaster is put on a person's chest, the warm spots are set in action. These latter also seem to be started off by various changes inside the body, such as occur in fevers and excitement.

The senses of pressure and pain may be best realised by taking any sharp point, or better a short stiff hair, and prodding the skin. Only at certain places is pressure felt, but these are much more numerous than the temperature spots, and vary from sixty to about nineteen hundred to the square inch on different parts of the body. Pain spots are harder to show, but with a sharpened horse hair they may be felt.

Now if the hand is placed in cold water which is slowly heated, certain curious things happen. The pain spots are excited both by a high and a low temperature, and the accompanying diagram shows this. At the side is a thermometer, at the lowest point of which, ten degrees, you will see that both pain and cold are excited, while of course there is no sensation of warmth. Going up the scale, pain is felt to about fifty-two degrees. Water below this temperature excites both pain and cold, but at fifty-two degrees and over only cold is felt. This combination of pain and cold makes us feel biting cold, such as when the arm is plunged into ice cold water. Going up the scale again the cold spots alone are brought into play between fifty-two and eighty-six, and at these temperatures we feel cold which is not biting or very unpleasant. The temperatures mentioned are the extremes for comfort in sea bathing or an ordinary cold bath.

Above eighty-six degrees the cold spots are no longer excited, and the middle column, representing warmth, comes in. Higher still, the warm spots are the only ones in action for a short space. This temperature gives a mildly warm sensation, as in a warm, but not hot bath. At a hundred and thirteen degrees, as may be seen from the diagram, the left hand column again comes into operation. The cold spots are once more aroused, this time by heat, and we have the sensation known as hot.

So that above a hundred and thirteen the warm and cold spots are both working. This happens in a hot bath when one often shivers and "goose flesh" appears. This arousal of the cold spots by heat is called the paradoxical cold sensation, because it is contrary to what might be expected. If the temperature rises still further, pain enters in again, giving burning heat. Above this point all three columns are affected, heat, cold and pain. Here is one of the many occasions when we have to stand aside and marvel! We have the three sense organs which come into play when, for instance, we place our hand in water. But nature has arranged that we can distinguish at least five different kinds of

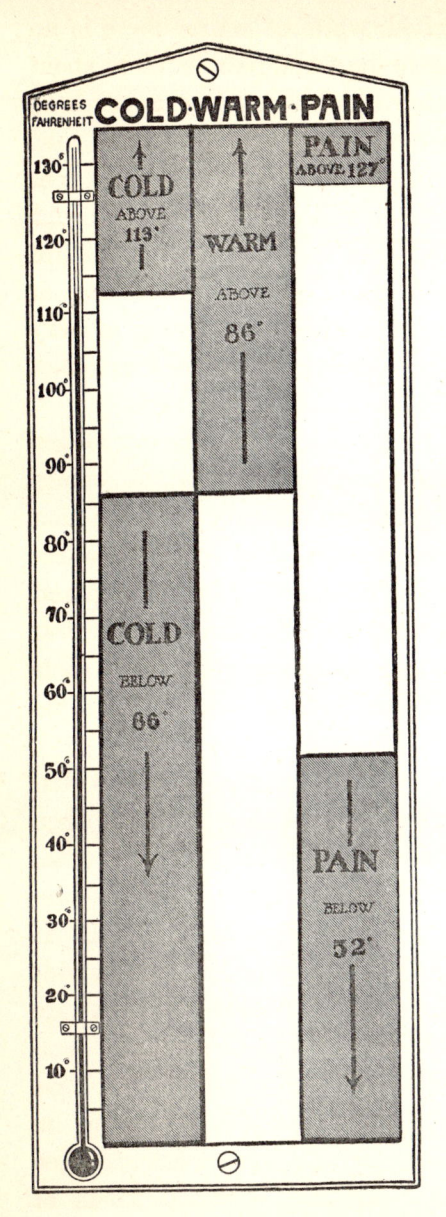

This Diagram Explains Why We Shiver in a Hot Bath

The three columns correspond to three separate organs or receptors which are found in the skin, and which are called into play in estimating temperature. From the right-hand column, corresponding to the pain organ, it is seen that a temperature below 52° Fahrenheit or above 127° calls out the sensation of pain. The organ of warmth is called into play above 86°, while the cold organ is set into operation by two classes of temperature, namely, those below 86° and those above 113°. It will be seen that, any temperature above 113° excites both the cold and warm organs. Consequently, when we get into a bath of, say, 120°, our skin is registering cold as well as warmth, and we shiver. It may also be seen from the diagram which of the three organs are in operation at any other temperature, from zero to 130°.

temperature with them. And to do this she has used the ingenious expedient of causing organs which really register opposite stimuli to be set in operation at the same time. Truly is the paradoxical sensation of cold well named!

The skin really then contains a number of different sense organs forming a kind of mosaic, and not merely one organ of touch. The number of these spots varies in different parts, as we have already seen in particular cases. Those parts which are most sensitive to pressure, such as the hand and the tips of the fingers, are less sensitive to temperature. For this reason, nurses are advised not to test water for bathing with the hand, but with some other part of the body, such as the elbow. Of course, also, our hands are more used to higher and lower temperature. Where there are hairs on the body, these also set as detectors of pressure, but in places such as the soles of the feet, where there are no hairs, the special organs alone are used for this purpose. Those parts which are most delicate in this respect we generally cover with clothing, although the face is left uncovered. The fact that the face is a very sensitive part of the body is perhaps some argument for the beard!

(h) THE COMPASS OF THE BODY

Turning round and round, and motion up and down in an elevator, is registered mainly by a small apparatus that is connected with the ear and arranged so that motion can be felt either upwards, towards the front, or sideways. It is a unique kind of compass, so constructed that it can register every possible variety of movement.

Part of the inner ear not yet discussed is an apparatus known as the "semicircular canals." Suppose that one took a glass tube, and bent it to the shape of an U. Now suppose that this tube is filled with as much water as it can hold, leaving open the two ends. As long as the tube were kept still, the water would stay without spilling. If, however, the tube were moved, water would spill.

Now motion in some directions would affect the water in the tube more than in others. Thus, if one started to run rapidly and suddenly along the line formed by the tops of the U, thus U, a considerable amount of water would be jerked out, but if one ran at right angles to this, in a direction coming out of the paper to the eye, very little spilling would take place. If the tube were taken up in an elevator and kept perfectly upright, practically no water would be lost, however suddenly the motion began, while if the elevator started suddenly downwards, water would spill. Thus, motion in two directions would move the water. Motion at right angles to both these directions would not much affect it.

The semicircular canals consist of three such tubes, arranged at right angles, as at the corner of a room where the walls and floor meet. Motion in the direction that has not much effect on one of these tubes is registered by the other two. Thus there is no movement which does not cause a disturbance in one or other of the three tubes or canals. Motion which is not in the direction of any of them affects them all in part.

Let us see this elaborate apparatus in action!

The rotation in the liquid of the canals is registered by a number of fine hairs, connecting with a nerve. When we move, the liquid in one or more of the canals is disturbed, and the pressure on the hair starts an impulse in the nerve. If, however, we continue moving, the liquid takes up the motion of the surrounding tube, and no pressure is exerted

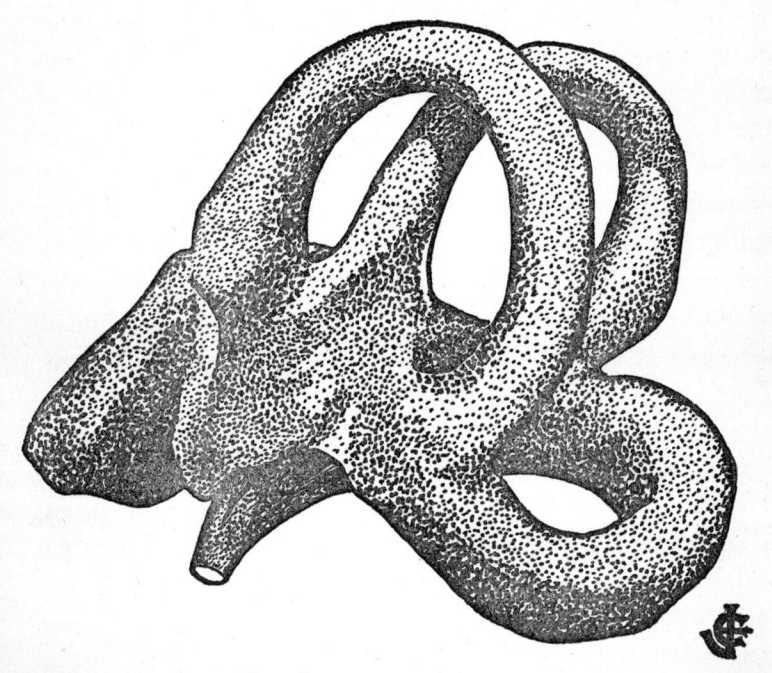

The Compass of the Body

A small apparatus, part of the inner ear, by which motion is registered. The three semicircles, arranged almost at right angles to each other, are full of liquid. When we start to move from rest, the liquid in one or more of these canals is disturbed. Tiny hairs register the disturbance, an impulse is started in the connecting nerve, and the body makes the appropriate adjustment. The three canals together take up not much more space than that occupied by a large pea.

on the hairs, and so we no longer have any consciousness of motion. In the same way, by starting very carefully with the U tube full of liquid, a very high rate of speed may be obtained without spilling the water. Such a tube might be carried with perfect safety in a swift and even-moving automobile, and if we closed our eyes in the same car we should likewise scarcely be conscious of any motion except for the noise. This would be because the liquid in the tube we carried and the liquid in the semicircular canals were both of them at rest relatively to the sides of the containing vessel.

This seems to have an interesting result. As far as the bodily conditions are concerned, there seems no limit to the speed at which we may ultimately be able to travel through space. As long as the starting and stopping are sufficiently gradual, there will be no discomfort in traveling at rates of speed that seem impossible today. Nature has set no limit in our bodies to the rate at which we may travel, providing that proper precautions are observed. The men of the future may well devise means of locomotion that by comparison would make our aeroplanes seem like stage coaches.

Now the nerve connecting with the semicircular canals does not go directly to the cortex of the brain, and so we have no direct sensation from the hairs that register the movement, as we have in the case of sight and hearing. But a connection is made with the nerves belonging to the muscles that move the body, and so, when we lose our balance, or move in any other than the proper way, a message is sent to correct this. So that these small tubes, all three of which taken together occupy a space not larger than that taken up by a large pea, are among the most important structures of the body; acting, as they do, like a compass, or like a gyroscope on a torpedo, and infallibly detecting and correcting the movements of the body when it goes off the course.

During the war, the enormously increased importance of flying made it very desirable to find out exactly how sensitive was this natural compass. And today, after the war, the problem is still of the utmost interest for aviators. Men in whom the canals do not work properly and those who cannot use them with discretion, find flying dangerous. When they are above the clouds, they are not able of themselves to tell whether they are moving to the right or left, upwards or downwards. Even with perfectly normal canals, this is sometimes extremely difficult. When the aviator is in a cloud, his plight is even worse, if his natural compass is not functioning aright. Experiments have therefore been made with the object of finding out in detail about the working of the organ.

Among the many scientists who have investigated the human compass is Professor Dodge now of Yale University. He has devised an ingenious instrument that photographs the action of a man's eyes while he is turning around. This instrument tests the compass. It shows exactly what is going on in the brain when rotation starts and when it stops, when the man can see and when he can see nothing. It shows the smallest amount of rotation that a man can perceive, the effects of training and the confusion that results when he does not move as he expected to move. It shows the lag of the compass, its reliability and its faults.

Some very curious things happen to a person who is placed on the chair and turned round very slowly: As he is moved gradually faster to the right, he reports that he is moving to the right, and then after a time he says that he is standing still. It is almost ridiculous to see a bearded man being turned rapidly round and round, and all the while quite certain that he is not moving at all. Then, as he is slowed down, he reports that he is moving to the left, because the pressure of the liquid is in the opposite direction. When he finally comes to rest, he thinks that he is still moving for a short time, until the fluids have also come to rest. Then he thinks he is moving to the right again, because of what seems like a kind of reversed action. Then he says he is at rest again, and sometimes even thinks there is yet another motion to the left. Thus a person who is gradually started moving and again brought to rest reports no fewer than seven changes of motion, all but one of which are false. Some of these illusions are very similar to the results of the experiment on the eye with the green leaf, and are also called after-images.

If one sits, as I have done, with the head down during rotation in Professor Dodge's chair, and then suddenly raises the head, a curious thing happens. The liquid in one of the canals is suddenly jolted, and the effect is as though a severe blow had been suddenly dealt with a pillow. So strong is the action of this tiny mechanism. It is possible that dreams of falling out of bed are often due to the turning of the head on the pillow, which results in a similar jolting of one of the canals.

The same small organs can also make themselves unpleasantly felt in seasickness, although this is due in part also to digestive disturbances. Many people cannot swing without becoming sick, again, perhaps, because of the over-stimulation of the semicircular tubes of the ear. Children who turn rapidly round and round are sadly perplexing the natural compass, which is quite unable to deal with the situation, and sends out signals of distress.

In a full account of the workings of the canals and their surroundings I would have to tell of what happens in disease and how, when one of them has been destroyed in a pigeon, the bird cannot keep head straight in one direction, or turns somersaults backwards, according to the tube that is affected. And I would have to describe many other interesting experiments and results. But enough has been said to give an idea of this wonderful compass of the body.

(i) IS THERE A SIXTH SENSE?

It used to be said that a human being had five senses, and mysterious references were often made to an unknown sixth sense which was ascribed sometimes to savages, sometimes to wild animals, and sometimes even to women. But if count be made of the senses that have been described, it will be found that a sixth sense has already been mentioned and several more than six, if we include the four different senses in the skin. In fact, there are more senses at the disposal of the human body than were ever imagined.

Instead of the five senses of the school books, there are really ten or more, including the four senses once classed as "touch." If each different kind of sense organ were considered as providing a different sense, we should have to say that there were some *forty* senses! Some of these unsuspected senses will be described in this and the following section.

A woman once came into a London hospital carrying a baby. This unfortunate child was in continual danger of being dropped on the floor as the mother moved about the room, for every few minutes she had to look at her child to make certain what position it was in. When the doctor spoke to her, the baby fell, according to the story.

The muscles by which she held the child were lacking in what is known as the kinæsthetic sense, the word being taken from two Greek roots, meaning perception of motion.

Embedded in the muscles and tendons are small organs responding to pressure, very much in the same way as the pressure organs of the skin respond to external pressure. When a muscle contracts, pressure is exerted on these organs and a nerve impulse is started. Many of the muscles work in opposite sets, one set, for instance, stretching out the arm, and another bending it, so that in almost every position of the arm one or other of the sets of sense organs is being stimulated. Consequently a normal person generally knows in what position his arms are lying without looking at them. Similar organs are also to be found hidden deep in the tendons, and in the joints and bones.

There are the organs which give us our general ideas of the nature of solids and liquids, our broad notions of the properties of matter. A book has weight. The weight is registered by the kinæsthetic organs. A fence cannot be walked through, nor a house. The fact is first announced by the same structures. A puddle or a heap of leaves can be walked through. The kinæsthetic organs tell us of the resistance that they offer. And when the kinæsthetic knowledge is combined by the central brain with the knowledge of appearance and form that the eye gives, the child's education is well begun.

We have seen that whenever a change takes place in a muscle, of such a kind that this becomes longer or shorter, or alters its shape in any other way, organs are in action. A sensation then results, very much as a telegraph operator will give a signal to a man at the other end that the line is working satisfactorily. Now this message from the muscle may, in its turn, start a new movement, and the second movement, a third, and so on, so that the body, left to itself, can often execute a whole series of actions when once a start is made. A person brushing his hair or sweeping a room can go on perfectly well while talking, leaving the body, like any good subordinate, to carry out the action, after, we may say, the order has been given.

So numerous are the internal receptors that some of them may be destroyed or put out of commission without seriously affecting an action, the work being done by the remainder. Without them we should nearly be helpless, and in fact, they seem essential to most of our every-day actions, while if we were suddenly deprived of all our other senses, we could probably get along with the kinæsthetic sense alone. A famous psychologist, Professor Watson, states that "even an extremely fine singer's voice is little disturbed" by cocaining the larynx, which puts out of operation many of the organs in the skin, "but does not affect the sense organs in the muscles and tendons."

Thus, just as large business sometimes has two systems of communication, one to receive orders, and if necessary to take them to the highest authorities and send back instructions, the other between the departments, so that these can keep in touch with each other and the business may operate harmoniously as a whole; in the same way, the body has two systems of receptors, the one to receive stimuli from the outside world, so that the proper adjustments may be made, the other to receive stimuli from within the body, providing checks and regulations for whatever actions are being performed, and helping to carry out and repeat actions once begun. These two systems are sometimes called extero-ceptors and proprio-ceptors, meaning receivers from without and within, the former including the "five senses," sight, hearing, etc., and the latter the sense regulating the muscles and tendons.

In addition, there are other organs that take stimulus from within the body, but not very much is known about them. There are the receptors which tell us when we are hungry, when our breathing is disturbed, and so on. Interesting experiments have lately been performed to show that the feeling of hunger, or rather sensation, as it should more properly be called, comes when the walls of the stomach contract. A small balloon of rubber was passed into the stomach and blown up through a rubber tube that came out through the mouth. Any air that was forced out of the balloon could be registered by an indicator at the end of the tube. The subject was asked to say when he had the sensation of hunger, and it was found in every case that air was then coming out in rhythmical puffs, showing that the stomach was contracting in regular waves, in preparation for the food that ought to be filling the void! The other internal receptors, which are concerned when one feels vaguely well or ill, sleepy or energetic, are still awaiting investigation.

This is all that we shall have to say directly about the particular sense organs or receptors. All of them serve the same purpose, to carry messages of disturbances from one part of the body to a more central part, so that the proper adjustment may be made. Sometimes the disturbance is outside the body, as in the case of smell, sight and hearing, sometimes within it, as when hunger is felt. The organs are placed for the most part where they will be of use. The eye is in the highest part of the body consistent with good protection, and not on the knees or elbows. But, where organs such as the pain spots are not needed, they are not found. Surgeons report that certain internal parts of the body are quite insensible to the pain of the knife, although, of course, they are sensitive to pains of the natural kind. A knife in the appendix is an emergency not contemplated by nature!

(j) WHY WE CANNOT SEE THE STARS BY DAY

Sensations cannot be measured exactly. It is impossible to say whether the sun is a hundred or ten times as bright as the moon or a star. What has been done is to find out just how much stronger the light must be so that we can notice the difference. This just noticeable difference is found to be proportional to the light already present.

Two men were once arguing about the lights on two lighthouses. One said that the light on the first was twice as bright as the other, because it could be seen twice as far out at sea. The other man, who knew something about the lights, declared that it was four times as bright, because it was listed at four times the candle power. Which of these holiday-makers was right?

In the year 1860, a great German scientist made a long series of experiments to find out, as he put it, what change in sensation is produced by a change in stimulus. Professor James, in his "Principles of Psychology,"* has translated the remarks of a great contemporary on this problem. "Every one knows that in the stilly night we hear things unnoticed in the noise of day. The gentle ticking of the clock, the air circulating through the chimney, the cracking of the chairs in the room, and the thousand other slight noises, impress themselves upon our ear. It is equally well known that in the confused hubbub of the streets, or the

*Published by Henry Holt & Co.

clamour of the railway, we may lose not only what our neighbour says to us, but even not hear the sound of our own voice. The stars which are brightest at night are invisible by day, and although we see the moon then, she is far paler than at night. Everyone who has had to deal with weights knows that if to a pound in the hand a second pound be added, the difference is immediately felt, whilst if it be added to a hundred weight, we are not aware of the difference at all."

One and the same stimulus produces an entirely different effect according to the stimulus which is already present. The problem, then, came down to this. What is the smallest weight which when added to a weight of one pound, will be felt as an increase? What will be felt as an increase to two, three, four pounds and so on? In the same way, how much candle power must be added to a light of one, two, three, candle power, for the eye to notice the difference?

The necessary weights and lights, might be expected to vary, for, as we have seen, in a noisy railway station it is sometimes nearly impossible to hear a voice which is perfectly clear in a quiet room. The additional sound of the human voice produces hardly any noticeable effect in the one case, and a well marked sensation in the other.

A truly remarkable thing emerged from the experiments. It was found that if a light of one candle power was increased by anything less than a hundredth part of a candle power, no difference could be detected by the eye, but an increase of this amount could just be noticed. If, on the other hand, to a light of ten candle power was added the same hundredth, no difference could be seen, and this added hundredth could be considerably increased without making the slightest difference to the eye. It was not until one tenth of a candle power had been added that any difference was noticeable! And if the original light was of a hundred candle power, one whole extra candle power had to be added.

These are proportionate increases, and the same is true for weights, sounds, sensations of pressure, and so on, though the fraction is not always the same. For weights it is one fortieth; one fortieth of an ounce must be added to an ounce before the difference can be felt, one fortieth of a pound to a pound. Later experiments have, indeed, shown that the matter was not quite as simple as was at first thought, but by and large the law stands today for moderate intensities.

This has some surprisingly curious results in every day life. The counsellors of a certain English watering place once decided that the water front was not well enough lighted. Feeling themselves competent, as many counsellors do, to decide upon any question without expert advice, they voted that each light in that area should be increased by fifty candle power. The result would not be at all what they expected. The small lights would indeed have been considerably increased in brightness by such an addition, but some of the very large lamps would have been practically unchanged, and the good money of the tax payers would have been thrown away. Fortunately, attention was called to the absurdity before it was put into effect.

The same law applies in many other situations for what are called "middle ranges" of sensation, when the stimuli are neither too feeble nor too intense.

The stars are invisible by day, while by night they become clear. This is because the amount of light they give is small, compared with the sun, so that the increased illumination is not large enough to have any effect. But when a person goes down into a well, the sun's light is shut off, and, relative to the light in the well, the starlight increases, and the reflected light from the dust in the air is mostly cut off. A perfectly definite sensation results. This result is also very much helped by the shutting down of the iris in daylight. The same thing may be noticed about the striking of a match or the light of an automobile or lighthouse lamp, which seem all of them curiously dim and ineffective by day.

The same law helps those who sit in the cheaper seats at concerts. The difference between the singer's pianissimo and fortissimo is very much greater in the front seats than in the back, and it might be expected that by the time the sound reached the fiftieth row it would have been distorted beyond recognition. But Weber's law again steps in to our aid, and decides that if all the sounds are reduced proportionately in loudness, the same effect will be produced. This is what generally happens, and one can hear quite well in the back rows, although the gradations of loudness and softness heard are really not what the singer produces. In the same way, shutting the door of the phonograph cabinet reduces all the sounds proportionately, and does not impair the music. But some telephones, especially when they are slightly out of order, seem to transmit the high tones, which we generally use when we shout, differently from the low ones, with a correspondingly unnatural result.

It becomes clearer now what should be the answer to the question started by the tourists about the lighthouse. They were confusing two things, the amount of light given out by the lamps, and the effect that was produced in consciousness or their brightness. It does not follow that, because one light has twice as many candle power, or even carries twice as far as another, it is twice as bright. These things have to do with stimuli, not with our states of consciousness when we are stimulated, such as is brightness.

In fact, a very strong sunlight would make the two lights indistinguishable, and it would be possible to say that they were then of equal brightness, for brightness depends on *what we see.*

So that, one who hears this argument, may well ask whether the moon or the sun was shining when the comparison was to be made, because it would make a difference.

And this question, it is to be feared, will only infuriate the disputers!

Chapter V

CHOOSING WHAT SHALL PULL THE STRINGS, ATTENTION

(a) THE STREETS THAT ARE IN ONE STREET

ONCE three friends, by profession, a doctor, a real estate man, and an artist, were walking together down a busy street. When they arrived at the home of the doctor, where they were to have supper, the small daughter of the house asked the artist to tell her a story.

"As I passed down the road today" said the artist, "I saw outlined against the sky a big dome, whose colour was of dark red gold, and which gleamed still redder by the light of the setting sun. And as I watched, a light appeared at the foot of the dome, and then another and another, as though the evening breeze were blowing a thistle-down of flame from point to point, and then the whole street broke out into brilliance, and I could see the red dome no more. And I thought how I would like to make a picture of all this, that I might show it to all who think the city is not beautiful."

Then the child thought for a time, and as children do, turning to the real estate man, asked him to tell a story in his turn. And he said,

"I can also tell a story of a street. I was passing down when I heard two boys talking about the businesses they were going to have when they grew up. One was going to have an ice cream stand, and he was to start it at a place where two streets came together, just by a subway entrance.

'Then the people from both the streets,' he said, 'will buy ice cream, and the people who use the subway as well.' That boy had the making of a good business man, because he saw the value of a position, and had chosen the best place in the street for his business without being told. I should not wonder if he grew into a very successful man." This was the real estate man's story.

The doctor's story was about a store window. "It was full from top to bottom with bottles of a patent medicine that guaranteed a cure for all kinds of indigestion, and there was a long list of fearsome sounding things that would happen if one did not take a cure in time. I saw men and women stopping at the show window, and I knew they were wondering whether the medicine would do them any good. I could see that what they wanted was not Gloria Gland Extract, but two medicines that cannot be wrapped up in a rainbow-and-gold paper, and they are fresh air and sleep. But I could not tell them."

"Was that the drug store on Charles Street?" asked the child. Her father nodded.

"And where was your street?" she asked the real estate man.

"Charles Street" was the reply.

"Mine was the same" said the artist.

This is a child's story, with a psychological moral.

The three men had been along the same street at the same time and had looked at exactly the same things, but they had seen three different streets. The street of the artist was a place of beauty, where lines and forms and colours came together to make a picture. The street of the business man was a place of lots and sites and locations, where Opportunity lay for those with eyes sharp enough to see it. The street of the doctor was the abode of men and women who had made themselves sick by their own folly. The copper sky was present to the sight of the other two but they did not notice it. Each failed to notice what was very plain to the others. With the same surroundings, their attention was on different things.

At any instant, there are innumerable stimuli coming to every one of us from the outside. Of these, by far the largest number pass unheeded, and only a few of them do we select for attention. You who are reading this book are thrusting away from consciousness, and refusing to react to, a whole host of messages from the outside world.

There are first of all messages from the muscles and tendons all over the body, which tell us the position of our limbs. Then there are the sense organs on the skin. The reader has, in the last few hours, probably not noticed whether he has been feeling warm or cold, unless the temperature has been uncomfortable. But thousands of temperature spots have been sending in their impulses, only to be disregarded, like much of the news that reaches a newspaper office. Wherever our clothes touch, the pressure spots have been busy, and especially that part where the greater portion of our weight happens to be supported at the moment.

How long is it since you thought of the pressure on the soles of your feet? And yet the messages from the many pressure spots there have been conscientiously delivered, week in and week out, only to be disregarded in favour of something more important. It does not matter, generally, that there is a feeling of pressure on the feet, and there is, as a rule, no necessity to take any special means to meet the situation which the pressure registers.

In the same way, there are certainly many sounds falling upon the reader's ears, which he also disregards. There is perhaps the ticking of a clock, or the distant rumble of traffic, or the sound of someone strumming a piano, none of which is heard unless by what is called a "nervous" person.

If the reader will listen a moment, and count how many sounds there are in the room which he had not noticed while he was reading, he will be surprised at their number. Always there are innumerable sounds, that are not observed until the attention is specially called to them, and the poet Keats has finely used this fact at the end of one of his sonnets.

> "Hark, hear ye not the hum
> Of mighty workings?. . . . .
> Listen a while, ye nations, and be dumb."

In the same way there are odours that are not noticed unless they become important enough for action to be taken on them, or for them to enter consciousness. I may pass through a city where nine hundred and ninety-nine odours assail my nostrils, as happened to the bishop in the story, and may pay attention to none of them. But when I reach home and there is a slight smell of escaping gas or of burning, I immediately give attention and take steps to meet the situation.

Attention is thus selection from the thousands of stimuli that come to us from the outside world. The stimulus or group of stimuli which, at any particular moment, controls action, is the centre of attention, and flashes out clear in consciousness. Add up the countless stimuli from the skin and muscles, the ear and the eye, and it is easy to see what a vast number there are to be selected from, and how few, comparatively, are chosen. It is attention to this or that kind of stimulus that makes one of the chief differences between men of different professions and types. What decides which stimuli shall be attended to or selected?

This will be the subject of the next few pages.

(b) HOW THE ADVERTISER GETS HIS MESSAGE READ

The following advertisement appeared in two different journals. The names and products are changed.

THE LABORATORIES OF THE GREAT EASTERN CHEMICAL COMPANY CONDUCT ELABORATE SCIENTIFIC RESEARCH, MUCH OF WHICH APPEARS TO BE USELESS AT THE TIME. BUT MOST OF IT IS ULTIMATELY USED, AND EVEN THAT WHICH TURNS OUT TO BE OF NO PRACTICAL ACCOUNT ADDS TO THE STORE OF HUMAN KNOWLEDGE.

The second advertisement ran:

THE PRODUCTS OF THE GREAT EASTERN CHEMICAL COMPANY CAN ALWAYS BE RELIED UPON FOR ABSOLUTE PURITY, AND MAY BE USED IN PERFECT SAFETY BY THE MOST PARTICULAR. THAT IS BECAUSE OF THE HIGH STANDARD MAINTAINED AT OUR LABORATORIES, WHERE THE MOST SKILLED CHEMISTS ARE WORKING FOR YOUR SAFETY AND CONVENIENCE.

Why did the Company mention in the one case their advancement of knowledge, and in the other the high standard and safety of their products?

This we shall try to answer in this chapter. But first, there are other questions that should be raised.

A blind man cannot notice the sunset, or read an advertisement, nor a deaf person give attention to the sound of the wind. There are innumerable things about us that the form and nature of our sense organs will never allow us to know. As I sit writing this, ether waves of all lengths go sailing by me at an incredible speed, which, acting through my sense organs, ultimately give rise to the states of consciousness called heat and light. The longer waves, sent out by the wireless stations, which make the ether round like a choppy sea, can never affect us, unless we turn them into sound. In the same way, we are, in the main, unconscious of the presence of electricity, although many feel uneasy before a thunder shower. It has already been seen that animals appear sometimes to possess sense organs unknown to us.

The nature of our receptors determines, to a large extent, what stimuli shall be selected. Many stimuli we *cannot* perceive. But even of those stimuli we *can* perceive, we only select a few. What determines which ones?

Now the two main things that cause one particular stimulus, or group of stimuli to stand out from the total situation, are movement and intensity or size. A lecturer whose talk is interrupted by a loud noise, such as a pistol shot, or the booming of a big clock overhead, would not find it necessary to beg his audience to pay attention to the interrupting sound. The sound itself would compel attention. People are born that way. Similiarly when some students let the smell of bad eggs into a political meeting, the intensely nasty odour compelled the attention of everyone in the hall. Everybody notices a flash of lightning, or the bright light from burning magnesium or fireworks. All of these things present a very intense stimulus. Advertisers often try to use this principle, by showing brilliant lights. The man who advertised his wares by shouting out descriptions of them through a megaphone at the top of his building was endeavouring to secure attention by *intensity of stimulus*.

In the same way, a thing that is unusually large attracts attention. Most of us turn to look at a very tall man on the street. More people read a large advertisement than a small one.

Most important is movement. If an animal is in the woods, and all is still about him, he may not notice a hunter a few yards before his eyes. But let the hunter move any visible part without making a sound, and the animal is off like a flash. This works for the animal's protection. Things that are motionless are, in the long run, less dangerous than things that are moving.

The same is true for human beings. A column of men in movement will be seen by a man at a much greater distance than if they were still. A shooting star will be seen and pointed out, when the sky is full of other stars just as bright but apparently motionless. It is probable that moving bodies are more easy to see because the image which they cast on the retina affects a larger number of neurones, the messages from which help each other, like a team of men tugging at a rope. One of the men alone may be quite unable to move the rope, but all together they do it easily. Advertising men again, those shrewd practical psychologists, know the value of motion. The moving signs on Broadway almost force the attention of the passer-by, however old an inhabitant he be.

Movement is change of position. Change of any kind seems to attract attention. If a familiar object is moved from the room one will very often notice the gap, while before, one hardly even knew what was in the gap. If a man shaves off his moustache or has something done to his front teeth, it often happens that his friends will know that there is a difference without being able to decide what it is. A clock or watch that suddenly changes its rhythm will immediately draw attention. Anything that disturbs or adds a new factor to the present situation is likely to be noticed.

These kinds of stimuli will be selected for attention by all of us, because we have inherited a nervous system arranged in certain ways, and which works in a certain fixed manner. Other stimuli will be selected or passed according to the previous EXPERIENCE OF THE INDIVIDUAL. This experience may be recent or of long standing, and it is called by different names accordingly.

Experience of recent date, may give rise to an *attitude*. Thus, in one well-known experiment, a person is shown a number of pieces of paper of different colours and shapes. These are uncovered for a moment, and at the same time the person is asked what colour he sees. Of course, he can say fairly closely what colours were present. If he is then asked what were the shapes of the pieces of paper, he cannot tell with nearly the same accuracy. The stimulus of the spoken question provides the necessary experience to cause him to pay attention to the colours, rather than their shapes or sizes. In this case the experience is nearly simultaneous with the situation.

Suppose now that the instructions had been given before the experiment, either immediately, or a day, week or month, preceding. In this case the cause of the selection would rather be called an idea. Thus if a man, going to a certain town, was told that he would sooner or later meet a certain person and was asked to notice whether this person was a trifle lame, he would attend to this detail, selecting it from all other details. It might be a day or a year before the meeting occurred, but provided, as we say, that the instructions were remembered, the reaction would be modified by the previous little bit of experience. If, after giving the report, the observer was asked the colour of the same man's eyes, he would probably be unable to answer. When a man is wanted, the police send out a description of him over the country, drawing attention to the right points, and thus aid in the detection of the criminal.

But there are certain details about a man that only a trained eye can see, such as symptoms of certain diseases, or little betraying details about his clothes. If a layman was sent into a roomful of people and asked to notice how many looked as though they might have Bright's disease or neurasthenia, the chances are that he would not be very successful. That is because his training and education have not been of the right kind. But training and education are only previous experience, spread out and more or less carefully arranged. A medical student will be told what things to look for in Bright's disease, and later he will be shown these things in actual cases. It is thanks to this experience that he is able to be on his guard for certain details in other people.

In fact, it is fair to say that his past experience has completely changed his selection of stimuli when he meets another person.

Practically every piece of experience affects our selection of future stimuli, or changes the relative strength of stimuli that will turn up again in future situations. When we have been for a holiday with a man who owns a fine flock of sheep, we notice, through the window, on the return journey the sheep to which we should otherwise have been indifferent.

A man returning from a fishing trip or who is an ardent fisherman will scan the face and appearance of another carrying fishing tackle much more carefully than one whose chief interest is golf. One who is just engaged to be married will look at the rings on the fingers of other ladies, comparing them with the one he has bought. A student at a university had been in the habit of taking a certain journey in the train every day on his way to school. Not until he had taken a course in geology did he see that a certain rock, which he had passed many hundreds of times before, was of peculiar formation. The experience of the class room, which can be reduced in the long run to certain stimuli falling on the eyes and ears, (but in the old days, alas, on other parts also!) had caused him to single out this one feature of a situation already well known to him. If he had been asked a question about that rock, he could have given the proper answer, and the reaction would then have been completed, which in many cases does not happen.

All this is used by advertising men in many varied and ingenious ways. First, to take a piece of experience that has just occurred. On a set of steep stairs coming up from a subway in London where there is no elevator, the words "For breathlessness take so and so," are printed between the steps so that no one can miss them. Most people become breathless hurrying up the stairs and the advertisement is immediately singled out.

In the same way, experience of a short time before is used to secure attention. What are called topical advertisements are of this and the first kind; for example, if there has been a great fire, the fire insurance companies skilfully use that fact by mentioning it in their advertisements. After a very successful play, a book of the same name is apt to be a success. Even a song or an ice cream may thus become popular. If the Prince of Wales has visited a place, the shoe stores will advertise that he is wearing their brand of shoe. If a comet has been visible, advertisements are apt to appear containing a reference to it.

In the same way, special happenings in the world at large are cleverly utilized to help sell goods. Thus, after Dempsey beat Carpentier for the heavyweight championship of the world, an advertisement appeared stating that the victor had taken a certain patent medicine. Other advertisements describe how some one in the same or a neighbouring town has been cured by a certain kind of electric battery. This is apt to be more successful than an account of the cure of some one in a distant city because it more nearly touches the experience of those for whom it is intended. Sometimes, however, for obvious reasons, the cure is reported to have taken place across the continent. The earlier or more organized experience that we call education is also put into service by advertisers. An appeal to buy will be expressed very differently in a paper that is read by college men from that in one intended for those still at school. Different ideas and different facts will be used and different things stressed.

This brings us to the two advertisements quoted. The first was intended to be read by college students; these, after their four years of college experience, would be impressed by the claims of a company professing devotion to knowledge. The other was written for an intelligent class of readers, but one whose interests are mainly of a practical nature. To tell the college senior that the products of the firm are pure and safe does not make very much contact with his immediate past experience. To tell a business man or housekeeper that the company pays men to advance knowledge would probably provoke a smile, even if the advertisement were read through, which probably would not happen in many cases.

Each advertisement used the particular experience of the readers for whom it is intended. And each, in that respect, is a good advertisement, for it gained attention.

In exactly the same way, advertisements in technical magazines are differently worded, with different facts, from those in general magazines, even though the same product may be advertised.

An advertisement, to be successful, *must touch the past experience of the reader*. This principle is recognized by advertising men, though they often express it differently. It is the first consideration in successful selling of every kind.

(c) WHAT IT MEANS TO GO TO COLLEGE
TRAINING ATTENTION

A great deal has been written of late to show that the college trained man or woman receives, on the average, a much higher salary than the high school graduate, and that the high school graduate receives more than the boy or girl who has merely passed through primary school. This is meant to prove that the training which comes from education increases a person's earning power.

Now this is perfectly true, but in many ways it contains a false argument. Take two boys, one of whom is industrious and intelligent and who attends to his job, while the other is stupid, lazy, and can be led astray by anybody promising him a good time. There is no doubt which of them will be likely to do well in school. John, the intelligent boy, will probably stand somewhere near the head of his classes and will be urged by his teachers and friends to take as much education as possible, while James, the stupid boy, will struggle through his school work, each teacher in turn being glad to get rid of him. He will probably never even qualify for higher work. Ten years later, one will have a profession behind him, while the other will in all likelihood be in a blind alley.

John doesn't become a doctor simply and wholly because he has been in high school and university.

Of course, this training helps him. But his success is due also to the fact that he is intelligent and industrious, while James fails because he is dull and lazy. Even though John had no more education than James he would be the more successful in after life.

College men, on the average, succeed better than untrained men because they are capable and industrious. Because they have been capable and industrious they have tried to give themselves the best possible preparation for their life's work.

It is much the same thing as when two yachts are racing. The captain of the one that is left behind might claim that the other had caught a better breeze, while the truth is that the one is built so that it can catch a lighter breeze It is the bad workman that envies the tools of the good workman, when the latter has been clever enough to pick the best tools.

Izaak Walton, the master of fishing, was sitting one day at the same brook with his pupil. The master seemed to have all the luck and the pupil persuaded him to change tackle, but even with the master's rod the young man could catch no fish, while the master pulled out the fish under the young man's nose.

Education is the tool which the more intelligent and

industrious make for themselves. It works in several ways.

First of all, it enables man to select different stimuli, that is, to pay attention to different things. The artist and the doctor and the real estate man selected different things in the same street, and they would be able to deal with the points they had selected in a way impossible to the untrained man. Not only the course of their selection but also their power of reaction have been trained. The doctor could prescribe for the sick persons he noticed, he could do something about it. The artist could paint the sunset he had seen. Education changes both the situations which will appeal to a man and his response to them.

Even though it were unpleasant to the doctor on his holiday to jump out of his car to help a man whom he saw overcome by the heat, he would stop and give aid. If he were asked why, he would probably answer that he must be true to his ideals as a physician.

One of the greatest things that education gives is the ideal of service. This means simply that the educated man will see the larger situation and meet it in the larger way. No training is worth while that does not do this. Nurses, teachers, editors of journals who are worth the name, all have their professional ideals, which means that, regardless of their own feelings, they must meet the situation that their training enables them to see, and react in the way in which their training has shown them. A nurse sleeping in the next room hears her patient in distress. She knows it is her duty to rise, and if she is a good nurse she rises, however tired she may be. Another person in the same room might not have heard the sound of trouble at all, and, in any case, might not have considered that she ought to go and help.

So a college man who sees that his town is not working

the schools properly will turn out and try to do something to make them better, provided that he has been at the right kind of college and has been properly taught. His education helps him to see the contradictory facts of the situation, how the people are paying for the good of the next generation and how the next generation is not being helped. And if he is true to his ideals, if he meets the whole situation in the way his education has shown him, he will try to *do* something about the matter.

The uneducated man can neither see what is wrong, nor does he know the remedy.

Education gives vision to see life, not in small fragments, chief of which is one's own interest and pleasure, but to see it whole. The larger the field a man is in, the smaller appears the man himself by comparison. The larger the world a college man lives in, the smaller seem his own likes and dislikes.

So that the reason many employers like the better college men to work for them is threefold: They are more intelligent to begin with. They are trained to see more things. And in their larger world their own selves are less important.

Their minds and their ideals are different.

(d) ODDS AND ENDS ABOUT ATTENTION

There is an old story handed down from mediæval times that the devil very much disliked the Lord's Prayer because those that said it were doing him a direct injury. Whenever he heard anybody beginning it, he hurried up to tempt the one who was praying. Now personal attention to a matter of this sort by the devil himself has a very powerful effect, and consequently nobody was ever able to repeat the Lord's

Prayer through without some distracting thought entering his head.

Unfortunately for the truth of this picturesque tradition, the same distraction occurs whatever be the nature of the thing repeated, provided that it be sufficiently familiar. Attention is never constant, as it appears to be, but goes in waves. It is said that no one ever attends to a single thing for more than a second. Let the reader try to fix his attention on some one feature of the room in which he sits, such as a piece of pattern on the rug. He will find that, very soon, something else will begin to edge its way in. Nature never holds still the kaleidoscope of the conscious mind. Always she is turning it round and the fresh patterns appear. And this has the definite purpose of bringing to mind as many associations as possible. It is not the fact observed, but its meaning and associations that matter, and only by an automatic bringing in of associations can past experience be given full scope.

Another interesting thing to do is to take a sound or a light that you can only just hear or see, and attend to it carefully. This may well be done with a watch placed across the room in such a position that it is hard to decide whether one hears it or not. The sound will then come in waves. If now the waves be timed, and this can be done roughly by counting the pulse, it will be found that they occur at fairly regular intervals. These waves are probably due, in part at least, to some kind of change in the ear. Now it is very difficult to say just where the explanation lies for this and all the other changes in attention. But, at least, it is possible to deny the claims of certain money-making mystics who maintain that some occult power of Attention or Concentration may be developed by gazing at a black circle. What really happens in this case is a slight hypnotism, and it is certain that general concentration on one's work is not developed by this means. Indeed, there is a possibility that one who practices these exercises may make himself less able to concentrate on his work.

Another question that is often asked is whether it is possible to attend to two things at the same time.

The window thieves in New York used to have an interesting way of stealing. They would take a child eight or ten years old and tell him to walk past a jeweler's window. Then they would ask what was in the window and exactly where everything lay. On the first few times a boy was made to do this, no very satisfactory result was produced, but after a month or so's practice the reports improved. In the end a wonderfully accurate account would be given of everything in the show window, with exact details of number, size and position. This information was of very great assistance to the thieves when the attempt was made. A man would be sent to break the show window, followed by another, who knew from a diagram where all the valuable things lay, and would snatch what was wanted and disappear in the crowd.

The child who is thus employed makes a kind of mental photograph of the contents of the window, which, by practice, it is possible to retain for a while and examine at leisure. This is what then happens when we seem to be attending to a number of things at the same instant, and the picture is called a memory after-image. A memory after-image is also produced when the countryside is lit up by a flash of lightning, and one can notice things in the picture after all is dark again. Such imagery may rival the vividness of *reality*, when it is sometimes termed Eidetic from the Greek.

Those sleight-of-hand men on the stage, who "do seven things at once," are really only attending to one. The others they have practiced so that they have become habitual. Julius Cæsar is said to have dictated to seven secretaries at the same time. If the story is true, he thought so fast that he was able to pass his attention from one to another in succession and keep them all busy. He certainly was not attending to seven letters at once. The story seems in a way possible, in view of the ability of the executives of some modern businesses, who seem to have an incredible faculty of turning rapidly from one person to another, one department to an entirely unrelated one. Julius Cæsar was one of the greatest of all executives. Much the same explanation holds of those chess players who can play eight games blindfolded at the same time.

People are often met, and some of them ought to know better, who will tell you that they can work more efficiently if they have a slight distraction in the room. A lumber merchant once told me that he could not think clearly unless there was a buzz-saw within hearing. In the same way a good lady who took some children from tenements near the "loop" in Chicago, where the noise from the cars is terrific, was much disappointed to find they could not sleep in the country. They missed the noise!

Now my buzz-saw friend and the Chicago children were both victims to something very similar to a drug habit. These noises had become so habitual that, like salt, they caused discomfort when they were absent. And yet there is no reasonable doubt that they were harmful. They used up nervous energy that should have been employed usefully, and, although the effort to thrust them out of consciousness was not felt, nevertheless the strain was there.

But there seems little to say for the man who proposed to build a school next to a garage, *because*, as far as the author could make out, "the children would soon get used to the noise."

Finally: it must be remembered, when we speak of attention, that we are not explaining, but only *naming*. It seems certain that the name attention has been applied to a number of different activities. In fact one psychologist, Dr. Rubin has called it the "psychological maid of all work."

When the forty-foot pump did not work, Galileo declared it must be that "nature abhors a vacuum" only up to eighteen ells! We seem to be finding similar limitations to the use of the serviceable word attention!

Chapter VI

HOW THE PAST IS BORN AGAIN IN THE PRESENT

(a) SEEING AND PERCEIVING

SOME time ago a friend of mine showed me a book which he had just bought, and of which he was very proud. The book itself was rare, but that was not what seemed to interest him, but rather some queer unintelligible-looking marks on the corner of one of the leaves. When my admiration was asked, I could not honestly give it until my friend burst out with the words, "It is Charles Lamb's signature!"

Both of us saw the marks on the book, but he alone saw the signature of Charles Lamb. What had held an important meaning for him was to me simply ink marks.

In the chapter on the baby we saw how the child was at first bombarded by stimuli which started impulses in his sense organs, but which had no meaning for him. He had the same nervous messages from the eye as do you or I when he looked at a newspaper, but he could not interpret the messages. Certain nervous impulses were started in his hand and arm when he grasped a ball. Certain other impulses were started when he put the ball in his mouth; others, when he put it to his nose, dropped it on the floor, and held it before his eyes.

Now this means that there were at first present in the baby a group of relatively unconnected and diffuse states of mind. Just how clearly these were all connected up it is impossible to say. But the nebulous sensing of a child "moving about in worlds not realized" must be something very different from

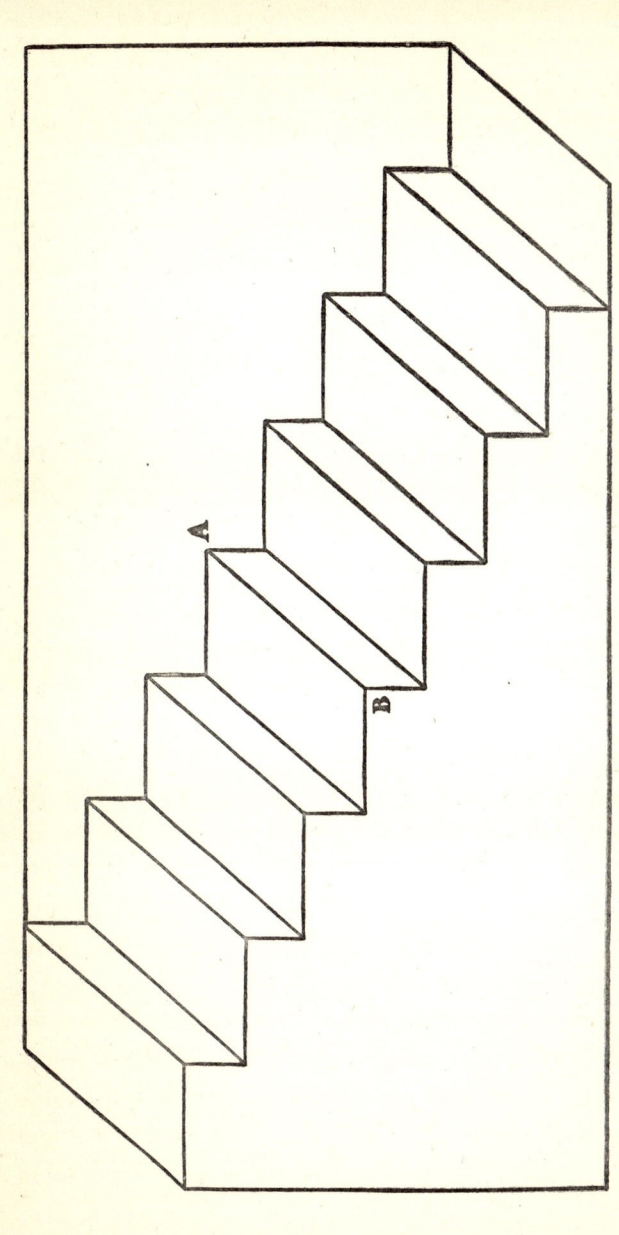

The drawing can be seen as a flight of stairs or as a cornice. Most people see the flight of stairs first, but the cornice can generally be seen by running the eye from A to B, and mentally "pushing" B inwards. It is nearly impossible to see what is actually there, namely three mutually parallel sets of straight lines.

We read past experience into the message from the retina. Gestalt psychologists think that perception of depth is here given directly, without the aid of experience. They claim that a figure in three dimensions is seen because this is the easiest way for it to be seen.

the clear cut perception you or I have of things, inadequate though even this is according to the poets and their brothers the physicists.

As time goes on, however, the world begins to join up and lose its chaotic character. Some say this is done by relating totally meaningless "sensations". Others that it is a process whereby vague form gradually becomes more complex and more detailed, much as a lantern picture on the screen may gradually come into focus.

If we wish we may contrast the totally meaningless "sensation" with the meaningful "perception". Or we may speak with the Gestalt group of the gradual growth of Insight. In either case we shall be in good company!

We shall speak of this "educated" state of mind as perception. An adult sees or hears practically everything in this way. So that there is a sense in which universal education is already accomplished!

Suppose one is viewing a table. We do not see the table as our eye really shows it to us, but as our past experience has shown us that it is.* We still see a square table whether we are sitting at it for a meal, standing in the room above it, or looking at it slantways from a chair. If anyone believes that he sees what his eye shows him and not what his experience tells him, let him try drawing from memory the table with four legs as it appears to one sitting on the floor in the room. Without special training or special gifts, the table will be drawn as it is, not as it is seen.

We see by means of the past as well as the present, through the day before yesterday and the year before last. We see, not what our eyes tell us to see, but what our experience has told us to be true.

*The Gestalt group attach less importance to experience. They claim that there are certain forms, such as right angles, that the eye tries to force us to see.

As a matter of fact, it is easy to convince oneself that one has never yet seen a square table top as it actually is. Most positions show it as a diamond of some shape or other, and the only possible way of seeing it square would be from a point at equal distances from all four corners and closing one eye. But even this does not give a square image. The retina, the sensitive part of the eye, is curved, and warps the image. It is not by means of the eye alone that we recognize squareness, but by fitting square blocks, and so on, into each other, and observing how they look. The play of young children with blocks, which seem to adults so elementary, and often so senseless, is really of very great importance.

The way in which we see, not what the eye presents to us, but the product of past experience, is neatly shown in such figures as that of the cornice. Here it is possible to see two things with only one image on the retina. The figure looks either like a cornice or like a flight of steps, and in both of these alternatives the experience of the person who sees the figure plays at least a part.

It is very nearly impossible to avoid bringing in one's past experience to interpret the present. As one gazes into the glowing embers in an open, old-fashioned grate, with a coal fire, patterns and faces begin to appear. The same thing happens with the clouds, especially at sunset, and with the pattern on the wall paper. Each person sees different things, according to his own particular experience, and it is exceedingly difficult to make other people see what seems perfectly obvious to oneself. It is interesting to make a large ink blot and pass it round a company of people asking them what it is like. Almost invariably the same blot will look like three or four different things.

Sometimes, however, past experience deceives us, and

the image cast upon the retina is misinterpreted, giving rise to what is known as an illusion. An illusion occurs when the wrong meaning is given to a stimulus. Thus, a certain showman once had a room with a swing in it so arranged that the room could be swung up and down. People were brought into the room and were set on the swing which was very slightly moved, in order to start the semi-circular canals working and help in the deception. Then the room was swung, gradually at first, and then, little by little, more, until it was finally turned right over, while the passengers in the swing moved only a fraction of the amount from their normal position. But all were convinced that they had actually been upside down at one time during the swinging. They had misinterpreted the visual images, thinking that these meant that they themselves were being turned over. Precisely the same images were produced on the retina in the two cases, and the meaning had always been motion of the individual concerned, never of the ground on which he stood or sat. The passengers were quite right in interpreting the stimulus as motion of the swing, for they had only their own experience to go on. And in the inconceivably greater proportion of cases their experience would have led to the right conclusion. Another instance of past experience leading to wrong interpretations is to be found in the well-known figure of the line with arrowheads on the ends. The line is judged shorter or longer according as the arrowheads turn outwards or inwards.

This is probably because we are estimating the areas contained, and not the lines, although other explanations have been given. Experience of similar lines in the past tricks us into believing that the length is shorter or longer.

There are many other illustrations of a similar nature;

some depend on the fact that we are apt to allow for perspective in the world around us, as in the case of the square table, so that if lines be suitably drawn, we may make a false allowance.

The exact explanation of all the illusions is hard to find, and many different opinions are held about them. The Gestalt psychologists claim that many of them are due to processes occurring in the apparatus of vision. Others claim that they are really mental misinterpretation.

It is often said that experience gives us habits of reaction and perception.

If that is so, many illusions are *bad* habits; for they result in the wrong reactions or perceptions.

(*b*) HABIT, EVERYBODY'S PRIVATE SECRETARY

It will be remembered that the nerves which carry messages inwards from the surface of the body and back are made up of a number of separate neurones or cells that specialize in communication, and that these work by relay, handing on the message from one to the other.

Now when one sends a telegram to some distant part, or dispatches a parcel across the continent, when once the message or your parcel has arrived at the main lines of communication, the rest of the journey is made quickly enough. To send a cablegram to Europe will take perhaps a couple of hours, while the actual passage across the Atlantic occupies less than a second. The delay takes place at the ends of the cable, the relay points. Very much the same thing happens with the relay points in the communication system of the human body.

Time is lost somewhere when a message is sent. Most of it is taken up with the points of relay. These are called

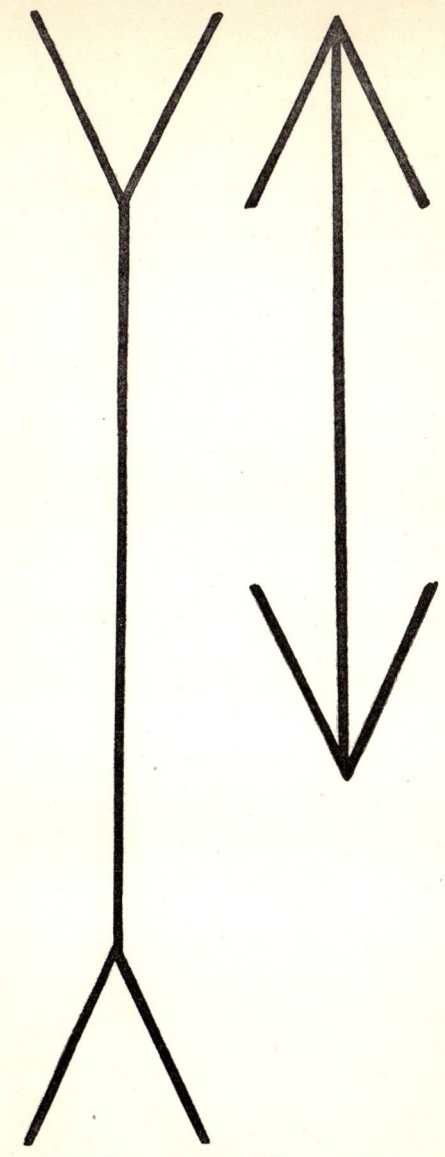

The famous Müller-Lyer illusion. The two lines are of exactly the same length. Why do they appear of different lengths?

synapses, from the Greek words, sun and hapto, meaning I join together. Now there is reason to think that these synapses may form a resistance which is gradually worn down by use. Thus a given set of nervous impulses will pass over the same group of neurones much more easily by repetition. This corresponds of course to what is observed with many of our actions. When any of us was learning to write, it took a great deal of trouble at first to make the hand move in the right way, even though we had the copy before us. After "practice" however, writing becomes easy. We say we have gained a "habit".

Yet it is not so simple. Practice does not always make perfect. Certainly it does not always perfect our mistakes, nor would we want it to do so. Synaptic resistance is then not always cut down by repetition. There are other complications also to the theory that habit runs like a street car, always on the same, gradually smoothening tracks.

The same habit may apparently use more than one set of neurones. Without further training an adult can write quite well with his left hand, about as well as an eight year old child. Here a different group of neurones is used. A chimpanzee taught to do a thing through one eye can do it through the other. A rat trained to run through a maze can also swim through. Here the nervous system seems to work not on fixed tracks like a street car but like a bus.

Thus we have something very valuable, a set of facts we *know* we do not understand. Iris, messenger of the gods, said Plato, is the child of Wonder. It is to be hoped that we shall soon understand how such a "pattern" can be formed and apparently pass over different neurones at different times.

But whatever it is that happens in the brain when we form a habit, there is no question of the *value* of habit.

When we have finished dressing, we walk to the door, turn the handle and walk downstairs to the breakfast room, all by habit. We eat breakfast with a knife and fork, by habit. A Chinaman eats his breakfast just as dexterously, with chopsticks, which habit has taught him to use, but you or I would find nearly impossible. Throughout the day, habit is at our elbow, saving time and energy, helping us to do all the little things that make up the greater part of the day's activities, and leaving us free to devote our attention to newer, more important matters.

Habit is everybody's private secretary, doing all the routine actions of everyday life.

William James, a great American psychologist, wrote a notable chapter on habit which was full of such practical advice that it was printed as a pamphlet and given to the freshmen at Harvard University.

First of all, he says, habit simplifies the movements required to achieve a given result, makes them more accurate and diminishes fatigue. These results can be seen from the example we have taken of learning. To one watching the contortions of a fourth grade child learning to write, the child seems to be employing the muscles of his face, together with both arms and legs. To the learner, and to older people, unaccustomed to the use of a pen, the writing of a single line means a considerable effort, and yet, although the letters produced are very much less accurate, such a writer is very much more fatigued than a practiced one. The same is true of learning any new task. The skilled automobile driver makes fewer movements, drives more accurately and is not so tired at the end of the day. The poet Horace says that black care sits behind the rider. The skillful horseman carries Habit as a third passenger.

Habit also "diminishes the conscious attention with which our acts are performed." The learner has to keep his attention carefully on what he is learning. One who rides a bicycle for the first few times has to make a conscious effort to turn the wheel in the proper direction to avoid falling. The early lessons on a piano seem to contain so many directions, each of which must be carried out carefully and conscientiously, that the unfortunate pupil wonders how anybody can remember them all at once. The beginner at chess or bridge or any other game of skill is overwhelmed by all the rules, and never does a doctor so admire a great surgeon as when he sees his first dangerous operation, when the surgeon, without apparent thought, makes a stroke which could only be taken by the younger man after careful reflection over the textbook. No man skilled at a trade needs to put his constant attention on the routine work. If he does, the job is apt to be spoiled. There is a rhyme about the centipede that walked splendidly until some inquiring person asked him how he walked and which leg went first. Then the unfortunate insect found that his legs twisted into a tangle, and what had been an easy matter when he let habit take care of it had now become very difficult when he gave it his conscious attention.

This is a most psychological rhyme. It contains a profound truth which is illustrated daily in the lives of all of us, for exactly the same thing happens if we pay conscious attention to any well-formed habit, such as walking. A person who has become "self-conscious" about his or her dancing at once becomes awkward. Handwriting that is done with particular attention to the formation of the letters is often not so good. Many performers grow conscious in public of the movements they are making. This means that something will interfere with a perfectly good habit. And just as a good secretary resents interference by the chief in matters of which the secretary usually takes care, in the same way Habit seems to resent interference and the work is not so well done.

Good instruction aims to make desired movements automatic. A good teacher of the pianoforte tells his pupils to listen to the sound of the music they are playing, thereby diverting conscious attention from the actual movements of the hands and fingers. The marksman is told to keep his eye on the target, and the batsman at cricket to hold his eye on the ball. In this way, the habits already formed are allowed the opportunity of working with no disintegrating influence to spoil the job. Critics have said that good art is often unconscious, and this, if true, can only mean that the artist has his technique so perfectly under control that he does not have to think about the means of obtaining his effects, but only about the effects themselves. Certain it is that the poet or author often does not know why his work is good so well as those who take it upon themselves to explain the work of art to others.

How to break a bad habit? This is also discussed by James, in his remarkable chapter, which the brief account here given is meant to induce the reader to read for himself. Later, in the book, there will be shown the methods which have been developed since James's time for dealing with undesirable habits, such as biting of fingernails and fears of lightning and other things.

Habit is the poor man's private secretary, and a good, bad or indifferent secretary, according to training. Train your habits well, and they will stand you in wonderful stead. Let them receive more authority than is good for a subordinate and they will ruin everything.

(c) HOW WE REMEMBER

Memory always seems to be more mysterious than anything else in our life. We live through an experience, it is past and gone. And yet we can re-create it, bring it back again to mind. We pass through a street, once, twice or thrice. Never in ten years do we go near it again, and yet on passing down the street after ten years, we go unerringly to the right house. Something seems to be stored in the body or the mind. It is as though the mind were a well, in which were dropped the pictures of all the places we have ever visited, and in which lurks a guide that whispers directions for repeating all the actions we have ever once performed. A mystery indeed.

And yet the mystery is not really so mysterious as it might seem. In fact, far from being any special "faculty" that is used on special occasions, memory is of precisely the same nature as any other kind of intelligent living. It might, indeed, almost be said that memory *is* intelligent living; living by means of past experience. If an individual is in any particular situation, the higher his type of nervous system and the better it is working, the more of his appropriate past experience will be brought up to aid him. Suppose I am told that Mr. Smith is coming tonight and I wish to remember what he looks like. Now at some previous time I have heard the words "Mr. Smith" pronounced at the same time as I have seen the gentleman in question. If then, on the second occasion, my nervous system is working properly, at once on hearing the words "Mr. Smith" the same picture comes up again.

I say "I remember what he looks like."

But this is only bringing up appropriate experience out of the past. The proper connections have been made. The right stimulus calls up the proper piece of past experience.

This is all that memory does and is. To remember is to be able to use past experience. And past experience, to be available, must not only be stored, but must be tied to the right stimulus.

Suppose again, I revisit a place where I have not been for many years and take the right turnings for my destination. Then I am said to remember the place. The sight of the streets and houses serves as a stimulus for the correct response. On the other hand, it may not be necessary to go to the place to remember it. I can say to a friend, "Think what Main Street looks like," and an image will be called up in his mind. Whether I go to the street or whether I imagine it, in either case I remember it. In each case the proper stimulus is necessary before I remember, that is before I can take advantage of previous experience.

In order to remember anything, we have to make certain, first that we have the correct response and then that the response is tied to the right stimulus. Lastly, the right stimulus must be given to bring out the response again. In practise, the main difficulty lies in making certain that the right response will follow a certain stimulus, and all kinds of methods have been invented to tie the two up together. Better than all memory systems, in general, for this tying up of response to the stimulus, is learning in the proper way. First of all, interest increases memory. Benvenuto Cellini, that amazing mediæval artist, states in his autobiography, that one evening in his early childhood he was sitting with his father by an open fire, and that he asked what was the small animal in the flames. Thereupon his father dealt the astonished boy a sound cuff on the head, saying "This I do, my son, not because there is any evil in thee, but because that which thou hast seen is a salamander." The father had wished the boy to remember the incident all his life, and had taken this rather drastic means of securing interest. Benvenuto was not incapable of an occasional lie to adorn his story! But this story has the sound of truth about it.

Anything that increases interest makes for better memory.

All the details of an interesting event will be recalled, whether the interest be due to emotion, pleasure, novelty or anything else. People always remember all the insignificant details about surgical operations which they have undergone, the picture on the screen round the bed, the exact appearance of the room where the anæsthetic was given, and so on. But it is not necessary to go to the length of a surgical operation in order to produce interest. Competition makes interest, as can be seen in the case of the small boy. He will remember every small detail about the teams with which his own school comes into conflict, their weight, age and records of last season. Other things also, for one reason or another, hold a great interest for him. It may be automobiles, or it may be radio. On such things his memory is apparently infallible. One reason why the boy and girl are often thought to have better memories than their father and mother is that they are more interested, less shopworn in the mart of life, than are their elders. And in the same way, the talented person who seems to remember everything is often found to be interested in everything. A man who is interested in people will remember their little peculiarities, one who is interested in locomotives will remember points connected with them. Instead of crying "I wish I had his memory" we should often, and more correctly, say, "I wish I were as interested in things as he is."

It might then be given as a first rule for improving one's

power of remembering any given subject, "Be interested in the subject."

It is perfectly possible to acquire an interest in anything. I once heard of a doctor's thesis that was written to describe the sizes of the grains in various kinds of sand. The author of the thesis would have found the size of a grain in a sand pile intensely fascinating, *because he had made a thorough study of sand grains*. It turned out that his work was of very great practical importance for the manufacture of cement. And this is not an exception. Any subject will respond in increased interest if only sufficient study be devoted to it. The more a person knows of a thing, the more interested he is in it, and the better he remembers. So that if a better memory is desired for facts connected with business, the rule is to learn more about the business. If a doctor wishes to improve his memory for the affairs of his patient, let him take more interest in them. If anyone wishes to remember better what is being done in current literature he should take a real interest in literature, not in what other people think about him for being ignorant of literature. Nature cannot be tricked. Each thing that is really learned provides a peg to hang other things upon. The more one knows, the more interesting is one's subject to him and the more and better pegs he has to hang new facts upon.

Only do not make the mistake of thinking that people who have different interests from one's own are necessarily uninteresting. The professor whose work seems so "dry-as-dust" may live within a veritable romance of his own subject. Rather than be contemptuous, one should be envious, because the other holds the only key to a fairy-land denied to most of us.

The next thing, if one wishes to improve one's memory for a given subject, is to be certain that one understands the general principles on which the subject rests. Here a technical training is a help. Very many, of course, acquire this knowledge of their work without such a training. But training makes it possible to obtain the benefits of other people's experience in a shorter time. A man who thoroughly understands the laws which govern the rate of exchange of the dollar, and can link up each variation with some political or other event, will have a better memory of actual changes than the one who simply tries to retain the different rates like flies on a flypaper. The photographer who really understands the theory and possibilities of colour printing will remember the name and the details of a new colour-photography process much better than one who is relatively ignorant of what has already been done.

Of course every man engaged in a trade or profession must have some knowledge of principles. To this extent he remembers things in his own department better than the layman. But, speaking in general terms, the higher a man rises in his profession, the more fundamental will be found to be his knowledge of the principles of his work, and, in general, the better memory he will be found to have in his own field. The high officials of our large corporations have a memory that is almost uncanny for the facts which affect their business. That is the reason why they are high officials. Of course, such men often have an excellent memory for unrelated facts also. But this native capacity is enormously helped by their grasp of fundamentals, and by the way they have mentally organized their subject.

Each fact is like a peg for another fact to hang upon. Each principle is like a cloak room with a thousand pegs.

(d) REMEMBERING SCHOOL LESSONS

Memory of such things as school lessons depends very much on the method of learning. Of course, the pupil who is really interested in the subject will remember it best, and, as we saw in the first chapter, interest can be created.

A good many pupils who maintain that they cannot take an interest in a certain thing really do not want to be interested. And again, the last section shows that learning to understand a thing will result in a better memory of it than just learning to say the words.

In addition to these general points about remembering, there are certain rules which will be found especially helpful by students of all ages, from primary school up. For the human mind works in the same way, whether the person who owns it be in a primary class or the post-graduate class of a University. The same rules hold good for students of a musical instrument, or of such things as typewriting or stenography.

First of all, it is better to distribute practice when learning. Suppose, for instance, that I wish to learn to use the typewriter or the ukulele. It will be much better for me to spend two half hours a day for forty-five days, than to try to cram the learning into nine days, by practicing five hours a day. Actual experiments have shown a difference of twenty per cent in favour of the distributed practice.

In the same way when learning an assignment of school work, if an hour can be allowed, it is better to divide this time into forty minutes practice one night and twenty minutes the next morning. Three twenty-minute periods would probably be better still provided that the interest could be kept up. In typewriting, the best method of practice at the start seems to be to work for three or four half-hour periods a day. The same division of time is used by a good many of the best pianoforte instructors.

A second thing that helps in learning is to have a thorough knowledge of four things about the lesson. First of the purpose of the thing that is being learned. If the adults of a family would consider how meaningless to a child are many of the things that have to be learned at school, they would have more sympathy with a child's distaste for school subjects. Suppose that the father of a twelve year boy could suddenly be taken out into a country of giants, who would by physical force compel him to learn by rote such things as a table of logarithms, or the Chinese weights and measures, and that this process were to continue forty weeks in the year for ten years. He might then begin to have an idea of how a boy regards his education during the period from six to sixteen years. All learning that has no meaning wastes energy and induces habits of boredom. No assignment should be given whose purpose is not clear to the pupil. Any parent has the right to complain if lessons are being set and tasks given that seem to have no use and no application.

Knowledge of progress and errors is also necessary for the quickest learning. In certain factories it has been found of the greatest help to have each man's output noted and recorded day by day. Good teaching does not allow any subject to be monotonously learned, without any record of improvement. One experimenter found that results were improved by eighteen per cent when progress was known.

Particularly is this important when a pupil begins a

new subject. Such a study as German or Latin or algebra is often very discouraging at the start, because, for a month or so, every day seems to bring new rules, against which the pupil seems to make no headway. And when there seems to be no progress, progress is actually hindered. The apparent standstill is in danger of becoming very real, and each new lesson is remembered with more and more difficulty. It is here that a mother or other older person can be of the greatest use, using her affection and knowledge of the child to point out the daily improvement. In the same way, no good teacher allows a pupil to go on making the same mistakes. No mother can expect her child to show improvement in such a thing as speech or handwriting, unless the bad points are continually and carefully noticed. It is found that even in the University it is of no use to tell a student to improve his English compositions. Unless he is constantly and persistently told where his mistake lies, no amount of fault finding will do any good. He must be taught. The same thing is true of accent in speech.

The fourth thing that should be known when learning a lesson is the time when the work is to be reproduced. There seems to be a different feeling and a different method of attack when a thing is being learned for a longer or a shorter time. Children at school, of course, generally know when the lesson is to be, and they are apt to learn their work for the purpose of the lesson, rather than with the intention of mastering the material. Here again, a parent can be of the greatest possible use by giving the right attitude.

If the material is to be learnt by heart, it is very important not to try to learn by sections but as a whole. Thus if it is several stanzas of a poem, this should be read through and through as a whole, not first one stanza and then another. In this way, each line and each stanza becomes linked up with the whole poem, and it is not necessary to link up each separately by a separate learning As a child, I remember well knowing the separate stanzas of my pieces, but not knowing the order in which they came! Experiments have shown that those who are quickest at memorizing poetry and other similar matter almost always adopt the method of learning by wholes. When a difficult part is met, this may be specially singled out for additional repetitions. It is thus possible to reduce the time of learning by anything from a third to a half.

These rules will seem to be helps to learning rather than to remembering. This is as it should be. Learning and remembering are so closely connected that any improvement in the one generally implies an improvement in the other. Better remembering almost always means better learning. Better learning means better remembering. There is no royal road to memory.

Teach the child or yourself to learn properly, see that he has the proper interest, that he is not working in the dark, but has the proper understanding of what he is learning and why he is learning it; see that the delicate work of remembering is not hampered by insufficient sleep or over-excitement, and his memory will be at the highest pitch of efficiency.

We can learn to remember if we remember how to learn.

(e) MEMORY SYSTEMS

It is said that Lord Macaulay was able to read the front page of a newspaper, advertisements and all, and reproduce the whole page afterwards, word for word. Lord Tennyson had such a good memory that he oftentimes did not know whether he was quoting or composing, so well did he remember poetry that he had once read. Each of these men was naturally gifted, but no possible training could have given them this unusual power of retention. We have to take our natural retentiveness, and make the best of it.

This will come as a great disappointment to many, who have the secret feeling that it ought to be possible to take one of the advertised courses and thereby produce for themselves an infallible memory. But it must be borne in mind that when we remember a thing, there are involved the three processes of learning, retention and recall. Learning can be improved, as we have seen, and this improves recall. But it seems quite impossible to improve the middle factor, retention. We all have a certain retentiveness that is natural to us and to our nervous organization. This we can develop to its natural limit, or spoil by abusing our body or mind. But we cannot increase it.

So that in strictness, memory, like matter, can be economised but not increased. It is easier to add a cubit to our stature than to add an inch to our natural power of retention.

This does not mean, however, that the memory systems advertised are of no use. Properly employed they have their place. Personally I have never been able to obtain much benefit from them, but I have known many who found them very valuable. It may be that my own failure was due to the fact that I did not spend the necessary time to make myself perfect in their use. Perhaps the kind of work which I do does not lend itself to memory systems. In any case, it must be remembered that no system can ever give the best kind of memory, which comes from thorough mastery and understanding of one's profession or business. But even to one who thoroughly understands his work, and is intimate with its every detail, there come occasions when it is desirable to remember a list of unconnected points. There are certain times when knowledge does not help much.

One man, for example, finds it useful in his business to remember the names of his different customers, and finds this difficult because they are so numerous, and because he sees some of them only once a month. Another wishes to remember without notes half a dozen successive points in a speech he is to make. There seems no doubt, from the reports of those that have used them, that memory systems can help in these cases. Of course, the same results could in each case have been attained by simply giving the proper kind of attention to the thing to be remembered. But the fact remains that many people do not give the proper attention. They have to be taught to give it. The better memory systems claim that, after a while, it is not necessary to use the system. If that is so, the course has accomplished the very valuable work of training a man so to give his attention that for all intents and purposes he has improved his memory for things of a certain type.

The systems may be divided into two classes. There are those that depend on verbal association, and those that rely on key words, with visual pictures. Let us take an example of the first. Suppose that you wish to remember the following list of purchases.

Butter,
Steak,
Potatoes,
Floor wax,
Writing paper,

Shoe laces,
Hair tonic,
Pipe cleaners,
Talcum,
Hair nets.

If one used the verbal-association method, butter would be connected with the steak by cow. Steak and potatoes hardly require any connection. Potatoes are generally in a sack, which lies on a floor, thus connecting with the floor wax; floor wax makes the floor bright and glossy, like the best quality writing paper. Writing paper is used for writing legal deeds, and legal deeds are binding, which connects with shoe laces. Shoe laces become stringy when wet, and so does hair, bringing us to hair tonic. Hair tonic makes hair clean, connecting with pipe cleaners. In a pipe bowl there is fine white ash, like talcum. Talcum connects with toilet, brushing the hair and hair nets.

Thus the list as remembered by one who practised this system would read,

BUTTER .. milk .. cow .. STEAK.
STEAK, POTATOES.
POTATOES .. sack .. floor .. FLOOR-WAX.
FLOOR WAX .. bright and glossy .. WRITING PAPER.
WRITING PAPER .. legal deeds .. binding .. SHOE LACES.
SHOE LACES .. stringy when wet .. hair .. HAIR TONIC.
HAIR TONIC .. cleans .. PIPE CLEANERS.
PIPE CLEANERS .. pipe .. white ash .. TALCUM.
TALCUM .. toilet .. brush hair .. HAIR NET.

It must of course be remembered, when criticizing this list, that practice is given by the lessons in forming new associations, so that these become very easy to make. One who was expert in the system would doubtless devise very much more satisfactory links than those given. For instance, the link between steak and potatoes is not very good, because there are other things that are commonly ordered with steak in a restaurant. It is quite possible that any one using this method to memorize the list might come home with electric light fixings, from the association between porterhouse steak and fixings.

Perhaps the reader can improve the chain words. It is useful practice.

In the second type of memory system there is a framework of words, to which the objects are added by means of a mental picture.

One of these key lists, a very simple and short one, is as follows:

1. Myself, I.
2. Tootoo, Locomotive.
3. Pawn shop balls.
4. Golfer (foursome).
5. Hand, five fingers.
6. Sick, hospital, etc.
7. Dice, "seven-come-eleven."
8. Ate, restaurant.
9. Nein, a German.
10. Tent.

Suppose, now, it was desired to remember the same list of things by this method. I would make a picture of myself with my pockets full of butter, and the butter, perhaps, running over in the hot sun. The locomotive might be pictured running over an enormous piece of steak. Instead of three golden balls there would be three potatoes hanging outside of the pawn shop. The golfer would be trying to make a stroke on the waxed floor and falling down ludicrously. The hand would be pictured as a fist coming through a large sheet of writing paper. The sick man would be tied to the bed by shoe laces. Four bald men are casting dice for a bottle of hair tonic. A man sits in a restaurant, eating pipe cleaners served like spaghetti. A fat and perspiring German walks along the street talcuming his face. A large tent is pictured with an enormous hair net hanging in the doorway.

Thus, each of the key words, which have to be learned first, is associated in a mental picture with one of the articles. Of course, the more elaborate systems have many more than ten key words, but the principle is the same. With a little practice it will be found that the list given can very easily be used to remember a list of ten articles, which need not be recalled in the same order. Thus, the person doing the trick would be able to say immediately that number seven was hair tonic; number three potatoes and so on, which is not possible by the other method. The systems have similar devices for remembering faces and names, and also for figures.

I have seen a roomful of people surprised by and entertained by a young man who asked for lists of ten objects, each of which was given by a separate person. Such a list might be: toothbrush, Ford car, dictionary, lawn mower, turbine, pencil, chair, razor, aeroplane, triangle. These were repeated at intervals of a quarter of a minute. Then a second list was given of the same character. After that, both lists could be repeated, or the name of any object in either or both lists given by its number. Thus it might be asked, "What is number seven on the first list and number two on the second?" The answer would be given without mistake as "chair," and whatever was the corresponding object in the other list.

It must, however, always be remembered that such systems cannot give the best kind of memory, which comes, it has been pointed out, from a thorough understanding of the subject. Nor can they make the ordinary person's power of retention equal to that of the specially gifted. As to the merits of the two methods given in this chapter, this seems to depend on the individual. I have known people very successful with both. The first method, which relies on linking up the names verbally, has been extensively practiced in England. Perhaps this is because the education in that country, being, for many, of a "classical" nature, gives more practice in the use of words.

(f) "THE FIRST THREE LESSONS SENT FREE"

This heading suggests a very common trap to catch the unwary. Suppose it is French or Stenography that a person wishes to learn. Looking in the newspaper, he sees somewhere an announcement something like this.

"You can accomplish marvellous results even in three lessons. You can learn to name in French the objects in the room in this short time. Send for the first three lessons, which will be delivered free, and if you are satisfied with your progress, remit us five dollars for the rest of the course."

The inference expected and desired is that if such results can be accomplished in three days, what cannot be done by six months' study?

Alas, the result will probably be that there will appear

as much improvement in those first three glorious days, as in, perhaps, two weeks of study later in the course!

Learning follows the law of diminishing returns. If a man puts two weeks' work on his field, he obtains a crop, of sorts. If he puts another two weeks' work, making a month in all, he obtains a better crop indeed, but not so much better as might have been expected. If he gives twenty weeks' work, it will probably require an expert to see how his crop is an improvement on that of the man who put in only eighteen weeks.

Each additional period of work brings in less returns. And in the same way, each additional period of learning brings smaller results. What is called the "curve of learning" rises sharply at first, and then gradually the slope is less and less.

The first periods of practice produce much more effect than the last. For example, when a skilled typist tried to increase his speed, it was found that the first five days' work raised the rate from three hundred and fifty words an hour, the original speed of the operator, to four hundred and sixty, a net increase of over a hundred words an hour. From the fortieth to the forty-fifth day, there was an increase in speed of considerably less than fifty words an hour. The next five days showed still less improvement, not more than fifteen or seventeen words an hour. The limit had nearly been reached. It is safe to say that, using the same methods, another month's practice would hardly have repaid itself. The same length of time, five days, had produced increases of speed varying from a hundred to seventeen words.

Progress in learning is never smooth. Always there are times where one seems to be making no headway. These are the times when despondency and discouragement are apt to set in. The course is given up. The teacher is changed. Just what the plateaus are, as the standstills on the curve of learning have been called, has been the subject of considerable controversy. Many explanations are given, but into them we shall not enter. Generally it has been said that there is a more or less mysterious process of settling down, by which habits already present have to be worked up before others can be acquired. If a person is learning Latin, he cannot make much progress in translation until the declensions are thoroughly mastered, while one who is learning the piano cannot become at all proficient until the position of the notes, printed and on the key-board, is perfectly familiar. Others again say that the level places, or the periods of no apparent improvement come through lack of interest. Any teacher can bear witness that there are mornings when the attention of the class is nearly impossible to secure. These mornings are often the product of "the night before," when there had been an election parade or a dance or something else that has proved too interesting to admit of good school work the next day. Often the weather will produce an apparent listlessness. Some indeed claim that a class is an excellent barometer, and that they can tell what the state of the weather is by looking at their class without going outside.

All these things will make pauses in learning, which, if the curve of progress were drawn, would result in socalled "plateaus," or level places. It is quite certain that the plateaus are nothing mysterious. They are due to checks that for one reason or another are bound to occur. They represent simply the fact that the individual always meets with impediments that prevent his progress from showing the smooth, unbroken slope that is ideal. A good teacher will realize what is happening, and somehow or other prevent the standstill. Perhaps that is one of the most important things the teacher does, to keep the mental traffic moving and prevent stagnation.

One encouraging thing that comes out of the study of progress in learning is that almost everything we do can be improved, if we give conscious and intelligent attention to the improvement. Professor Thorndike of Columbia states that in his experience, no "Mental function has ever been deliberately practiced with an eye to improvement, and with the proper opportunity for the law of effect to operate," without some improvement taking place.

We all waste ourselves and our vital forces. We live, probably, in a state of mental and physical efficiency far below the forty per cent efficiency of some of the locomotives. Very few of us practice the daily occupations of everyday life. And yet Professor Thorndike found that seven hours spent on practice in such an activity as mental multiplication of three figures by three figures more than doubled the speed!

Perhaps the education of the future will be able to turn our day into two, three days, or even a week, by teaching us how properly to work the everyday affairs of life. Certain boys of my acquaintance cut down the time of their dressing in the morning by one-half, as the result of thinking out the best method and practicing it. Hardly one of us, probably, reads as efficiently as he should. Scientific management has shown that the methods of the average craftsman are incredibly wasteful. The output of a bricklayer was greatly increased simply by telling the man what to do and making him practice doing it. Even such an operation as loading a truck with pig iron was enormously bettered by doing the thing right and practice in doing it right. An experiment with girls engaged in folding handkerchiefs in a factory showed an improvement of three hundred per cent in the number of handkerchiefs folded!

This last miracle was brought about simply by allowing a minute's rest every five minutes!

No business man that I know has ever deliberately practiced the dictation of letters. Yet there is no question but that such practice would pay for itself many times over in time saved.

Undoubtedly the schools of the far future will teach us how to save ourselves in living. The man of the future will accomplish far more with far less effort. Dr. Thorndike now tells us that we can go on learning without much decrease in efficiency right into middle age. More than ever the future man will prolong his education through life.

Instead of "picking up" his skill in the everyday tasks of life, he will be instructed in the best methods. He will live better because he has been *taught* to live.

(g) TESTING THE IMAGINATION

A simple experiment of Professor Pillsbury's will help the reader to understand this chapter. Let the reader call up to his mind the water rushing from a faucet into a sink. Does the sound of the water at once thrust itself forward? Or does the visual picture come first, with the sound following by an effort?

Those who *hear* the water and then see it by an effort are apt to be of what is called the auditory type of memory. These people remember and think in sounds. The ones who *see* the water and have some difficulty in bringing up the sound are generally of the visual type. Of thirty people there are usually about two or three who, in this experiment, can hear the water much better than they see it. Some have to force up the picture with considerable effort.

Many see and hear the water about equally well. They are generally of the mixed type that thinks and remembers by a combination of images given by hearing and vision. There are other types also, such as the "kinæsthetic," that remembers things in terms of muscular movements, and perhaps also the verbal type, that reduces everything to words.

The most notable investigation into these images, which are really perceptions produced by some other than the original stimulus, was made by Sir Francis Galton, the eminent English scientist, about forty years ago. Sir Francis Galton sent round to a number of people, distinguished scientists, a list of questions with the purpose of finding out how clear were their mental pictures or images. They were asked to think of their breakfast table as they sat down to it that morning. Such questions as these were asked about the mental picture.

Is the image dim or fairly clear? Is its brightness comparable to the actual scene?

Are the colours of the china, etc., quite distinct and natural?

Can you recall with distinctness the features of all near relations and many other persons? Can you at will cause your mental image of any or most of them to sit, stand or turn slowly round? Can you deliberately seat the image of a well-known person in a chair and see it with enough distinctness to sketch it leisurely (supposing yourself able to draw)?

A request was also made to call up certain things and consider whether the image was very faint, faint, fair, good, or vivid and comparable to the actual sensation: the list was, the beat of rain against a window pane, the crack of a whip, a church bell, the hum of bees, the whistle of a railway, the clinking of teaspoons in saucers, the slam of a door.

The answers from a hundred people were classified. On the first question, which asked for the clearness of the image, the man who reported the clearest picture of his breakfast table replied, "Brilliant, distinct, never blotchy." The man who scored seventy-five in clearness reported, "Fairly clear, illumination of actual scene is fairly represented. Well defined. Parts do not obtrude themselves, but attention has to be directed to different points in succession."

The middlemost man reported:

"Fairly clear. Brightness probably at least from one-half to two-thirds of the original. Definition (*i.e.* sharpness of picture) varies very much, one or two objects being much more distinct than the others, but the latter come out clearly if attention be paid to them."

The man who scored twenty-five per cent replied:

"Dim, certainly not comparable to the actual scene. I had to think separately of the separate things on the table to bring them clearly before the mind's eye, and when I think of some things the others fade away in confusion."

The lowest man said:

"My powers are zero. To my consciousness there is almost no association of memory with objective visual impressions. I recollect the table but do not see it."

By this scale it is possible roughly to score one's own power of making mental pictures. If the reader's recollection of the breakfast table is about that of the seventy-five per cent man, he can score himself seventy-five. If it is between this one and the middlemost, the score is sixty-seven, and so on.

The fact that people vary so much in this power of making mental images came as a great surprise to the scientific world. Sir Francis Galton claimed that the power was higher in the female sex, and among young people. Some young children seem to have it very well developed and cannot even distinguish what is real and what is imagined. With practice, the pictures can be made very much more clear, and this commonly happens to those using the second kind of memory system described in the last chapter.

An artist, of course, generally has very clear memory pictures, while a musician has generally an unusual power of recalling sounds. Whether this is due to natural gift or training it is hard to say.

Probably both are to some extent responsible. Most of the great composers have been very highly gifted in this way. Beethoven, deaf and composing symphonies for full orchestra that he could never hear, and Mozart writing out the long, elaborate music of the Sistine Chapel from memory, must have been able to recall sounds with a clearness that the ordinary person cannot conceive. But strong auditory memory does not make a Mozart; there seems to be no relation between clearness of mental pictures or images of any kind, and intelligence. Galton, indeed, claimed that the habit of scientific thinking dulls the pictures of the mind.

Thus it may be literally true that Science clips the wings of Imagination.

(*h*) THE GIFT OF FORGETTING

There is a fairy tale that describes how a young man was given the power of hearing everything that everyone said in the world about him. At first he found this gift amusing, but after a time it became so unbearable that the young man prayed for the blessed gift of ignorance. Gossip is entertaining when it concerns oneself, but only when it is possible to select the times and seasons for it. Memory is useful. Without it we could not possibly use past experiences. But universal memory of everything that has happened to us would soon be unbearable, because much of our past experience is of momentary importance only.

Indeed, a universal memory of everything in the past would be as absurd as a universal joint in the knee. We have to select what it is profitable to remember, just as nature has selected certain very limited ways in which the knee moves. To remember everything means to retain all the insignificant details of yesterday, the day before yesterday, and the year before last; what we had for dinner on January the twelfth, 1923, and the exact words of the conversation at that interesting meal; what coloured tie or blouse we wore on that day, and how many times we lifted the fork to our mouth. It means recalling who left the table first, and exactly what passed through one's mind as they did so. And this is only one day. For every day of our lives we should have to remember all these things and more, just what the weather was, whom we saw, and just what we were thinking about at every moment of the day. Truly, forgetting is a gift; not one in a hundred of these things is worth remembering because not one in a hundred of them can be used to help us on another occasion. One may see at any time those who apparently have a nearly universal memory for trifles that are of no importance. They are all gathered together in one place, where they can tell each other what they had for breakfast this day ten years ago, how many flies they killed three days later, and what kind of weather the farmers prophesied the next week. It is an interesting place. The unkind call it a lunatic asylum.

We select what we shall remember, just as we select to what we shall attend. As a general rule, the events and the experience of a recent date are more important than the more distant. It is of greater importance for me to remember that it is raining this morning, or that it was wet yesterday, than the state of the weather a year ago. If I meet a man in the ordinary way of business, it is very important for me to remember his name during the time he is talking to me, but it is not so important to remember the names of the casual acquaintance made in hotel lobbies, and the types of complexion of all the partners with whom I have ever danced. Speaking very generally, the recent is the important, and nature has arranged that the recent is remembered, while the more distant is usually forgotten.

Elaborate experiments have been made to find out how rapidly this forgetting goes on. It is found that it is very rapid at first and gradually becomes less as time goes on. One investigator, working with meaningless syllables, found that fifty per cent was lost at the end of eight hours, most of which was recovered by the next day, and that the fifty per cent was permanently lost at the end of six days. Others, with different material, found only twenty per cent lost in twenty-four hours, and seventy-six per cent was lost after a month. Very much less was lost between the twenty-eighth and twenty-ninth day than between the first and second day. In fact, if a curve were drawn showing the rate at which we forget the happenings of today, a very steep drop would be shown at first, sloping off less and less as time goes on, until in the end a day or so makes very little difference. This curve is called the curve of forgetting.

One of the interesting uses to which psychology has been put is the proposal to send out what are known as follow-up letters according to this curve of forgetting. It is clear that if a customer receives a letter on, say, the first of the month, it is by no means certain that this should be followed up at regular intervals by other letters. Rather, the dates of the follow-up letters, if these are to arrive at the point on the curve where they will do most good, should be very carefully worked out.

Professor Freud, of Vienna, founder of Psychoanalysis, has some interesting ideas about forgetting. He claims that we remember the pleasant and forget the unpleasant. An illustration will show best what he means.

A certain lecturer, of English extraction, had to talk one day about the complementary colours, red and green, blue and yellow. On reaching the lecture room, he began to speak of the pairs of colours, but found himself quite unable to recall which colour went with red. Both blue and yellow came to his mind, but he recognized that these were the wrong names. Finally, he had to look the point up in a book, to the amusement of the audience. This occurrence was very disquieting to the professor, who knew the colours as well as his own name, and had lectured about them many times. Accordingly, he set out to discover the reason.

The explanation was a strange but perfectly satisfactory one from Freud's point of view. Just before the class began he had glanced over the morning papers. One of those contained an account of a disturbance made by a party of Irish Nationalists in New York. A green flag had been carried up and down the street, and several Englishmen had been insulted. Sympathizing, as he did, with the position of the Irish, this was all very painful to the professor, and as he came into the lecture room he had remarked on it. The colour green thus had suddenly become connected with a very unpleasant occurrence, and was therefore banished from memory.

It was purposely forgotten, according to Freud, because it was disagreeable, and in the same way, all forgetting, it is claimed, has a purpose, namely to suppress the unpleasant.

Very many other illustrations are given of the same thing. Freud tells of a lady "who, the day before her wedding, forgot to try on her wedding dress," and had to have it fitted later in the evening. The whole matter of the wedding was evidently distasteful to her, and she divorced her husband very soon after. There is, too, a standing joke about the bridegroom forgetting the wedding ring at the ceremony, and another standing joke about the unwillingness of many grooms to take the final plunge. These two jokes may very well be connected, for, as Freud would point out, there are no instances of a young man very much in love who forgets to take the newly bought engagement ring. Another similar story is of a man who was jilted in favour of an old friend. Try as he could, he was not able to remember the name of his successful rival, and had to ask other people to tell him. It was his endeavour to banish all thought of the other man from his mind, and he had begun by banishing the obnoxious name. My own mother, when I was a boy, used to say of anything that I had forgotten, "You do not want to remember it." Perhaps she was nearer the truth than she or I thought!

Now I do not wish to give the idea that Freud is right in everything that he says. It is quite certain that all cases of forgetfulness are not due to such a purpose of suppressing the unpleasant. In fact, certain researches that have lately been made claim to show that there is no more forgetfulness of the unpleasant than of the pleasant! But, in spite of these results, there seems much to be said for examining any particular case of forgetting to see whether it really meets the unexpressed wishes of the forgetter. Sometimes it is possible in this way to dig up a symptom of some liking or dislike that has been before unsuspected. If a constant churchgoer forgets the name of the new clergyman, one may be certain that the reverend gentleman is not very popular! If a doctor finds that an otherwise good payer has forgotten his cheque, he may be suspicious that the patient believes himself to have been overcharged. Suspect the strange mistake, and you may find out something, for in many cases, at least, the gift of forgetfulness is the shrouding of the disagreeable.

(i) THE FEELING OF HAVING BEEN THERE BEFORE

This is one of the baffling and elusive experiences of everyday life. We are in a strange place, perhaps on holiday for the first time at a hotel. Suddenly, without warning, a certain feeling of familiarity seems to create itself. At once we seem to know the whole scene, windows, doors, pictures, and view from the windows. We recognize the person with whom we are speaking, although, to the best of our knowledge, we have never seen him to this minute. We even recognize the words he is saying, though it is impossible to know what he is going to say.

We have the feeling of having been through everything before! Then, in a flash, the illusion vanishes. The room is ordinary again. The walls and windows have lost their intimacy, and a stranger is again speaking. The landscape is new and strange. The wheels of time are working once more.

A curious and startling experience every time it happens. What is its explanation?

Some of the philosophers thought that each of us has lived other lives before this one. For example, the followers of the Greek Pythagoras held this belief, and they thought that their master had passed through many lives, among others, that of a warrior at the siege of ancient Troy. In a later life, "he bore witness to his Trojan days," says the poet Horace, "by taking down his old shield. Nought had he given to dark death but his sinews and his frame." Those who made this legend, which is thousands of years old, had in mind these flashes of familiarity with the scene, which, of course, were experienced by mankind distant ages ago no less than now. The belief is held by some today. In his "Ode on Intimations of Immortality," the poet Wordsworth says for instance:

"Hence in a season of calm weather,
  Though inland far we be,
  Our souls have sight of that immortal sea
Which brought us hither."

The whole poem is full of references to the same belief, that we have somehow lived before on earth, and that at times we have a flash of insight into a past life. The feeling of having been there before is one of these flashes.

Another explanation, that sounds more scientific and less mystically interesting, has to do with the action of the brain. It will be remembered that the brain is in two halves, and that, in general, the right half of the brain controls the left half of the body, and vice versa. Now it has been suggested that in ordinary times, when, say, a room is seen, the message reaches the two sides of the brain at exactly the same time.

But suppose that for some reason or other, one side receives the message a little in advance of the other, then by the time the slow message arrives we have already seen the room and consequently have the feeling of recognition. The unfortunate fact for this interesting theory is that it does not seem to be true. There is no evidence that the messages do take different times to arrive, and, if they did, it is hard to see how the feeling of recognition could arise. The theory is given as a curiosity. We must look elsewhere for an explanation.

For a *full* act of memory there are necessary four things. First we must learn. The things which it is desired to remember must be experienced together, generally, with the stimulus that is to call them up, though sometimes the connection is made through intermediates. Thus, if I wish to remember the pictures in a certain gallery, it is best to see the pictures *in* the gallery. Secondly, I must retain the memory. Obviously, if there is no retention, there is no memory. Thirdly, when asked about the pictures, or when any other situation turns up that prompts the memory, I must recall the pictures by name or in any other way. Lastly, when recalling the pictures, I must recognize that I am recalling an actual experience, not inventing the name of a gallery and the titles of the pictures. The last process in memory is thus recognition.

It very often happens that we remember perfectly well but do not recognize. There are many well-worn quotations which have become part of the languages. These we are apt to use without realizing that they are quotations, and sometimes, with a conscious thrill as if we had originally said the witty thing. Much of the humour of certain people is of this type. They make a remark which, perhaps, Shakespeare heard one of his friends say, and believe it is their own. In the same way, young authors will often go through all the process of creation and produce an exact imitation of some one else's work. They have remembered but not recognized. In an earlier chapter reference was made to the memory of Tennyson, who often did not know whether he was quoting or composing. This was not really a perfect memory, because it lacked recognition.

Thus it is possible to recall without recognizing. Sometimes, however, occurs recognition without memory, and this is when a person thinks he has been there before. Suppose, for instance, that after I have visited the picture gallery I go to the next city where there is another gallery. Perhaps in some corner of a room there is some insignificant detail, such as a gilded cornice, that is the same as in the last gallery. This will be seen and recognized, but the feeling of recognition, instead of being confined to the one detail, may be spread over the whole room. In that case, I may not consciously understand just what brings the feeling of recognition, but feel that I am recognizing the whole.

To put the thing in brief, the "feeling that one has been there before" is due to recognition misplaced, because, while it really belongs to a detail of the scene, it has spread itself over the whole.

Very often, one who cares to take the trouble can single out this detail that has caused the illusion. Often it will be found to consist of an odour, which will entirely escape observation at the time. I have heard related a story of a man who, whenever he visited a certain house, was always vaguely reminded of something that had gone before. On thinking the matter over, it occurred to him that a trip in Spain figured somehow in the recollection, and then everything became plain. A feature of the Spanish trip had been the number of Cathedrals visited, and the Cathedrals were chiefly remembered in connection with the smell of incense. The lady of the house he visited was in the habit of burning incense, and the faint odour always hung about the house. This odour had acted as the bridge between the two scenes, and had brought the false feeling of recognition. We speak sometimes of a "familiar atmosphere." That phrase is often literally true. It is, indeed, just possible that the expression, "the odour of sanctity," originated with the faint odour of the incense in the Catholic churches.

(j) "IS TELEPATHY POSSIBLE?"

About the beginning of this century there appeared in Germany a phenomenon in the shape of a so called "reasoning horse." President Sanford, of Clark College, has given us an interesting description of "Clever Hans" as the animal was called. He was an eye witness, and heard the horse asked the questions and saw Hans give the intelligent-seeming replies. "The horse is a black stallion," he writes, "of trotting stock, about eight years old. He is spoken to in German, but without special emphasis. We are warned that he will not reply to questions addressed to him in French or Latin!

"His master, standing near him, addresses him in a kindly way and shows him an arrow, a circle and a square drawn on three little blackboards hung up conveniently, and asks him to pick out the arrow. Hans goes to the proper board." Later he is asked how many corners a circle has, and "very properly replies by moving his head from side to side." He then tells, by tapping off the right number, which of a row of gentlemen is the tallest, the stoutest, which are officers, which carry swords, and which has his arm in a sling.

But that is only the beginning. This remarkable animal can tell how much is four times four, and four plus four. He can work out problems in division and subtraction, indicating, for instance, what numbers go into 28. This last question is correctly answered by tapping 2,4,7,14 and 28 in succession. He can change common fractions into decimals, and vice versa. He correctly adds 2/5 and 1/2 by tapping off first 9, and then 10. He can correct his answers when he has made a mistake.

He says on which board a certain word is written, and the number of the board carrying cloth of a certain colour. He spells out the answer to the query, "What has the lady in her hand?" On one occasion the lady in question was carrying an umbrella, and Hans spelled out Schirm, tapping according to a system. He answers the question "between what figures will the small hand be when the time is five minutes after half past seven." He tells the value of coins, indicates the emperor's birthday, identifies people by their photographs!

But the most remarkable thing is yet to follow. He actually guessed the number of which a gentleman was thinking, without stating it. This he did with "astounding success."

"There are no restrictions as to the place we may occupy. We may come as near as we choose, and look on from any side. The horse is entirely free and is managed wholly by means of the voice, with frequent rewards in the way of bread and carrots. If he understands a question he signifies it, we are told, by nodding his head, etc."

A truly miraculous animal! And the miracle was attested by men of all walks of life, including horse-trainers and psychologists as well as the general public. The facts were observed by hundreds of careful and qualified witnesses. They have purposely been presented briefly and baldly, because they are startling enough to speak for themselves.

One doubt will already have crept into the reader's mind. Let us answer it at once. The owner of the horse, "a retired Prussian schoolmaster past sixty years of age, and dressed usually in a long, seedy overcoat, or duster, and slouch hat" was unquestionably honest. He would never take money. He refused all offers to go on the vaudeville stage, or to exploit the animal in any way. He seemed really to believe that his pet was endowed with some preternatural power of reasoning. And no evidences of fraud could be discovered by two highly qualified committees containing army officers, experts in horse training.

And here is another astounding fact. Besides working at the command of his master the horse solved problems for others, also men of unquestionable honesty! This seems entirely to rule out the possibility of fraud on the master's part. And if the explanation was telepathy, as many claimed, the telepathy was between an animal and not merely one, but a whole group of people!

Fraud being ruled out, there seemed then to be one of two things possible. Either the horse could reason, like Swift's Houyhnhnms in Gulliver's travels. Or one mind was able to act directly on another, which is what is called telepathy. The trouble with these explanations is that both are contrary to everything else that psychologists believe.

If a horse, with the known nervous system of a horse, with the physical brains of a horse, can do square root and tell the time of day, then the labours of generations of scientists, with their carefully recorded accumulations of thousands of facts, established in hundreds of laboratories, will have to go for nothing.

If a horse, without any physical stimulus or connection, can read the mind of a human being, and tell the number of which he was thinking, then we shall have to throw our books away.

Psychology is placed between the devil of telepathy and the deep sea of a calculating horse!

The latter possibility was the first to be ruled out by the scientific enquiry. It was shown, for example, that the animal cannot even read numbers!

When the numbers on the cards are visible only to the animal, and he alone knows the number asked for, he is correct in only four out of forty-nine times! When the answer is known to those present he is wrong only once in forty-two times! The same thing is true of his "reading." When the spectators knew to which of the cards he should go, he was *never wrong*. When they did not know, he was *never right*. When one number is whispered to him by one experimenter, and another by another, Hans almost got the right answer, when, in addition, some one in the room knew the answer. Otherwise, he was hardly ever right! It looks as though we shall have to put telepathy into our text books!

The experiment was then tried of putting blinders on the horse, so that he could not see the spectators. For the first time Hans is seemingly disturbed. He persistently turns his head so as to see the questioner. Even though the question was not asked, but only thought, provided that the *answer* was thought and the horse saw the man who was thinking it, the right answer was given.

Now this seeming enigma gave the clue to the whole

mystery. By carefully watching his colleagues, one of the experimenters saw that certain minute movements of the head and body were always made when Hans was answering questions. These movements were made by all those who had had success in questioning him. If the motions were made voluntarily, Hans would make certain movements, even though the wrong answer was thereby given. Those questioning bent over slightly in their natural interest, to see what the horse was doing. When the right number was reached, the head would be raised again, and the horse at once stopped moving! By observing these hardly visible movements of the bystanders, *"movements often as small or smaller than one hundredth of an inch in extent,"* Hans was able to tell when to stop. And thus he appeared to be solving the problem, or reading the mind of the bystanders, when he was simply reacting to small movements on the part of the spectators. In fact, he was a most wonderful "body-reader" but no mind-reader. As Professor Sanford says, he was interested in bread and carrots and he used all the means at his disposal to get them!

Later, indeed, the problem was taken up again by others with the object of showing that, after all, Hans could reason. Other horses were trained. One, in particular, was "especially strong in the extraction of roots!" He answered the following sums correctly: What is the fourth root of 614656? What is the cube root of 5832? He gave the solution of the equations $x - 48 = 46$, and $\sqrt{x} + 12 = 18$! The original committee did not examine the claims of this prodigy, but there seems no shadow of a doubt that the animal used the same methods as Hans.

Psychology can breathe again!

The example of Hans has been taken because it combines

two questions, the first as to the possibility of abstract thought among animals, and the second as to the possibility of telepathy. After the introduction given by the case of the clever horse, I can give what is probably the opinion of most psychologists on thought transference.

As far as we can see in the present state of science, the transference of thought immediately from one conscious mind to another, without any intervening material link, is an impossibility. Such attempts at transference as have been made under anything like strict conditions have always resulted in complete failure.

Thought, of the kind that is ours, seems to require a body and a brain, and it has to be set off by some physical change, generally outside us. The cases of human thought transference, which seem to be established, may very well have been due to some such thing as happened with Hans.

Let us take, as an example, some of the experiments described in Mr. Podmore's book, "Phantasms of the Living." This book contains perhaps the most scientific account yet published of what is generally called thought transference. The experimenters in the cases taken were people of undoubted integrity. The testimony of the witnesses seemed at first sight absolutely conclusive. And yet the evidence they give for telepathy does not seem, on examination, to be of such a character as to justify us in rejecting the results of the labours of generations of psychologists.

On one occasion a person goes out of the room, while those left decide upon an object which the absent one shall name on his return. Perhaps a quotation will show better than anything else what happened.

"Each went out of the room in turn, while I and the

others fixed on some object which the absent one was to name on returning to the room. After a few trials the successes preponderated so much over the failure that we were all convinced that there was something very wonderful coming under our notice. We began by selecting the simplest objects in the room; then chose names of towns, names of people, dates, cards out of a pack, lines from different poets, etc., in fact any things or series of ideas. They (the children) seldom made a mistake."

Of course, it is impossible to be absolutely certain of the reason or the explanation of a thing unless a careful scientific investigation has been made. But if one thinks of the enormous development of human intelligence compared with that of the horse, a difference which is so great that the horse's power of thought is probably not much more than ours has ever been since we were born, it is easy to see that the "Clever Hans" trick would be easy to an intelligent child.

Not only would it be easy, but a much more complicated trick would be easy. And it might be impossible, after practice, for the child to say exactly what were the clues which led him to the right object. In just the same way, the reader of a book will often say that he received a certain "impression" from a book. Or one skilled in observing men will say that he knows what kind of a man he is watching, without being able to say why or how he knows.

It is notable that, careful and precise observers as they were, the authors of the book state "nor were there any effective means taken to block the percipient's channels of sense," and again that "such simple objects would not demand an elaborate code." It must be admitted that it is difficult to imagine how cues could be used to aid in selecting a card from a pack when the children received their message from *strangers*. But the cues which Hans took from strangers would be difficult to believe had they not been seen.

And it is not so hard to believe that the children were guided by some kind of clues as to think that they actually received the thoughts of another directly in their own minds. Let it be remembered again that no scientifically controlled experiment has ever demonstrated the existence of transference. Both at Stanford University and at Harvard experiments have been made. The worker at the latter place, a brilliant young scientist called Troland, found that his subjects guessed right exactly the number of times which pure chance requires. Accordingly he declared that his experiments had "proved the law of chance."

One other experiment was given by Mr. Gurney, which from its peculiar character is worth describing. In this case one person sat at a side of the room with an easel before him, on which was drawn a simple figure. The other person, a woman, was at the other end of the room, blindfolded, until she said she was ready. In two or three minutes she requested that the blindfolding should be removed, and then drew a picture that was startlingly like the original. The position of the easels made it impossible that she should see the first drawing. Fraud was out of the question,

Another mystery, until we remember that the lady had not had her ears plugged up!

The reader will say that it is impossible for a woman to *hear* what kind of a drawing a man is looking at, and to hear it so well that she can reproduce the figure. It does seem impossible! Now it is true that she could not hear what the man was looking at, but she could hear what his reaction was to the drawing, whether his breathing was easy or laboured, whether he was easy or uneasy in his movements and so on. That is the way in which a mother hears whether her baby is sleeping well or not, by observing slight changes that would be lost on everyone else.

And here comes out a startling fact. *The pictures thus drawn and reproduced had almost all of them a sexual meaning,* according to the interpretation of some of the newer psychologists!

Let us see what this seems to mean! The explanation which we shall advance is not, of course, given as in any way scientifically valid, which would be impossible at such a distance of time and space. It is offered as a very tentative substitute for a view which seems to contradict the results of generations of scientific workers.

Somehow or other, the mood of the man, which suggested the picture he drew, communicated itself to the woman, through his motions and his breathing, which she was able to hear. This mood, thus taken from across the room, was reproduced by her in the picture, which, unknown to her, was a definite symbol of what she felt.

The "atmosphere" of the room was that of mixed company, which everyone knows is different from the "atmosphere" of a room containing only men or women. The mutual atmosphere, which each sensed, suggested to each the drawings, which were not "transferred."

Again, an impossible-seeming thing, for a mood so to communicate itself. But something very similar is always happening when a mother lies uneasy in her sleep because the baby is tossing on its bed, when a political speaker "senses" discontent among his audience, or a teacher "feels" that the class is hostile. We all "sense" the mood of those around us. We none of us know the exact signs by which we do so, though the signs are there.

In fact, in the experiment described, much the same thing happened as though a clock in the room were ticking in regular beats of five. Anyone there who was asked to think of a number for the purpose of transferring it to the mind of another, would be apt to think of the number five. And in the same way, the person who was trying to guess the number of which the other was thinking, would probably also think of the same number. And thus there would be a pretty case of thought transference!

Such is a possible explanation of these remarkable drawings. It is difficult to see how the astonishing similarities shown could be brought about, even by this means. But this is no harder to believe than the feats of Hans, which *were* observed.

It seems then unnecessary to bring in telepathy, when we remember the following things: First, that the larger part of the drawings are of an undoubted sexual character, and it may be that an expert on these things would pronounce them all to be so; secondly, that the communications in question all took place between a man and a woman; thirdly, the fact that the "drawings generally run in lots. A number of successful copies will be produced very quickly, and again a number of failures," which seems to show that some kind of "atmosphere" was necessary. In face of these facts I for one would refuse to accept the hypothesis of transference until the experiments were duplicated with the ears of the lady stopped up, as well as her eyes closed, and pictures brought in from outside were reproduced.

If, in the future, those who are working on the problem

can show us cases of thought-transference which will pass the tests of science, this will make necessary a revision of many of our ideas. It may be that this revision will, at some future time, be called for, but at present, sufficiently cogent cases seem to be lacking. What new ideas we have seem to come through a physical stimulus of some kind or other, and not directly from another mind.

Chapter VII

MAN THE MASTER

(*a*) WHY NO ONE HAS EVER DRAWN A CIRCLE

THERE is a famous story of the Carthaginian general, Hannibal, who was trying to invade Italy over the Alps. The passage was hard and very rough, and on the way he encountered rocks which proved to be impassable for his army. Perceiving that the obstruction was composed of chalk, the resourceful general poured over many gallons of vinegar, which so softened the cliff that the men were easily able to make a passage. The tale has been denied by many, but the wonder stories of the ancients have a knack of coming out true!

When he saw the rock, Hannibal said at once that it was chalk.* And he had learned that chalk was softened and dissolved by strong vinegar. This is a piece of what we call general knowledge. The fact that Hannibal can say, "Chalk is dissolved in vinegar," gives him the power to do certain things to ANY PIECE OF CHALK IN THE WORLD.

Now it is possible to use the same piece of knowledge for many ends. Cleopatra, dissolving the pearl to impress poor Antony, used the same general fact for quite different purposes, for, of course, pearl is the same substance as chalk. Hannibal might have gone to Africa and picked up a piece of chalk, with the full assurance that he could make it disappear in vinegar. The chalk was in his power. Or he might have visited the mysterious shores of Britain and astonished the natives of Dover by dissolving a part of their

*An eminent geologist now tells me that the geology of this story is wrong!

cliff. The key to all these situations was one piece of general knowledge. All chalk is soluble in vinegar.

Such knowledge is beyond the power of all but human beings, because it seems that only our kind can see such a piece of rock and decide what makes it what it is, and what is just accidental. The dog knows that a particular morsel is food, but his nervous system is not so constructed that he can separate the goodness or badness of the food from the food itself. He knows what food is bad, but he does not know why it is bad. And this renders such thinking as he has much less powerful as an instrument of adaptation.

In this respect he may be compared with the man who must remember a pack of cards by some individual detail on each card, because he cannot recognize the heart and the spade as the same on the cards of the same suit.

The dog has to deal with the world by particulars because he does not recognize and separate the essential parts of things. We are here speaking relatively, of course.

Now the startling thing about Hannibal and his chalk is that he never had a piece of chalk before his eyes! And yet he saw hundreds of tons of chalk! This is how it comes about. By chalk he meant, let us say, a rock of pure white, of a certain density, and which dissolved in vinegar. Now no piece of rock that he ever had in his hands absolutely fulfilled those conditions! No piece was ever absolutely pure white all through.

No piece ever had *exactly* the right density, for the dampness of the air and other impurities would interfere with that. No piece ever dissolved in vinegar with *absolutely* no residue, so that it would not be possible to say of any particular piece that it was really soluble. And yet, of course, for all practical purposes the chalk was chalk!

We may go a step further. Nobody, even with the aid of the most advanced chemical science, ever had a piece of chalk in his hand. If this seems incredible, let someone try the experiment of sending up to any of the well-known chemical firms for a sample that absolutely fills all the requirements, that is to say, that is absolutely pure. A tube will come back, costing more or less money, according as the buyer is more or less particular. On it will be read, "Contains not more than .5 or .05 or .005 per cent of impurity," according as one has paid a higher or a lower price. No chemical manufacturer in the world would maintain that what he sold was chalk, in the strictest sense of the word. If he did, he would be laughed at. The way in which this is put by scientists is that CHALK IS A CHEMICAL CONCEPT, AND NO CONCEPT CAN EVER BE REALIZED IN PRACTICE.

In the same way, a circle is a concept of geometry. Nobody ever drew a real circle. All of us have *seen* one. It is impossible to draw a real circle, because even the finest draughtsmanship, viewed under the microscope, is like the edge of a saw. Even the finest and straightest line must be drawn on something solid, which is made up of molecules in perpetual motion, so that the line we see is really a chain of tiny, rapidly moving particles, themselves made up of groups of almost infinitely small somethings, these again whirling on their diminutive orbits with astonishing speed! So that our apparently straight and fairly drawn line or circle is really far from straight and even.

But the circles we draw are near enough for all practical purposes, just as are the pieces of chalk we find. While the concept is never actually realized, yet what we actually deal with is so near to the concept that the difference does not matter. And the fact that we are able to form, or separate out, the concept of circle, enables us to deal with every individual circle in the world, and to make better adaptations to situations into which a circle enters, although we know that the concept, like the end of the rainbow, never will be held in the hand by mortal man.

A concept is then a handle that enables us to deal with an infinite number of things of the same kind. It is never found, but what we find is always near enough. It multiplies a million times the power of adaptation, and gives dominion over the infinite realm of particular things. From each one of us there stretch out, like invisible tentacles of Mind, these lines of force, touching all things of which we have knowledge.

Truly, a marvelous advantage over the brutes, and a stupendous instrument of thought, of power to counter environment!

(*b*) THE ROMANCE OF THE CONCEPT

Such a thing as a concept, the use of which, for our thought and action, was shown in the last section, would seem as far as possible removed from romance. And yet, so strangely have things worked round, that the speculation as to its nature is connected with some of the most romantic figures in history.

The whole story hinges on the question, "What is a concept?" In the last section we tried to show the advantage that the concept gives to human thought, how, by knowing something about the properties of a chemical which never can itself be actually realized, we win a power over myriads of pieces of matter throughout the universe and thus enormously increase our power of adaptation to the world. How the concept helps us is plain. What it is, that is not so plain.

In fact, the nature of this open-sesame that casts its spell over such millions of things has puzzled thinkers almost from the beginning of thought.

The earliest people to discuss the question were the Greeks, a number of centuries before Christ. After many years of speculation, there arose among them the great Plato. Plato was, by profession, as we should say, a philosopher, which means a lover of wisdom. But he might have been a poet, so delicate were his perceptions, and so exquisite the beauty of all that he wrote. And at heart he was what we call today a mystic, for he believed that this world was but the shadow of another higher, more celestial land, to which the good man might rise at moments of exaltation. His answer to the question, "What is a concept?" was that it is the only real and true thing. That we have the concept of a table, which includes, and is the original, of all tables. The other tables, he would say, partake of the real table, which is the concept. If we can know the original, we then know all tables, and we actually came to know the type—arche-, or original, type—in heaven, which was once our home. Heaven, or "the heavens," as the Greek has it, contains the pattern of all things on earth. Hannibal would have obtained his knowledge when, before he was born, he was wandering through the celestial land where dwell the types. When he came to earth, all that was necessary was to recall this knowledge by instruction or some other way.

This is the theory of a mystic. Whether Plato really believed in heaven, as he described it, we find it hard to say. But his way of looking at the problem has found many modern followers, who, of course, omit the part of the theory that has to do with life before birth. They say that Plato was speaking in parables, that all he really meant was that the concept is the one real, unchanging thing while all around us is impure, liable to change, subject to death. The chemical concept for chalk never changes and is always pure. Any sample that we see is always changing, by growing damp, and in other ways, and is never pure. What more natural, then, than to imagine a place where everything was pure and unchanging—"the world of thought"?

The next great figure in the controversy was also a Greek and a philosopher, the great Aristotle. Now Aristotle was in many ways the exact opposite of Plato. He was at heart a scientist, and his mind was tied down strictly to earth. Aristotle was one of the first men to realize the value of coöperative research, and, in the manner of the modern university seminary, he had his students out making scientific observations, which they turned into the central college. In this way he wrote, and had written up, surveys of the forms of government of sixty or seventy of the cities round him, a truly remarkable piece of coöperative study. It is possible to see how careful and minute were the observations of these workers by the fact that one of them noticed that the bee goes to only one kind of flower on a journey, and that another accurately described the distribution of hairs on the lion's tail!

Such a man, whose aims were those of practical knowledge, would not be likely, in his theorizing, to agree with any such mystical doctrine as that of the poet Plato. In fact, knowing the man, it would be almost possible to predict his criticism.

"The ideas, as you call them, which you say dwell in heaven, are not really separate things," he said. "They are in no sense real *separate substances*, such as could dwell in heaven or anywhere else."

"To talk about patterns, and to say that the things around us that are not ideas, *partake* of the ideas, all this is to talk nonsense," says the scientist, "and to use metaphors which belong to poetry." Thus the man of science against the poet. But Aristotle himself was able to substitute nothing of any great value for the theory which he tore down. His own explanation of the nature of the concept was as much open to objection as the one he criticized, and he has shared the fate of many critics whose criticism is remembered, while what they offer of their own is forgotten.

The next important chapter came centuries later, long after the birth of Christ. Aristotle had denied that the Concepts or Ideas were separate substances that could exist in heaven as the pattern for things on earth. But he had claimed that, none the less, they have a real existence. The concept of a circle, which is never found but which all circles approach, is just as real as the multiplication table, although neither of them can be actually held in the hand like a book or a pencil. A thing may be real, and yet be intangible, as is the influence of the Press or the law of gravitation.

And Aristotle had claimed that the concept was real in this way. But there came men who disputed the word of the sovereign Greek and claimed that the concept was in no sense a real thing. Some even maintained that the only thing real about a concept was the name, that the name circle was our way of describing a number of things, and that there was nothing more to the concept than this. That was indeed bringing down Plato's heaven to a name!

The cudgels were taken up this time by one of the romantic figures of the world, Abelard, spoiled child of society, monk, founder of the University of Paris, who set by the heels the learned theologians of the day, in character "ambiguous as a riddle," and who was one of the great lovers of all time. The story of the love of this brilliant man for his pupil, Heloise, is one of the most affecting in the world. Their marriage, kept secret for a while, and therefore misunderstood by her uncle, who took a terrible revenge on the brilliantly arrogant young man, all this makes one of the touching, and, at the same time, one of the most horrible stories of all time. Abelard retired to a monastery, Heloise to a nunnery, and there exchanged letters of penitence. . . . .

It was this Abelard who took up the doctrine of the concept, maintaining that, even though it were a name, yet it was more than a name. "It is," he said, "the basis of all knowledge, which a mere name could not be. One who has the concept of circle does more than name all the various circles of the world. The concept is a name, together with something else that the mind has given it. There is similarity in all circles, but this similarity is a product of the mind and does not affect the real circle."

Here seems an abstract enough doctrine. But see whither it leads. I have a concept of man. This means, according to Abelard, that all men are the same, as being men, just as all circles are the same, as being circles. A democratic doctrine, it seems! But Abelard lived in a feudal age. And so one can hear him saying:

"But this sameness is the product of the mind. It does not affect the real existence of the man."

What is given to democracy with one hand is taken away with the other!

Now I have given a brief account of what certain men

have thought about the concept, because of the three unusual figures with which the controversy was connected, and to show an example of the way in which, by the patient labours of many and the brilliant flashes of a few, we have arrived at our present ideas about the mind and its working. Thousands of men have pondered over the mysterious concept. At the time of Abelard, the controversy was at least fourteen hundred years old! In the words of John of Salisbury, a writer of the twelfth century, quoted by Professor de Wulf, "The world has grown old treating of it, and has taken more time for its solution than the Cæsars took to conquer and govern the world."

Much of the argument on one side or the other of this famous question will have seemed to be a splitting of hairs. The men of the ages that came after Abelard are said to have exercised themselves discussing how many angels could stand on the point of a pin! Undoubtedly, there is much that savours of word-jugglery in the interminable arguments about the reality of the universal. And the reason is that the men of that time conceived of the mind as something shut off, and working upon the body, which, in turn, works on the world. A concept seemed to be in the mind. How, then, could it ever become connected with things in the world?

If, on the other hand, a person believed that the concepts were somehow in the outside world, how could they be connected with knowledge, which is clearly in the mind?

Today we have learned, thanks to the labours of those who came before us, to regard a human being as living within an environment, all situations of which he tries to meet. And psychologically a concept may be regarded as simply meaning that one has the power to meet any one of a thousand situations, at the proper stimulus. Thus the concept is connected up with action, not with the mystic and detached Mind of the older thinkers. As to what the concept really is, apart from what it helps us do, that is a question for the wise. And one thing is certain. We would not like to be forced to make a public defence of even this modest position against the brilliant Abelard.

(c) HOW WE REASON

Ordinarily the actions of a full-grown human being run along fairly smoothly. By the time we leave school, most of us have acquired enough habits to take us through the average situations of everyday life. It will be remembered from the earlier chapter that there are habits for dressing and undressing, habits for smoking, writing, turning over the pages of the books we read, and so on. Doughty, the Arabian traveller, describes the clumsiness with which the unlettered Arabs turned the pages of his books . . . they had not acquired the habit, which is at the command of practically every adult of this country. Suppose, now, that a situation arises that cannot be met directly by habit. Perhaps there is a hole in my favourite tie, and I may wish to put it on so that the hole does not show.

Here is something new, not altogether possible to deal with by routine. It is what we call a problem, and when the human organism meets a problem, it has several alternative methods of action, any one of which may be chosen. In the problem of the torn tie, first, I may go away, leaving the problem unsolved. The tie will then be thrown away, and a newer, less pleasing one taken. Or one element of the situation may be disregarded, leaving the situation not really met. I may simply tie up the wornout piece of neckwear, hole and all. Or finally, a definite way of meeting the situation may be thought out, and the problem solved.

I may devise some means of tying that will keep the hole covered. And this is reasoning, which in the main is *the process of meeting properly a situation that, for some reason or other, brings the person to a standstill.* He wants to go on but something in the situation stops him. He "reasons," to get him out of the blind alley.

To take another example. Once two boys who were walking in a pleasure park came across an ornamental pond. The pond was in the form of a square, and it had a square island exactly in the middle, twenty feet each way from the bank. Now in the island there was an apple tree, with large and succulent apples, but the boys had no means of crossing over except two twenty-foot planks which they found on the bank. How did they get the apples, without wetting themselves?

There are several things that complicate the situation in which the boys find themselves. First, there is the attraction of the apples. Were it not for the water, the boys would go straight forward and pick the fruit. The sight of the apples would act as a stimulus for action of a very definite kind. On the other hand, the sight of the water restrains them from action! They do not want to get wet.

So that this situation is self-contradictory to the boys. If they are to solve the problem, they must get the apples and at the same time not wet themselves. They can, of course, leave the problem unsolved, and go away apple-less. On the other hand, they can jump into the water and swim across. That is "cutting the Gordian Knot," but not solving the problem. If the problem is to be solved, the final action must take into account every part of the situation.

To solve the problem, past experience comes into play. The various objects surrounding the pond call up different possible solutions, which are, one by one, rejected until the proper method is found. One of the boys will suggest trying one of the planks, for this has been found by previous experience to be a feasible way of crossing water. This is discovered not to work. Perhaps one suggests trying to jump. But this also is seen to be impracticable. A raft is perhaps also considered, but there is no wood to make it. Each of these suggestions is called out by some part of the situation, and again scored out by another part. The process of calling up associations and scoring them out is accompanied by the clash and interaction of nerve-impulses in the cortex of the brain. During this process the person is "conscious" of first one solution, then another. All are rejected, until the final solution is reached, which clashes with no piece of past experience, runs counter to no association called up by the situation outside. The whole thing is very much like the work of a locksmith, who tests out first one skeleton key and then another to find which one will fit. But the work of the nervous system, with its complicated receptors, its lines and organs of co-ordination, its possibilities of the most delicate distinctions, its wonderful skill in making the adjustments for which experience calls, is far beyond the capabilities of any locksmith.

Finally, as a result of this miracle of adaptation, the sight of the two planks suggests to one of the boys, out of his past experience, that one be placed across the corner, and the other placed from it to the island. This is found to work, and the apples are picked.

This is a simple example of reasoning, but it shows how the process is always carried on. There must be a problem, that is to say a situation which holds up the individual. Very often such a situation contains contradictory stimuli. In the example given, there are the water and the apples, but this contradiction is not always necessary. But always such a situation contains stimuli from which it is hard to combine a single course of action, and always the solution of the problem, which is reasoning, lies in allowing each factor in the situation to take its proper place when the final action is reached.

Let us find another example. This time take a man who glances at a chess problem before retiring, and works out the problem in bed. First of all, there is the situation on the chess board which only his past experience, in learning the game, enables him to understand. His aim is to set the white pieces on the board in a certain way, also shown him by past experience. He wishes to achieve "checkmate" in three moves, but this he cannot do at once because of the disposition of the opposing pieces. So he tries out first one move and then another, and the wrong moves register themselves as being in contradiction to something in the situation on the board. Finally, the solution comes. All the parts of the situation have been taken properly into account, each piece given due weight, and yet checkmate is achieved. Out of the conflicting parts of the situation a final course of action has been welded. The actual moving of the pieces may not take place until next morning, or perhaps never at all. In that case, the meeting of the situation might be said to be incomplete. But the process of adapting the action to the circumstances will have been in all essentials finished.

The very simplest acts of reasoning are almost always completed by actually performing the requisite actions. As the situations grow more and more complex, which means that the problems to be solved are more and more difficult, the intervening process between grasp of the situation and final action becomes more and more complicated and long drawn out, until finally it looms very much larger than the final action. A child wondering how to reach a high shelf will put the result of his conclusion into immediate practice. He reaches a chair. A man facing a difficult business situation may think a whole week and finally meet the situation by dictating a letter of half a dozen lines. A mathematician may write on a half sheet of note paper the solution of a problem that has taken a lifetime to solve. So far has action among us civilized folk been sicklied o'er with the pale cast of thought.

Such is Reason, the highest of the capabilities of man, yet differing in nothing but degree from the simplest intelligent action. There has been a good deal of discussion of late years concerning the method by which the various elements of the situation are finally combined to form the correct solution. It has generally been thought that first one *separate* solution is tried then another, until the final one is formed. This is implied in what has been written. The Gestalt psychologists however claim that we must think of all these attempts as aspects of one total attack on the problem. They would say that we have not a succession of trials and errors, but a unified set of actions with gradually increasing Insight. It is this Insight, the seeing of the whole situation in all its relations, that is here stressed. Insight may come suddenly, as happened to the chimpanzee with the bamboos, and it is this sudden clicking of all the factors that interests them. Many psychologists do not agree with them. But they have at least made us overhaul our ideas about reasoning and learning; which is high service!

Chapter VIII

THE BIRTH-GIFTS OF NATURE

(a) VICTOR, THE BOY WHO LIVED AMONG THE ANIMALS

This is the story of a boy who lived from early babyhood in a forest of the South of France, alone with the trees and the birds and the beasts. It shows how much we owe to the teaching and example of other human beings, and how little we learn when we have to teach ourselves by ourselves. And it shows how far from the truth are those sentimentalists who deplore the advance of modern civilization, and look back with longing to the good old times, "When wild in woods the noble savage ran."

"A child of eleven or twelve years old," says M. Itard, a French physician, who lived around the time of the French Revolution, "of whom glimpses had been caught several years before in the woods, was encountered towards the end of the Seventh Year of the Revolution, by three hunters, who seized him at the moment when he was clambering up into a tree to elude their pursuit. He was stark naked, and had been engaged in looking for acorns and roots to eat." The boy has since become famous as the "Savage of the Aveyron," from the name of the place where he was found.

At this first encounter with civilization, the boy was captured and taken to a hamlet near by, where he was placed in the care of a widow. At the end of a week, Itard tells us, he escaped and made off to the mountains, much, we may guess, to the worthy widow's relief. Here he stayed and wandered through the most rigorous cold of the winter,

VICTOR, THE BOY WHO LIVED AMONG THE ANIMALS

He lived for eight years as a wild boy. When found, he had twenty-three scars on his face and body. He is generally considered to have been feeble minded, but especially noteworthy is the fact that no one could tell, by the picture, that he was not a perfectly normal boy. The face might, indeed, remind one of several notable characters in history. Who are they?

which, to be sure, is not so cold in these parts as in this country, though cold enough for discomfort. With a ragged shirt on, he came by day to the outskirts of the villages, and went back by night to lonely places, "leading, in this manner, the life of a vagabond, until the day when he entered a human habitation of his own accord."

The boy was finally taken to Paris for observation. This is what Itard saw. "A child of disgusting filthiness, afflicted with spasmodic and often convulsive movements, rocking backwards and forwards incessantly like some of the animals in a menagerie, biting and scratching those who opposed him, showing no sign of affection to those who helped him: indifferent to everything, and giving attention to nothing."

In certain respects, he seemed, as Itard tells us, less educated than some of our domestic animals. He could not distinguish between an object in relief and one in a painting. His ear was "insensible to the loudest noises and the most affecting music." He could not speak, but continually emitted a monotonous grunt. He could not smell either perfumes or the stenches that his filthy habits left round his bed. He paid no attention to anything that was not connected with the most elementary needs of his body, and could not open a door or even climb on a chair to reach food. No signs had any meaning to him, and he passed, without apparent reason, from profound melancholy into peals of excessive laughter. As to his intelligence, it was, according to the clever phrase of Itard, nothing more than "an arithmetic of gluttony," and his "whole existence was, in a word, purely animal."

This is a picture of untaught man, of man with none but self instruction. It shows a state comparable with that to which you and I would be reduced, were it not for the education that comes from contact with a civilized environment and civilized companions. It is hard to discern the noble savage.

I have said *comparable* with the possible state of any of us, for it is generally considered that the child was of low original mentality. Even though he had enjoyed all the advantages of education and upbringing, he could thus, probably, not have developed into a man of any very high order.

When he was in the country, the most rigorous precautions were necessary to prevent his escape, so passionate was his love of the open and so keen his woodsmanship. He actually succeeded twice in slipping past the government guards of the institution where he was confined. And so like the beasts had he made himself, that he had great difficulty in walking with anyone. He preferred to trot or gallop! The state of his teeth showed that he was as a rule a vegetarian, which will perhaps give comfort to those who claim that vegetarianism is the natural state of mankind. But there seem to have been exceptions. "He was given a dead canary. In an instant the bird was stripped of its feathers, large and small, opened with a finger nail, smelt, and thrown away."

"On nights when there was a fine full moon, when the beams penetrated into his room, he almost invariably woke and stood before the window. He would stay there, according to the report of his guardians, for most of the night, standing motionless, his neck stretched out, his eyes fixed on the moonlit countryside, and wrapped in a kind of ecstasy of contemplation. The silence and immobility of the scene were interrupted only by the greatly quickened breathing of the boy, and a little plaintive sound that he made."

Such was this pathetic little child of nature.

The physician Itard, in whose hands the child was placed, made himself from the first his champion. While the other learned men who studied the child were inclined to consider him simply a case of low mental development, abandoned, perhaps, by his parents for this very reason, Itard took the opposite view. It became the doctor's endeavor to show that the boy's backward state was due to the way in which he had grown up, and in this endeavor he was at least partly successful. The task which Itard set himself, and to which the boy was a living challenge, was this: "To determine what would be the degree of the intelligence, and the nature of the ideas, of an adolescent who, from infancy, had been deprived of all education and had lived entirely separated from his kind."

The worthy man attained some success. At first the child had been almost unable to use his "sense of touch." The nervous messages which were started in his fingers and arms by what we call warmth and cold, softness and hardness, seemed to be nearly meaningless to him. But, after a time, he used this means of telling whether the potatoes were cooked. "Taking them from the pot with a *spoon*, he put his fingers on them several times, and decided from their hardness or softness whether to eat them or throw them back into the boiling water." His education is beginning. Carrying things seemed to be a puzzle. He would sometimes let the object drop and study attentively the end of his fingers. He had to learn the meaning of pressure on the finger tips, and in his past experience that particular sensation had too often meant harm. After a time, he began in every way to improve what Itard calls his sense **discrimination** which means that he began to make correct interpretation of the nervous messages that were started by the new environment through his receptors. Many of these messages had in the past meant nothing, had been accompanied by nothing significant. They had consequently led to no action, or as we might put it, had led to no learned reactions.

One day a practical joker fired a gun off near him. To the astonishment of everybody, the boy took absolutely no notice, because such noises, if he had ever heard them, had never meant anything. But once when he was on a walk with friends, he suddenly darted forward a considerable distance, and returned with an acorn, which he had heard drop! It had been in his poor existence, vital to him to be able to interpret the noise of falling fruit. Consequently the sound, by training, had set off the proper action.

Play he would not. All attempts to interest him in the proper pastimes of his age failed, except when the games were directly bound up with his feeding. Necessity is a stern master. A boy who has been in the woods fighting, singlehanded, against the forces of nature cannot afford the luxury of play. An afternoon's amusement means a half day's starvation. Candies and sweet things a stern regimen had also made distasteful. In fact, one of the difficulties of his training lay in the fact that it was almost impossible to devise any means of reward. So hard had been his life, and so sparse had been his pleasures. But little by little he began to show a softening of his unnatural sternness. Indeed pathetic scenes are somewhat later related of his affection for those who loved him.

One day, when he had escaped in the road, "on seeing Mme. Guérin, the housekeeper, he burst into a flood of tears," the effects of which lasted several hours. When M. Itard comes in to see him, he embraces the doctor, and sits him down beside him on his couch. Sometimes he jumps up, laughs, and claps, and "places himself opposite me to caress my knees in his individual way, which is to feel them, and press them vigorously all over for several minutes and sometimes to press his lips to them two or three times. People may say what they like," says the kindly doctor, "but I admit that I lend myself without ceremony to all these pieces of childishness."

How the boy was little by little trained to use simple speech, how he came to answer to the name Victor and to use a few simple words, how M. Itard taught him to recognise the word "milk" and to fetch the letters forming it when he wished to drink, this is all described in Itard's report. But attempts at further education were not so successful. In a report to the Minister of the Interior, five years after his first account, the doctor confesses to a disappointment. The pupil can now recognise various sounds of his new environment, and has begun to know what people want by the sound of their voice. He can now also read a number of words.

But he never grew to be an ordinary man, and was always in a state of apparent feeblemindedness. So deep was the influence of those terrible years of his childhood, spent alone in the forest with, perhaps, an inferior mental equipment to start with. His pathetic case can teach us, as Itard puts it, that "This moral superiority, that is said to be *natural* to a man, is only the result of civilization, which lifts him above the other animals by a great and powerful force."

And this is, perhaps, a blow to our pride, and yet a

source of pride, that we have taught ourselves to be men and not animals.

(b) THE INSTINCTS OF MAN

Victor, the boy of the last chapter, had to rely almost entirely on the stock in trade that nature had given him at his birth. It is true that he taught himself many things such as to know the sound of an acorn, to recognise the position of things from the way they looked to him, to smell his food before eating to find whether it was good. But these things, important though they are, did not avail him much in the everyday life of a civilized community. He had learned some things, but not very much.

It has often been said that Victor was to a large extent the child of instinct. What is an instinct? And to what extent may it be said that there are human instincts? These are questions that will be discussed in the next few sections.

Now it has been seen that a child, by virtue of being a child, inherits certain bodily characteristics, such as synapses or joins between neurones with certain resistances, and certain arrangements of nerves. As a result he can do certain things without learning them. When a finger is put into the mouth of a new-born child the baby makes the sucking motions. This is because nervous impulses are started in the mouth, which are conducted along the proper paths, through the proper synapses, and ultimately set in motion the muscles that do the sucking. The child's body is arranged in such a way that the impulses are guided along the right paths.

But here is a fresh thing. Instead of a comparatively simple action, such as sucking, it appears to happen that whole masses of actions are thus fathered by nature. Instead of a single reflex, a combination of reflexes may apparently be inherited.

Such a combination has been called an instinct. An instinct depends, then, not on the inheritance of a simple bodily structure or arrangement, or a simple action, but on a combination of structures in the body, thus making possible a more complicated *unlearned* reaction.

A reflex depends on the inheritance of a simple arrangement of structures and of resistance in the synapses. An instinct depends on the inheritance of a complicated pattern.

Of course, this is difficult enough. It is hard to see just how an openness of the synapses, however finely shaded, can account for such marvels as are accomplished by the insects. There is the well-known case of the wasp that lays its egg on a grub, which will be necessary as food when the eggs have hatched out. But as these do not hatch for some time, the grub is first paralyzed by stinging. The result of this action is said to be that numbness but not death will follow. Thus the meat is kept fresh until it is needed. How an openness of the synapses, however wonderfully arranged, could account for this, it is difficult to see. The matter is certainly much more complex than would appear from this very simple statement. But the explanation given seems to be less improbable than any other and seems to agree best with the known facts, which is really all we have the right to ask of any explanation!

Now we have seen that a very large part of the actions of a human being are performed with the help of habit. These things have all been learned. We learn to write, to eat properly with a knife and fork, to perform our business and social routine of every day. But an instinct, if instincts we have, is by definition unlearned.

It would then seem comparatively simple to settle the vexed question of what are the human instincts. All that is necessary is to find those reactions that are originally given by nature to an adult, as contrasted with those that each of us has to acquire for himself. Complicated enough, but quite a clear cut problem.

But wait. The imp of doubt whispers. "Does not a man really acquire everything himself, reflexes and all? Contrast John Smith at thirty with the same individual at the beginning of his life. Not at birth, for he is already nine months old at birth, but at the instant when he begins to be a single individual. This is the moment of fertilization, when the male and female elements unite. From that time forward, everything that goes up to make the body of Smith is taken up from the surrounding environment, which, to be sure, must be highly selected. If then we contrast the tiny, relatively formless fertilized ovum with the fully developed adult, possessing an astonishingly complex bodily machinery, a fully developed personality, and an elaborate system of habits, everything has surely come from environment. The cells making up the bodily mechanism are fashioned of material taken from environment; so, in particular, are the nerves; and the experience that we have seen to play such a large part also has its rise in external events. Nothing is then *innate*, really *indigenous* to a human being. Certainly not the reflexes, for they depend on nerves and other structures, every particle of which has been taken up from without. Certainly not our hair colour nor our fingernails. These come likewise from substances which have at some time been taken into the body. The only place from which a lady may take her complexion is the environment, whether she applies it indirectly through the bodily processes, or directly from one of those neat little compacts." Thus the demon of doubt.

It is then certain that the material of the body is taken from environment, but what determines what kind of a body will be made from this material? *The character of the individual at the time of fertilization.* Here is a leaf of lettuce. Smith eats half, and in due time material from that half becomes part of Smith's body. The other half is eaten by a caterpillar, and goes to form a butterfly. Each individual has taken very much the same substance from the world outside, but has done very different things with it.

Every individual is the joint product of himself as originally constituted and an environment of a specific nature. Change either, and the individual at maturity will be changed. Those who spend their energy arguing as to whether "heredity" or "environment" is the more important might just as well argue as to whether the length or the breadth of a rectangle matters more, or whether the convex or the concave side of a curve makes the shape.

Human nature needs nurture; but there must be human nature to nurture. The cradle is not empty.

It is not so easy now to decide about the instincts. Clearly an instinct is not really independent of environment. It has been gained by the individual, who has to acquire the bodily structure that has made it possible. This acquisition has come by help of the environment, just as learning has come by help of the environment. Thus we cannot say that an instinct is something originally belonging to us, while learned action is acquired.

Now we ordinarily assume a certain standard environment. Human children must have air to breathe and an earth to stand on. They must live in a temperature not much above a hundred degrees Fahrenheit, and not much below zero. They must have access to water and certain "food stuffs", etc. Granting such standard conditions, a human fertilized ovum will develop a bodily form which we consider to be the standard human body. It will act in certain standard ways when standard stimuli or situations occur. These actions we call the reflexes; or, if they are more complex we call them instincts.

On the other hand, the more gifted creatures have in their power to acquire other more flexible reactions, in cooperation with their own changing environment. These, which are over and above the standard acquisitions, we think of as individually acquired or learned actions.

Everyone develops the proper internal machinery to enable him to digest. Otherwise, he would not be alive. Few people develop the ability to eat rice with chopsticks, to eat spaghetti like an Italian. These actions depend upon the acquisition of the necessary bodily machinery, just as does the ability to digest. Here the bodily structures are less permanent, being built up in the central nervous system, which seems to be a specialist in rapid modification. Like any reflex, however, they are brought about by both organism and environment, the two reacting on each other. They are acquired by the activity of original nature working in environment.

Thus reaction of all sorts is possible because of the appropriate bodily machinery. This bodily machinery is built up by the interaction of the organism and its environment. Some of this machinery is a permanent part of the structure, like the ceilings and plumbing of a house. Reactions brought about by this kind of bodily machinery are ordinarily called reflexes, or, if they are of a more complex nature, instincts. Some of the machinery of the body, however, is of a more temporary kind, less deeply imbedded in the permanent structure, like the pictures on the walls or the apparatus in the doctor's consulting room. Bodily reaction brought about by this kind of mechanism is called learned reaction. Thus the much discussed difference between instinct and learning is really a relative matter, and indeed many, if not most actions, seem to be a mixture of the two.

(c) IS THERE AN INSTINCT OF ACQUISITION?

Consider for example the activity of walking. We have, indeed, to "learn to walk," but it seems very probable that this learning means that the proper connections are not yet made in the nervous system.

There are on record cases of children who have been sick during the time when they would normally be learning to walk. With returning strength, one day they have simply risen from the bed and walked across the room. Left to itself, the nervous system of a child seems to grow in such a way that walking is possible. But a child might be left all its lifetime without being able to go through the multiplication table. That is the difference between an instinct, or something that is built into a child as it grows and something that requires special "experience" or "education."

Another similar activity that has lately received much attention is the so-called "Wandering" or "Hunting" instinct. This has been used to explain the behaviour of a certain class of boy and man, who never seems contented to stay at home, but must always be wandering away.

Now it is of very great importance to decide whether there is really such an instinct of wandering, because, if there is, our treatment of such persons must be entirely changed. Suppose, for instance, we take the true case of the young boy who would never stay at home at night, but used to be found on street cars speeding away from the city, and brought home by police officers. A mistaken social worker might well attribute this to the "Instinct of Wandering," and try to treat the boy accordingly. Of course, if there is really an instinct behind the boy's roaming, the proper thing to do is to try to divert it into other channels. An instinct cannot be suppressed without serious damage.

In this case, then, it would have been proper to say that the boy ought to become a sailor or a travelling salesman, where his instinctive tendency would have proper play. As a matter of fact, it was found that this particular youth, so far from roaming instinctively, that is to say, without being taught, had been given this habit by another boy, who had made him restless by various vicious suggestions. Anyone who had tried to make a sailor out of the lad might well have done him harm. In order to understand the boy's conduct, it is not enough to say the magic words, "Instinct of Wandering."

And just as a deeper examination showed in this case that the wandering had been *taught,* and was due to something entirely removed from an "instinct," so in every case it will be found that there is some special reason for the running away. Either the person is a social misfit or he is in unhappy circumstances, or he is vicious by nature or by association with some vicious person, and finds a better opportunity away from home. There seems no reason to believe that the tendency to run away is an instinct or untaught reaction.

The "Instinct of Hoarding" is also a very popular phrase.

This instinct is said to account for a large part of the actions of civilized man. Those who amass millions are said to have a double measure of this original tendency. The school boy with his collections of birds' eggs, postage stamps and stones, and later the collector who scours the world to buy Chippendale chairs or Australian boomerangs, is said to be following the same tendency.

But I do not believe that there is any such instinct.

What seems to be an innate tendency to acquire or collect springs from various things. Often it comes from personal pride or the wish to make oneself as important as possible. A young child may be seen to put on his father's shoes or hat for the purpose of making himself look bigger. In the same way, he will refer to books and other things as his books, that he may seem bigger to himself and to other people. If anyone takes things which the child considers his, this is considered as an insult. To say that the favourite book belongs to someone else, means that its enjoyment is to be taken away. The statement is thus met with indignation. In the same way, when the boy grows older, the collection becomes part of his own personality. A good instance is the wall which is said to have started the fatal quarrel between Romulus and Remus, founders of Rome.

Romulus had built a wall, and Remus showed his contempt by leaping over it. Thereupon Romulus was so moved to anger that he slew Remus. Romulus took this leap as a direct insult to himself, as indeed it was intended.

In just the same way, to laugh at a boy's coat or his watch or his father or mother or anything that is his, is the same as to laugh at the boy. These things are regarded by him and his friends as part of the boy himself. So, a collection is thought of as part of the boy's own personality, and the one who has the largest or best specimens gains glory thereby. Sometimes, indeed, the object is found interesting in itself, as in the case of the small boy who had a passion for locomotive catalogues. In this case, again, there is no instinct of acquisition, but simply an interest in certain things.

In short, as stated above, there seems to be no instinct of acquisition. The tendency to acquire and collect is to be explained by such things as self-pride and competition. One who watches children can see the idea of possession being taught, and the good mother takes care that the sense of possession, with the sense of responsibility that goes with it, *is* taught. The bank account of the grown man is in almost every case a means to an end. A man collects a big balance, just as he collects a beautiful wife or a big house, to increase his self-esteem and to impress his neighbour, not because of any "Innate acquisitive tendency."

(*d*) WHY PEOPLE GET MARRIED

It is related that there was once a mother who was alarmed by a suspicious quietness in the nursery. So she called the nurse and cried, "Mary, go and see what the children are doing, and tell them not to."

This may seem to the inexperienced an unnecessarily unpleasant way of doing things, but, as all mothers know, it was probably entirely the right thing to say. We were all of us, in our childhood, little bundles of self-centredness, to whom life in any kind of society would have been impossible, even though we had understood what society demanded of us. When we wanted a thing, it was very hard for us to understand why we should not have it. And even when we were old enough to understand that it belonged to someone else, it was hard to give in gracefully. The reason was that we had learned to do things, but had not learned to hold off from doing things that are frowned upon by others. We had learned to stretch out the hand for candy that we wanted, but we had not learned not to stretch out our hand because it was someone else's candy.

These restraints upon action are called by the psychologist, "Inhibitions," and he says that, in childhood, we have not yet acquired the social inhibitions. Much of our early education consists in learning not to do things, because there are other people in the world whose interests would be harmed. The seemingly unsympathetic mother was, in all probability, perfectly right in assuming that the suspiciously quiet child was doing something that damaged someone else. Most things that a child wants to do, *do* damage some other person or his property!

Now one of the most important tendencies that we have to learn to check, is what is called the "Instinct of Sex." This section is entitled "Why People Get Married." But the puzzle really is, how anyone can avoid getting married, for the instinct of sex is so strong and so insistent, that it seems difficult to explain how anyone of adult years can learn to control it.

That there is such an instinct is, of course, beyond question. One of the things that we do not have to be taught is the attraction that normally draws opposite sexes together. Special training is not necessary to set off the sexual responses. Like stomach or eyes, sex is part of the permanent structural equipment of every child. Attraction of boy and girl, man and woman, is as innate in all of us as is hunger, for instance. We get married because we were born that way!

Indeed, the urge of the sexes is one of the great compelling forces of society, and next to the desire for food and drink, it is probably the most compelling. Not without reason did the ancients attribute their most disastrous war to Helen, of "The face that launched a thousand ships." And although it seems today the fashion to say that this war was due to bread and butter reasons, called by historians the economic motive, yet I, for one, am prepared to take the account of those who lived near those times.

It is easy to see why nature has arranged for this extraordinary force. In the march of generations, an individual may come or go, so long as the race goes on. If there is a race, there will always be individuals. And the attraction, whose purpose is to see that there will be a next generation, must be powerful enough to overcome even the strongest wishes of the individual. That is why so many young men, and women too, "make fools of themselves" over a member of the opposite sex. According to their fathers and mothers, who look at the good of their children, they do make fools of themselves. But if one could ask Mother Nature, who is wondering what is to become of the human race about the year three thousand, she would probably be of the opinion that things had happened very well.

To keep under guard such a tremendous urge as this between the female and the male, there is clearly necessary a social restraint of the most drastic and powerful nature. Indeed, our restraint on all things connected with sex would probably strike a stranger in our land as one of the most impelling forces of society, and, at the same time, as one of our curiosities.

Curious it is, looked at from the broad point of view, that we should be so reticent about a thing that is evident at every turn of the street, at every place of amusement, in every scene of family life. But this reticence is only a part of the great restraining barrier, which is a fundamental necessity of our civilization.

Another part of the same barrier is marriage, which protects the children by protecting the mother. The great problem is to give the powerful sex impulse as free play as possible, and, at the same time, to provide for the children without placing all the hardship on the mother. In very early times, no one cared particularly about the hardships which the mother endured. Later there came into being the state of society called matriarchy, which was possibly due in part to something like a trades union protest on the part of the woman. For as the Greek poet said, woman is a "banded race." As knowledge advanced man took more responsibility for the care of the children, until we have the civilized marriage of today, in which the man is equally responsible with his wife for the bringing up of the family.

But this has meant a tremendous curbing of the instinct of sex. The trouble is that not one man or one woman is attractive to an individual, but almost every man and every woman provides some kind of sexual stimulus for every member of the opposite sex, and the restraining force of custom has to be brought in to check the impulse. Where there is no check, civilization such as ours would be impossible.

Many people will, of course, claim that sex leaves them indifferent. In particular will those who are happily married, or in love, be inclined to think that, apart from one particular person, all members of the other sex are, to them, alike with members of their own. But if they honestly look into themselves and observe the impressions that an unusually attractive man or woman makes upon them, they will find that there is a difference. And if they carefully examine their attitude when they are talking to any member of the opposite sex, they will find that there is always a slightly changed viewpoint, which is unmistakable when it has once been noticed.

Now those who say that people of the opposite sex are indifferent to them because their affections are already fixed upon some one person, are to be congratulated. Their love for the one has practically succeeded in checking the primitive responses to members of the other sex. They have succeeded in setting up a strong barrier of restraint or inhibition, which now plays a large part in their happiness. But those who make the same claim, and who are not happily married or in love, are often not honest with themselves. These people are apt to be prudes and puritans because the restraint or inhibition they have put on themselves has grown to unwieldy proportions. These are the people who never marry and "hate" men or women. They are the misogynists and the criers of "Down with men."

Such cases are really abnormal, and abnormalities are common among those whose instinct of sex cannot find healthy expression. Indeed, only a robust personality can avoid growing "peculiar" in celibacy.

Old maidishness comes very near being a disease. But then, all old maids are not old maidish.

(e) FALLING IN LOVE

In the last chapter reference was made to the present family system. Now a great number of books and articles have lately been written to show that the custom of today, by which two people live together and have children, and between them care for the family, is unnatural and contrary to the way in which men and women are built. We saw that every man has an attraction for every woman because he is a man, and similarly every woman for every man. Therefore, it is argued that to tie down one man to one woman is contrary to the laws of nature, and that the restraints which civilized man here puts upon himself are harmful.

Now there are a great many points to be taken into consideration on this difficult problem. But, in general, the argument just put forward is as false as anything could possibly be. To begin with, it has never been shown that normal restraint or inhibition does the slightest harm to the nervous system. On the contrary, a great English scientist, Professor Sherrington, tells us that in the simpler processes which he has investigated, inhibition is never observed to harm and that it seems, indeed, to put the nervous system in a better position for further action.

Further, monogamy, or the marriage of one wife to one husband, seems, in the light of recent work in psychology, to be an absolutely scientific solution of the problem, and absolutely in accordance with the real nature of man and woman.

To explain how this comes about it is necessary to go back to the experiments of Pavlov, the Russian scientist. Pavlov, it will be remembered, showed a light to a dog at feeding time. After a few repetitions, he found that saliva flowed in the animal's mouth when the light was shown without any food. This reaction was called a conditioned reflex. Falling in love is something like this but considerably more complex. The original stimulus, which calls out the feelings and emotions that make a man so happy and miserable, is the sight of a particular lady. After a time, however, anything which he can possibly connect with her will have nearly the same effect. He will treasure up handkerchiefs, flowers and letters that she has touched. Even her telephone number glows with a mystical halo! All these things are stimuli which have taken upon themselves entirely new responses, just as did the light with Pavlov's dogs. If there is any reader who is suffering from an unhappy love, let him console himself with the thought that a large part of his unhappiness is due to nothing more romantic than a set of reactions of which we may see a simple example in Pavlov's dogs!

Now a person who has fallen in love in his early manhood and ultimately marries his first choice has formed a bond that is practically indestructible between one woman and certain responses.

Consequently, although other women can never, as we have seen, leave him quite indifferent, yet this effect stops off very short. The full effect of the stimulus of sex is inhibited, as we say, by the attachment which he has for his wife. Exactly the same thing happens in Pavlov's laboratory. At first the dog's saliva flows at the sight of any light, but after a time this action only occurs when a light of a particular brightness is presented, and scientists claim that this narrowing down of the stimulus is due to inhibition or checking of the other reactions.

That is to say, a man who marries without sowing wild oats, as it is called, is making normal married life normal for him, by narrowing down to one person the stimulus which will set off certain feelings and emotions. A man who has not confined these emotions to the one who is to be his wife is practically making certain that all women will continue to affect him strongly after matrimony and is sowing the seeds of an unhappy life.

Thus the old theory that reformed rakes make good husbands is given the lie direct by sober scientific experiment. Nothing could be farther from the truth than this statement.

Nothing is clearer than the fact that promiscuity before marriage is the most certain way of causing married life to be an intolerable burden, and of making conjugal fidelity an impossible restriction, where other women call with the same voice as the wife, or the lure of other men is the lure of the husband.

Science, looking from the unexpected quarter of a laboratory in Russia, smiles upon the old-fashioned marriage!

(f) IS FIGHTING INEVITABLE?

After this discussion of the urge of sex, let us return to the consideration of the human instincts.

The reader will remember that we found ourselves obliged to reject several of the tendencies often classed as instincts. They were actions that could not be considered to be due to a mechanism built permanently into the human frame, but were more or less temporary acquisitions. A "normal" human being can exist quite well with no urge for acquisition, but he cannot live without the urge for air.

Consider now the activities connected with clothing. Undoubtedly among all kinds of animals there is an unlearned process by which the animal's body is protected against the cold. Birds are covered with feathers, animals with fur or hair, and the process of growing these things is entirely unlearned by the animal in question. But when we come to look for any real instinct of clothing in man, it is hard to find it.

Now according to the well known physiologist, Professor Cannon, the body is so constructed that it keeps constant, in an extraordinarily accurate way, a number of factors within itself. For example the alkalinity of the blood is kept constant within amazingly narrow limits. So much so that if there is more than an almost undetectable variation the animal dies. The volume of the blood is kept constant in the same way. Those who are interested should read Professor Cannon's lately published book.

Now one of the most obvious of these constant factors is that of temperature. The temperature of the nursery may rise ten degrees, but if little Johnny's temperature rises to 108.6° Johnny is already past the doctor's ministrations. The temperature of the human body is kept within narrow limits by a very delicate and highly complex apparatus. Certain lower forms of life do not possess such an apparatus. Thus you may see a snake that has ventured out of a hole too early or too late in the season moving in a much less lively manner than in the heat, and this is no doubt due at least in part to the fact that the chemistry of his body is slowed down by the cold.

Such dependence on external temperature is avoided in the birds and higher animals by the temperature-preserving apparatus. Part of the mechanism for the maintenance of temperature is the feathers or hair already mentioned, the rest is of a chemical and nervous character. So efficient, indeed, is the fur of the fur-bearing creatures that with all his power of artificial production man finds himself turning to the skins of animals to keep him warm!

Let us take now an animal such as a mouse living in a cage. The fur provides insulation, but even so the animal's body is ordinarily much warmer than the room, and heat has to be supplied by the operation of the natural thermostat. If then the air grows cold, a second line of defence is called into play. The animal builds a nest! Nest building in mice has been observed by Professor Richter of John Hopkins to be part of the means by which the temperature of the animal is maintained. Thus one should hardly call this activity an instinct. It is here part of the means of preserving the bodily temperature, very much like, say, slapping the sides in a human being. Whether in the mouse nest building is "learned" we do not know; even if it is not, it is probably better not classified as a separate "instinct."

Much the same is true of clothing in a human being. Victor indeed had on a tattered shirt, but we should probably not on that account attribute to him an instinct of clothing. Every mother knows that a child is in respect of clothing a little barbarian, and has to be taught what the adult community regards as decency in the matter of self-covering. Victor's shirt would be for warmth not decency, and his wearing it almost certainly self taught.

Of course, in the adult, clothing is complicated by a good many other factors, such as self adornment. But in general there seems to be no purpose served by setting up a separate instinct for it.

Much the same may be said of fighting. Part of the general machinery for preserving life and limb seems to consist of certain defensive and offensive postures. Thus the tortoise pulls in his legs when he is tapped, the snail withdraws its horns, and so on. There could probably be found also offensive actions and postures, actions designed to modify the dangerous situation. Such, in a small way, is the scratch reflex in the dog. All such should be classed as part of the general defensive machinery of the body, which we know is so organized that its reactions do, as a matter of fact, tend towards the animal's survival. When a tortoise withdraws into its shell it is logically truer and less likely to lead to unjustified conclusions to say that we have here an instance of the particular organization which has brought it about that tortoises are now living, rather than to speak of an instinct of withdrawal or a defensive instinct.

This brings us to the crux of the question of pugnacity. There has never been shown to be an instinct of fighting, meaning by this an innate disposition to attack other human beings by physical force. The more we know about the human body, the more impossible such an instinct appears to be. There are many mechanisms, some working more, some less, directly towards the preservation of the general bodily state of the organism and for the perpetuation of the species. That there should be a special built-in mechanism for the destruction of other organisms of the same species *as an end in itself* is scientifically unthinkable. This seems to be true even of animals, who are said under ordinary circumstances not to kill other members of the same species for the sake of killing.

"Dogs delight to bark and fight." They have generally been taught. So teach a child and he will consider the slaughter of his own race a glorious feat. So teach a nation and it will count as its most meritorious achievement the slaughter of citizens belonging to the nation across the way.

"Ten thousand Frenchmen gone below.
Praise God from whom all blessings flow."

(g) WHY IT IS IMPORTANT TO KNOW WHICH THINGS ARE INSTINCTS

The reader will have concluded from the last few chapters that, while we have been tearing down many of the instincts, we have built up little in their place. Now this is perfectly true. A number of those who have studied the human instincts are today boldly asserting that there is no such thing as a human instinct. Others claim that there are two instincts, others allow a few more, while still others give a list containing twenty or thirty or more. In the main, there is in progress a great scientific house-wrecking of instincts, and very little house-construction. Even those who agree to leave some instincts, do not agree what instincts to leave, and thus is confusion worse confounded.

Now the question of how many instincts there are in human beings, and what are the instincts, is of very great importance in practical life. Upon the answer to it depends the whole conduct of our system of education. For anything that is learned may by proper instruction and environment be prevented from being learned. And on the other hand, anything that is innate can only be modified or, at the most, prevented from working by withholding the proper stimulus. Thus, the instinct of sex can be dwarfed or curbed in its operation by living on a desert island in the manner of Robinson Crusoe. But it will probably never be finally rooted out. A pretty woman would have caused Crusoe even more excitement than did Man Friday. When, as in the case of sex, the machinery for an action is built into the very foundation of our nervous structure, it would seem impossible ever to sweep the action completely away.

Can the Ethiopian change his skin or the leopard his spots?

On the other hand, with an activity such as fighting, or the aggressive use of physical violence, the story is quite different because we have reason to believe that these activities are learned. And here it rests with educators to teach or not to teach. But until scientists have decided much more certainly what is, and what is not, an instinct in the young human being, the educator can never be quite certain that he is taking the right attitude in any particular case.

Two things are certainly instincts; namely, the instinct

of sex, and some kind of impulse of self-preservation, the urge "to continue in one's own state of existence," as a great philosopher has put it. Sometimes these are called the instinct of the Race, and the instinct of Self. Just how much we are able to accomplish by their means without teaching ourselves, we do not know, nor how these two forces furnish the motive power for so many dissimilar actions.

Perhaps in twenty years' time we may know!

(h) WHY A CHILD FEARS THE DARK

One thing which very many people are quite positive they have never been taught is the fear of certain things, particularly of snakes and of the dark. A distinguished scientist, Galton, had a strange loathing and horror of the peculiar movements of a snake, and he was never able to rid himself of the emotion. A great scientist described how he was quite unable to avoid flinching from the dart of a snake in the zoölogical gardens, although he knew perfectly well that the glass between them was safe. Very many people from the most ignorant to the most highly cultivated, confess to the same fear. Personally, I feel a slight uneasiness when I am close to a snake, but that is all. But I remember that when I was a boy I was entirely free from any such aversion, and indeed snakes seemed then to us to have a fascination all their own. I cannot but believe that somehow or other I have learned in the interval to fear the snake. Many children are unwisely told gruesome stories in which snakes play an unpleasant part. In my own case I do not believe that this was the cause for my dislike, but I seem to connect the sinuous movement of these animals with bodily dislocation and contortion, and vaguely with entrails. If the reader who fears snakes will search his own mind, he will possibly find some similar connection.

It is interesting that among the Greeks and Romans of ancient times there seems to have been no fear of snakes, of the kind that many experience today. These races were, of course, also indifferent to many scenes of bodily tortures and suffering that would strongly affect most of us, so that it may well be that the connection with bodily writhing and suffering holds good in the minds of others as well as in my own mind.

The other fear that is said to be instinctive, or untaught, is the fear of the dark. Now it is quite certain that a very large number of children are taught to fear the dark. From my own childhood I can perfectly well remember the exact time and place of this vicious piece of education. A certain nurse girl, ignorant, as nurse girls were apt to be, had told me, shortly after she arrived, about the exploits of a nephew of hers. This remarkable young man, it appears, at the tender age of seven, walked through a churchyard at night on a "dare," whistling to keep his courage up. It occurred to me at the time that there was nothing so wonderful in that, for why, I thought, should any one be afraid of a churchyard? At this time the dark had no terrors for our small family. But later in the career of this accomplished story teller we were told the tale of a weird and wonderful ghost that appeared in some old house, and which disturbed our own rest for many nights after.

At that time I slept in a room with sloping walls, at the top of the house. Today it makes me uneasy to go into an attic in the dark, though no other rooms have the same effect. I have been taught to fear a dark attic.

It seems probable that many cases of fearing the dark are thus due to some kind of teaching on the part of an ignorant mother or nurse. As Plato, one of the greatest educators of all time, has told us, "Some tales are to be told, and others are not to be told to our disciples from their youth upwards, if we mean them to honour the gods and their parents and to value friendship with one another."

This is, of course, not to deny that the fear of the dark will often begin without any such direct teaching on the part of an older person. A place that is light is not so likely to contain anything terrible. A place that is dark may contain the unpleasant. And in the dark one bangs one's head and shins, and has the feeling of helplessness if anything dangerous is really there. Both these things probably entered into the consciousness of the child who lately told me that "a big lion lives down those (dark) stairs." The point here is that the big lion was what inspired fear; if I had not taken occasion to separate the lion from the darkness in the child's mind, she would certainly have begun to fear not only the lion, but the dark which held the lion. And in this case, the child would have taught herself to fear the dark.

Chapter IX

PROTECTION IN ROUTINE AND IN EMERGENCY

(a) LIKES AND DISLIKES. THEIR IMPORTANCE IN BUSINESS

A DOG is running down the hill, looking, as dogs will do, as though he were going on forever to nowhere. Suddenly he stops, turns aside, and bends his head to what turns out to be a piece of meat. He snuffs the meat, and the man who knows dogs will tell you, from the way he holds his body and wags his tail, that he is pleased.

A musician is playing a sonata on the pianoforte. Page after page he turns over, rendering with the easy grace that shows the trained performer. Suddenly he stops. From the well worn music a piece of the sonata has been lost. The face of the performer wrinkles up, he turns red, shuts up the book, and walks away from the piano. He is annoyed, and feels displeasure.

A hungry baby lies in his crib, and the nurse comes in with the bottle. "Look how pleased he is," says the mother, and she is probably right. Undoubtedly the child is pleased, feels pleasure, at the sight of his food.

In all these cases, pleasure or its opposite is felt, and we are able to say that the person or the animal is pleased or displeased by watching its behavior. All of us know when the characters in the motion picture plays are pleased or displeased "from the way they act." All of us know when our family or business associates are pleased or not, from the way they behave and the way they talk. Pleasure is unmistakable, and behavior during pleasure is unmistakable except when it occurs in a person with a more than usually good poker face, who can conceal his feelings.

This pleasure is something quite different from anything that has as yet been discussed. We have seen the organism at work, have understood that its actions are the result of stimuli in the surroundings which, partly from what has been learned, partly from what comes naturally without learning, produce certain responses. This is the outside, or what might be called the moving-picture view. From the inside, we have a view that is entirely private, and according to which the person says he has certain sensations, that he is *conscious* of his surroundings, and, generally, of the means that he is taking to meet the situation. The two aspects are both necessary if we wish to understand the whole man in relation to his environment. But here enters what we call pleasure and displeasure. Pleasure is not an action, it is not a sensation, it is not an image. It does not seem to be in itself an adaptation to the surroundings, and yet it is connected with adaptations. The dog's pleasure as he smells the bone is not his action nor his sensations, but it is somehow bound up with them.

Pleasure is spread over actions "like the bloom of a youth." If strict attention is paid to it, it is likely to disappear. Everyone knows what it is, but it is hard, if not impossible, to describe; as hard, for that matter, as is any other simple fact of consciousness. It is . . . Pleasure.

But though, in a way, it is so mysterious when we try to describe what we feel, yet what it does is not difficult to understand. It may be said to show the first line of defence and offence of the organism against the environment. A dog smelling a bone that will furnish food feels pleasure. If the bone turns out to be covered with pepper or mustard or tar, he feels displeasure. Things that are good for him are in the main pleasant, things bad for him unpleasant. He is saved endless harm by the fact that harmful things are unpleasant. He is helped very much in his life by the fact that things good for him are pleasant. A dog to whom sulphuric acid was extremely pleasant would live a very short time if there was any possibility of his satisfying his craving. A dog to whom water to drink was extremely unpleasant would be at a considerable handicap; one who found extremely pleasant the contractions of the stomach causing what we call hunger would starve himself to death for the fun of it.

Thus pleasure and displeasure are apparently the conscious aspects of a process of regulation encouraging action that is correct, and discouraging action that is harmful for the organism.

Our pleasures are obtained in different ways. Some things are naturally pleasant, such as exercise of the body, taken in moderation. Others are naturally unpleasant, such as most pain. But another class of things becomes pleasant by association, as we say. This association takes place in the same way as Pavlov's dogs grew to connect a light with food.

Thus honey is to me personally very unpleasant. The reason is that, in my school days, a misguided school fellow took me to his home, where we devoured large quantities of the sweet. The next day we were both very sick. The feeling of unpleasantness was transferred from the nausea to the honey. The stimulus of the taste or even the smell, or sight, of honey now has the unpleasant effect. In the same way, a psychologist tells how he cannot read "The Three Musketeers" without an unpleasant feeling because he had once read it coming over the English Channel!

Almost everybody has these likes and dislikes, which can usually be traced back to some such association. It is interesting to make a list of them, and to try and account for them in one's past experience. Sometimes it is persons who become the "conditioned stimuli" for a feeling of unpleasantness. Thus, no one would be likely to feel very comfortable in the presence of a hangman, however estimable and pleasant a person he might be, so strong is the unpleasant association which he bears. A child will scream at the sight of a doctor, especially if he happens not to be very "good" with children. On the other hand, most of us have a distinctly pleasant glow of feeling for the man who writes out the check for our salary, the bearer of good news, or the minister who married us.

The practical importance of all this is very great, especially in the field of advertising and selling. I am in the habit of seeing every year a number of representatives of different publishers. Some of these leave what is known as a "pleasant" impression, others are relatively indifferent, others somewhat unpleasant. One man in particular succeeded in making himself unusually agreeable to me, and I find myself going over the catalogue of that firm, welcoming the chance to order anything from it. And it happens that the largest order I have placed this year was with his company.

Now it is quite certain that this man did not succeed in selling his goods to me because he was a pleasant man. But there seems no doubt that, in case of indecision, the feeling of pleasantness or unpleasantness that hovers round such a representative may correspond to a casting vote. All other things being equal, there seems no doubt that we are likely to buy from the man who pleases us best. And if this is true of such a thing as buying technical books, where the merits of the thing sold are so well known and so carefully examined, how much more it must be true of things where our knowledge is small and where we are somewhat indifferent as to which we shall purchase! Knowing that three or four restaurants are about equal in the value they give, I am more than likely to choose that one which has a cashier with a pleasant smile, and avoid the one with a waiter whom I dislike. Of several hotels in Boston where I have been accustomed to stay, and which are of approximately equal cost, I seem finally to have decided on one in particular. It is really somewhat out of the way for my general business, but I have an unusually pleasant remembrance of the room clerk and the man who works the elevator to my usual room. Most of us finally adopt a doctor or a dentist whom we like; it is an unusually rational person who will call a physician whom he dislikes for a slight sickness. And it is from the slight sicknesses that the doctor makes his living.

With the merchant's goods, whether they be books or clothes or medical attention, we buy the merchant's smile, and are often more willing to pay for a good quality smile than good quality goods.

One way in particular in which displeasure is apt to be aroused is by a thwarted activity. If the reader will pick out of the past twenty-four hours the things that have displeased him, he will find that a large proportion of them come from a hindrance of some kind. Few things are so annoying as being held up at the start of an expedition by some member of the family who cannot find his or her gloves or hat. To find a road barred or impassable, and to have to retrace one's course is always unpleasant, even though the ride is undertaken purely for the sake of fresh air. Hindrance is almost equivalent to annoyance. Particularly annoying it seems to be to have one's routine interfered with. If it is my habit to write letters at a certain hour, and a friend calls and prevents me, I find I am apt to be much more displeased than if the caller had interfered with a casual hour set aside for letter-writing. A caller who stays late and interferes with the routine of the house is always unwelcome. Any change from routine is resented, and this is only too well known by those who take over the management of any old established concern, whether it be a church, a school, or a business house.

This unpleasantness of disordered routine is as it should be. The larger part of our actions has become habitual, because the larger part of our actions is simply a repetition of what has already been accomplished. New situations are, one may say of extreme rarity in our everyday life. Having once solved the problem it would be useless to attempt to depart from the solution gained. Nature in man is concerned with efficiency, and efficiency consists in finding the best way to do a thing, *and doing it in that way.* I follow the grooves I have made, because progression in them is easier. As the humorist has put it, I am "in fact, not a bus but a tram." And when I go off the rails, there is as much discomfort as when a locomotive is derailed. The displeasure functions like an indicator which is put into operation when I am leaving the rails. The reason why prolonged reasoning is, to many, such an unpleasant process is that the essence of reasoning is a new reaction to a new situation. Old habits have to be broken up and combined in a disquieting way. Many popular periodicals fully recognise this fact. They have brought down to a fine art the process of presenting the same point of view again and again, knowing that what proceeds according to habit receives a pleasurable tinge, and what breaks, over the trammels of habit is distinctly unpleasant.

One thing has not been said about this curious pair of opposites, pleasure and displeasure, or unpleasure, as it is sometimes called by the more particular. They come from no particular sense organ, such as do many of the things that go to make up our consciousness. Visual experiences and visual images originate in the eye, kinaesthetic sensations, which come when we move the body, spring from their own organs. But pleasure and displeasure come from no such organ or receptor. They are something that is added to sensations, again like the "bloom" of youth. Thus, it is not really correct to speak of a sensation of pleasure. The term "affection" is used by psychologists, designating the way in which one is affected, pleasantly or unpleasantly, by the sensation. The whole thing, pleasantness, sensation, and all, is called correctly "feeling."

(b) HOW PAIN MAY BECOME PLEASANT

Let us begin this paradoxical sounding section with two statements of facts that we already know.

(1) Pain is a definite sensation like sight, and comes from a definite receptor or sense organ of its own, as explained in Chapter four.

(2) Pleasure is not a sensation, but may be attached to Sensation.

If the reader will grant these, he must come to the following conclusions:

(1) Pain is not the opposite of pleasure.

(2) Pain, like any other sensation, may become pleasant.

Let us take the first.

If pain is a sensation, of its very nature it is not, and cannot be, the opposite of anything, any more than sight can be the opposite of anything.

What is the opposite of sight? The question is absurd. What is the opposite of pain? The question is equally absurd, although practically everyone would answer at once "Pleasure." And the sin is not confined to those whose ignorance is excusable. A number of scientific books refer to the "pleasure-pain" principle, as though these two things were opposite, and could be put in the same class. The opposite of pleasure is of course displeasure, or "unpleasure", and this is by no means the same as pain.

Of course, this is not to deny that most pain is unpleasant. And here comes our second point. Nature has so ordered that harmful stimuli give the sensation of pain, and we have seen that one function of unpleasantness is to indicate trouble. Consequently, it follows that, for the sake of consistency, most pain *must* be unpleasant. But there are exceptions. The "affect", as it is called of pleasantness is sometimes, in fact, actually fastened to the sensation of pain, as it may be to any other sensation. There are, indeed, abnormal cases where the proper functions of these natural indicators have become twisted up, and all pain becomes pleasant. Thus many of the mediaeval ascetics, who flogged themselves "for the Glory of God," probably found a keen pleasure in their self-torture. There is an interesting experiment of Pavlov's where a dog was fed at the same time as an electric shock was given. At first the animal howled at the sight of the electrode, but after a time the shocking process became welcome, because it had become associated with something pleasant, namely food. Professor Sherrington, one of the greatest physiologists in the world, has compared this experiment with the ecstasy of the martyrs, who went to death and torture with a smile. Many more instances of "pleasant pain" could be given.

There seems in fact no particular reason why *any* pain should not be given a pleasureable tinge by proper manipulation.

A little consideration will show how this possibility *must* really exist, if pleasantness and unpleasantness are properly to perform their work. Pains come about when there occurs a stimulus that has, in the long history of the race, been harmful. In an inconceivably great majority of cases it has been harmful for the organism to have its body penetrated by some foreign substance. As a result, and without our having to learn it, we suffered pain when, at school, the boy behind pushed a pin into us. But there may be times in the history of the individual when it will be to his own advantage to be able to endure such a thing as a sword wound.

Something of the sort appears to have been the case among such early peoples as the tribes that worshipped Baal, who cut themselves with knives, and among the Mohammedans, who counted it a joy to be wounded and even killed in the defence of the faith. I myself have seen a German student with an unpleasant looking gash on the cheek, smiling with inward joy as he was taken away. And this was no pose, as he told me afterwards that it was one of the "pleasantest moments of his life." Among all these people, it was a distinct advantage to receive a wound that, by all the rules of life, would seem inevitably harmful. And because it was useful to them the pain was pleasant.

A famous case is to be found in the Flagellants, or floggers. They were a sect that grew up in Italy and Germany in the thirteenth century, and consisted of bands of ragged, filthy men, and women also at times, who wandered from town to town flogging themselves in public. They worked themselves into a frenzy of beating which so excited the spectators that the sect soon numbered thousands. In Genoa there were actual guilds of floggers, who marched through the streets scourging themselves, "with bishops and dignitaries at their heads." "Survivals of these customs exist even to the present day. A newspaper correspondent describes the observance at Grosseto, in Tuscany, on Good Friday, when a procession takes place of some thirty youths, their faces covered with linen masks, each armed with two scourges, one of fine wires, the other with knots in which sharp points are firmly twisted. With these, at command of a leader, they beat themselves on the bare shoulders, till the blood flows freely, the exercise lasting *for some hours,* and winding up at the church." So says Doctor Lea, in his History of Confession and Indulgences. The Catholic Church has consistently opposed these exhibitions.

Sometimes there are cases that are still more abnormal. One such person who had developed an unhealthy craving for whipping, connected in this case with various abnormal tendencies, says of one such castigation "I wanted it, I craved it" and "I enjoyed it thoroughly"!

It is not, however, necessary to go to these abnormal cases for instances where pain may acquire a pleasureable tinge. Everyone has felt the same thing to a lesser degree when there is some slight irritation at some point of the body. When a gum is swollen and the tooth is uneasy, it is a positive source of pleasure to press the tooth and experience the slight pain that follows. Particularly also is this true of irritations of the skin. The writer remembers once as a boy being afflicted with a most irritating skin disease, when it was exquisite pleasure to dig the finger nail into the flesh at that point, until the blood actually came. It is probable that such pleasure in scratching a part of the skin dates back to the time when man had to fight hordes of insects, and when it was to his advantage even to wound his skin, if only he thus rid himself of the stinging pest.

Other examples of pain that is pleasant are the feel of the cold air on the face during a brisk walk, the chill of ice cold water to the hardy swimmer, and the cold of the ice cream in summer. These all, as we have seen, set the pain spot in operation, and the pain is pleasant, because it is to the distinct advantage of the organism to endure it.

Perhaps, as our civilization becomes more and more a surgical one, there will result, by natural selection or otherwise a race of men who will regard a major operation without anaesthetics as an interesting afternoon's diversion!

In conclusion, there is one thing more which has to be said about this curious fact, that pain may on occasion acquire a pleasureable tinge. If such a bitter thing as a sensation of pain may become pleasant, then surely there is little in life that may not become agreeable. Some things, we are inclined to believe, can never be pleasant to us. They vary from person to person, and from one period of life to another. But as far as we can see, there is no reason why anything not harmful in the normal course of our life should be anything but pleasant. In particular is this true of children and their everyday routine. To one child, going to bed and sleeping is an everyday ordeal that puts the whole household in confusion and anxiety. To another, the daily going to bed is taken as a matter of course, and is as pleasant as rising in the morning. The difference is that in the one case the daily going to bed has been *allowed* to become unpleasant, through some kind of bad management, while in the other case an atmosphere of pleasantness has deliberately been fostered. The same thing is true of many other things that come up in the everyday life of childhood. By proper management, almost anything may be made pleasant. I have even heard of a children's dentist who was so popular that the children cried to go again!

Nature has given us the sugar coating. Why not put it round the pill?

(c) WHAT IS AN EMOTION?

In 1884 there appeared in one of the magazines an article which astonished the world of psychology. The article was by William James, the famous Harvard Professor, and was called, "What is an Emotion." It seemed to set the world upside down. There was bitter attack on it from every side, and the article was said to be absurd, paradoxical, and impossible. But strangely enough, the next year, there appeared another article, this time in Danish, and published in Copenhagen, which contained exactly the same view as Professor James', only expressed perhaps, more scientifically.

Let us see what this double bombshell contained.

Professor James had been studying the bodily effects

or accompaniments of emotion. Everybody knows, from external signs, when a man is angry. The face is flushed, the teeth are clenched, the fist perhaps drawn up ready to strike, and so on.

In the same way, we know when a man is in grief. "He walks slowly, unsteadily, dragging his arms. His voice is weak and without resonance.... He prefers to sit still, sunk in himself and silent.... The neck is bent, the head hangs ("bowed down with grief"), the relaxation of the cheek and jaw muscles makes the face look long and narrow, the jaw may even hang open." These are the outward signs of grief, as given by Lange, the Danish scientist to whom reference has been made, and quoted by Professor James. Important internal effects of the same emotion were also noticed by Lange, producing bloodlessness in the skin and consequent paleness and sometimes shivering. All these things had been remarked by psychologists of many generations, but no one had claimed for them, in any downright way, the importance which they assumed in the writings of these two men.

The older workers had thought that one first experienced an emotion, and then the emotion produced the bodily changes. James and Lange reversed this account. They claimed that the external stimulus which caused the emotion made the bodily changes, and that *our perception of the bodily changes is the emotion.* To take James' famous example. "We say we lose our fortune, are sorry, and weep, we meet a bear, are frightened and run." "The more rational statement," says James, "would be that we feel sorry because we cry, afraid because we tremble." The bodily changes come first, and the state of consciousness we call emotion follows them. In short, as one psychologist puts it, "The emotion is the way the body feels on such occasions." That is the famous theory that has come to be known as the James-Lange theory.

Now it is quite certain that the readers of this book will at first think this absurd, as did the psychologists of the '80's. But if the arguments of those who started the theory be examined, the theory will sound a little more reasonable. First of all, it was pointed out that all these bodily changes may be felt. We may be conscious of the contraction of the forehead in grief, of the sinking of the head, the hanging of the arms, the limpness of the muscles. Every part of the body is affected, and each part contributes its share to our state of consciousness. The reader may convince himself of this, the next time he is under emotion of any kind, by observing that all the parts of his body and their attitudes are helping to make up his general state of mind.

Secondly, if the bodily feelings are taken from the consciousness of an emotion, there seems to be nothing left of the emotion. James asks people to imagine away all the bodily feelings of laughter, or of grief, and to say what is left of the emotion. Anyone, as he says, who had absolutely none of the bodily accompaniments of fear, such as running away, quickened heart beat, shallow breathing, trembling lips and so on, could hardly be said to have fear, especially if he were also free from the internal agitations that usually go with the emotion. An emotion without any of these bodily symptons is like Hamlet without the prince. It seems simply not to exist.

Furthermore, there are occasions where the body is not working properly, and when the internal changes that go with emotion are brought about with no external object. In this case, we seem to have an emotion that is caused entirely by internal means. Thus, a patient may have fears or phobias, as they are called, which will come on at about the same time of the day, and will attach themselves to anything that happens to be in the neighbourhood. The writer remembers, during a mild nervous trouble, walking along at night, and suddenly being afraid of a lamp post! In this case, the bodily changes that accompanied fear had been put out of gear, and were liable to be started off as by a hair trigger. Some internal stimulus set them off, and fear was felt. This kind of thing seemed to show that fear reactions could be caused simply by internal changes.

But in spite of these facts, which were pointed out to them the critics were far from being convinced that the seemingly topsy-turvy idea was true. The flood of objections that was let loose came from two quarters. First of all were those who could not agree with James and Lange because of what they themselves felt during an emotion. These people argued that when they "saw a bear," they were frozen with fright, stood stock still for a moment, and then turned to run away. The fear came before the expression of the fear, so that James could not be right. But there was little difficulty in disposing of this argument.

"You do not," said these who sided with the two erring professors, "have any definite consciousness of the very important internal changes that take place on such an occasion. It is these changes that give the emotion its devastating character, and these that precede, by a fraction of a second, the conscious emotion. Then come the further bodily consequences, and you run away. In running you increase your fear, as every schoolboy can tell you who has started to run home at night in the dark. Consequently, the bodily changes, internal, come first, then the perception of them that we call fear, then further bodily changes, and further emotion."

On the other hand, there was a group of critics that asked how it could be that we are sorry *because* we weep, when everyone knows that we often weep for joy. If the bodily expression causes the emotion, how can the same bodily performance go with different emotions at different times? Here, again it was pointed out that the expression was different in the two cases, and apart from this the answer was that the central thing in the emotion is the internal effect, which cannot be observed from the outside. Now observe that the essential point of the difference depends on something that is really assumed, namely that there are different internal reactions for each emotion, and that the difference is enough to make the enormously varied experiences of emotional life. Nobody said what these internal processes are that decide whether one is to feel sorry or glad. Left in this way, most scientists were inclined to reject the theory as not proven.

The next step was taken by Sherrington, the British physiologist. He argued in this way. "If emotion is, in the main, the consciousness of certain internal changes, then if I make it impossible to feel any such internal changes, there should be no emotion possible." So he experimented on dogs, which had been so treated that practically all the impulses from the sense organs of the body up to the shoulders were barred from the brain. The animals still showed signs of fear, anger and disgust. The stomach, lungs and heart were also, in another experiment, barred from the brain, and still the animals showed emotion. These experiments, said Sherrington, clearly showed that internal, organic processes are not of any vital importance in emotion. As a result many psychologists concluded that the paradox of James and Lange had to be discarded.

But the matter was not to be settled so easily. It was seen that Sherrington had proved nothing beyond that certain external movements were unchanged in character. Externally, that is to say, the emotion was not changed. But on the question as to whether there was an actual change in the way in which the emotion felt in the consciousness of the dog, if he had any, the experiment threw no light. As we have seen, intense joy and intense sorrow produce, both of them, a paleness of the face. Sherrington's experiment might have transformed joy into sorrow, and yet, in this particular, he would have had to judge that the emotion was the same. The external signs are not the important part. It may well be possible to leave them unaltered, and yet fundamentally to alter the character of the emotion. But Professor Sherrington had performed an important service, by applying to the theory the touchstone of experiment. That is the path of all science, first a theory based on the known facts, and then experimental, controlled, testing of the theory, with its final acceptance or rejection.

The position in which the idea of James and Lange now found itself was rather curious. The main point seemed to many attractive but paradoxical. Those who disagreed were bound to admit that their objection was based mainly on the fact that the thing was not proved. On the other hand, they admitted, many of them, that the case *against* the theory was not proved. And the next turn that the theory was to take was still more curious. It was the strange fate of being upheld by one who maintained all the time that he was discrediting it!

Professor Walter B. Cannon, again of Harvard, began

in 1909 to publish a series of papers on the emotional states and their internal accompaniments. The most important of his researches concerned the working of certain small glands lying near the kidneys, and called the adrenal glands. These small glands were found to give out minute quantities of a substance which Professor Cannon has called adrenin, and the strong emotions, such as fear and rage, as well as very great pain were found to increase its flow. Now the amount of adrenin secreted was extraordinarily minute, and yet enormous effects are produced. In five seconds, the two glands together produce something under one hundredth of a milligram, or one three millionth part of an ounce. And yet this almost infinite small secretion can, it seems, transform the behaviour of a hundred and fifty pound man, seven billion times as heavy! It is as though, by the introduction of a substance equal in weight to one of its inhabitants, everyone in the city of Boston and ten thousand other cities was thrown into a turmoil!

The way in which the adrenin works is very interesting. First of all, it acts as a direct antidote to fatigue. This it does in two ways, first by bringing out sugar from the liver; and sugar is one of the great sources of energy for the muscles, as athletes know who eat it between races. It acts directly on the muscles, making them able to be used again at very short notice. So strong is this restoring action of adrenin that Professor Cannon has said that, what rest will take two hours to do, adrenin accomplishes in five minutes. Thus the muscles are restored and fresh fuel is given them.

The second thing that the adrenin does is to drive the blood from the digestive and other parts of the body, to the muscles moving the skeleton, which, it seems likely, an emergency will call into action. At a crisis, digestion may well be suspended, and it has in fact been shown that anger or fear will stop the digestive movements of the stomach. During emotion, power tends to be diverted from all channels except those providing for swift action to meet the threatening situation.

Lastly, the adrenin decreases the time of coagulation of the blood, hastening the formation of a scab. Thus, if the organism is wounded, as is more likely to happen in time of emotional stress, less blood will be lost, and wounds heal quicker.

Thus, the adrenin places the body under martial law, and puts everything into the condition most favourable for great muscular exertion. When stories are told of the wonderful things accomplished by soldiers in the heat of battle, or of wonderful feats of endurance, it is not necessary to assume, as is often done, some subconscious store of energy. Store of energy there is, but it is in the body, and is set free by the little adrenal gland. When this gland pipes the order for preparedness, at once the whole body is put on a emergency basis. Unheard of exertions are possible, a special fatigue elimination service is set up, wounds are quickly taken care of. A miracle of organization! And it is then we feel "angry" or "afraid".

Now these results of Professor Cannon on the work of the adrenal glands were exactly what was wanted to put the James-Lange theory on its feet again. The difficulty had been to put a finger on any bodily change that could account for what we can observe when we are under emotion. To say that the general disturbance of the intestines, or the changed heart beat, or anything parallel to these, could cause the terrific upheaval of which we are conscious when under emotion, seemed watery and unconvincing. But to consider the whole body as for a time placed on special emergency basis of one kind or another, this seems at least to fit in with "the way it feels." And although Professor Cannon claimed that his results made against James, yet he has really done James' theory a very good turn by showing the existence of these important internal disturbances, even though they seem the same in such opposite things as fear and rage. So that many of the psychologists of today are inclined, as a result of the discovery of the workings of adrenin, to think that something very like the rejected James-Lange paradox is true. And meanwhile, we wait for someone to tell us, just why anger should feel so different from fear!

The discovery will come, though, perhaps, not along the lines of Professor Cannon's experiments.*

(d) THE TWO WAYS IN WHICH OUR BODY MOBILIZES. EDUCATING THE EMOTIONS

Pleasantness and unpleasantness, pain, and emotion illustrate a fresh fact, namely that the body is organized at different levels to meet the situations in which it finds itself. Pleasantness and unpleasantness belong to an earlier line of defence. If a thing is good for us, in general it is pleasant and we feel attracted towards it. If it is bad for us, as most things are that cause pain, then we are usually repelled from it and we say it is unpleasant. If it is very bad for us, we show emotion, and in this case an entirely different organization of the body takes place. Let us explain this by an illustration.

Take a number of children and train them to sit and listen together to someone in a hall, or to engage in an orderly and quiet manner upon their own tasks in a class

* Many physiologists reject the findings of Professor Cannon, who again vigorously rejects the James-Lange theory!

room. This is what is done by a capable teacher, who, by interest or otherwise, manages to keep what is known as "good order." The children are organized into a class. Now suppose there is a sudden alarm of fire. At once, in a well managed school, the children all know exactly what to do. Ordinary work is suspended, and the pupils stand up and file out in the proper way to the proper place, the roof or the stair or whatever it may be. An emergency organization has been staged, the ordinary routine is broken off for the time being, and special steps are taken to meet the particular crisis.

Now very much the same thing happens in the human body. When the ordinary, everyday routine is adequate, the first organization, that of the class room, suffices. Pleasure and displeasure are bound up with the routine situations of life, and belong primarily to the routine working of the body. But here is a remarkable thing.

No one has to teach the body to organize its parts and the messages of its nerves. No one teaches the human class to keep order. Nature has schooled the cells and the collections of cells called the parts of the body to be a *child*, before ever a teacher schools him to be part of a *class*. No one has to teach him how to feel pleased or annoyed.

Suppose now that an emergency arises. At once a different organization is brought into force. The body behaves in the same way as does the well trained class of children at a fire alarm. Routine is stopped. Digestion is abandoned for the time being; the heart beats quicker, and so on. By concerted action, the crisis is met. But here again the body does not need teaching. Nature has completed the organization, drilled the class, assigned each group its duty. She has taught us how to be afraid.

Each of us carries, written out, orders for an emergency, which are put into effect whenever the routine organization is inadequate.

It can easily be seen, then, that one of the most important things we have to learn is how to use our own powers of protection by means of the organizations which nature has given us. It is impossible and unnecessary to teach a man to be angry. It is completely possible to teach him when to be angry. Someone was perfectly right and a very good psychologist, when he distinguished between unreasoning fury and righteous indignation. It is impossible to teach a child not to fear, and this would be undesirable if it were possible. But it is proper, and indeed essential, to teach the things that ought to be feared. A young child should fear to cross a busy road alone. The ordinary organization, with the consciousness of pleasantness and unpleasantness, is not adequate to deal with a situation where life and death may be involved.

As a measure of emergency, emotion should be a comparatively rare occurrence. The man who is furious at breakfast when the porridge is cold, and furious after breakfast when his train is late, and furious in the train because the window is down and so on through the day, is like a class that has fire drill every quarter of an hour or a nation that mobilizes for war every month. Ordinary business is impossible under such conditions, and in spite of the advocates of the crowded hour of glorious life, it is routine that keeps the earth turning. It is best, to be angry and to show other emotion at the right occasions, and then only. Just which are the right occasions, is for other and wiser people than I to decide. And this solves another puzzle.

Many psychologists, and in particular the followers of the Austrian physician, Freud, have lately been pointing out the evil effects of what they call repression. A repressed emotion is one that is bottled up. To live day in and day out with a person who inspires one every half hour with a desire to kill him, and to keep perfectly silent about it all; to watch, month in and month out, somebody stealing away the affections of a loved one, and to endure; to go to bed in abject terror of the dark and not cry out for fear of the word coward: — that is repression. It is far healthier in such cases, say these psychologists, to let the emotion take its normal course, to fight, to upbraid, or to cry out as the case may be. Repression of this kind has been proved beyond a doubt to have very serious effects. "Nervous breakdown", loss of sleep, and whole flocks of the most extraordinary symptoms may result. The body is disorganized, just as would be a class of children to whom the teacher was continually shouting "Fire", while compelling them to keep their seats. To express the emotion is certainly far healthier — for the individual concerned. But it is hardly so healthy for others. It seems a little one-sided to tell a patient to kill his aunt in order to cure his insomnia! Yet many such cases arise, where it is impossible on the one hand to counsel expression, because of the rights of others, while on the other hand the repression is doing harm to the patient. The dilemma is certainly a difficult one.

Such problems do not of course confront the ordinary man or woman, and when they occur they should be dealt with by an expert. But there is another aspect of the same thing which very vitally affects almost every household in the land, and that is the problem of the expression of childish emotions. If repression of emotion is bad, then it seems to follow that when a child becomes angry he should be allowed to rage and scream, throw his (or her) cup on the floor, and his hat at his mother, and tear his hair out by the roots. All this is expression of emotion, and, the theory is that if the tantrum does not "out" in the natural way, the childish individuality will be warped, and possibly nervous trouble set in. The logical result would seem that every house with children should be, if not a hell, at least a chaos, that so the individuality of the child may be preserved. Now of course the many eminent specialists who have devoted themselves to the study of the child along these lines would hardly take such an extreme position. But there are so many who profess a Freudian omniscience that it is worth while to expose this particular fallacy.

First of all, nobody, outside the few savages of Aveyron, has to live in a world apart from other people. The fact that there are others in the world, necessarily limits us, and it is part of our education to learn to live with other people. The practical problem is, then, not what might be the best thing if the world were made differently, but how best to educate a child to meet the conditions that are. Any tantrum, therefore, the expression of which interferes unduly with others, should be repressed, if that is the only way to safeguard the rights of others. A child can no more disregard the fact that there are other human beings in the world than he can disregard the fact that if he falls from a fourth floor window he will be killed. People are as much a part of his environment as pavements, and if he disregards either he will ultimately come to grief when the nurse happens to be away. No one allows a child to fall out of a window so that his individuality may be retained. The same point was pointed out to me recently by a very wise psychologist and father. He showed how wrong it is to take the attitude that one should never be angry with a child. "The child," he said, "has to learn that if he does certain things he will make people angry, and that is part of his education." And yet how many parents there are who feel somewhat self-righteous over the fact that they never punish in anger!

Fortunately there is a way of escaping this dilemma, that seems to arise between repression and harm for the child, and expression, with harm to other people. The escape lies in the proper education of the emotions. The maxim is, not to grow angry and repress the anger, but *not to grow angry at all where repression is to be necessary*. Anger is not wrong. Anger at the wrong things is wrong.

Such education, which provides that the natural mechanism of anger shall be set in motion at the proper stimulus, is an extraordinarily important part of our upbringing, and very few parents consciously face its problems. That it is in theory possible to cause any stimulus to set off the mechanism of anger or fear is shown by the experiments of Professor Watson on young children. Watson found that one of the few things which caused fear in a young baby was the sudden clang of a metal bar. So he first of all took animals such as cats and rabbits, and brought them up close to the child in its cot. Baby was delighted at the curious jumping sight. Then a white rat was brought up and at the same time the objectionable clang loudly sounded. Baby began to cry. This was repeated a few times, and then the rat was brought up without the clang of the bell. Cries came again, and the child showed every evidence of terror. He had been given a conditional, or associated, fear reaction, the first or primary stimulus being the unpleasant sound, the second the sight of the animal. By association, the second stimulus was made to gain strong emotional power. When this emotional reaction was firmly established it was set off by a rabbit and finally by a fur coat! From these and other experiments, it is obvious that an extensive emotional education of any child is entirely within our power. We can teach a child the right kind of occasion for the emergency mobilization of his body.

The proper answer then to the perplexing choice between repression and expression of emotion is something as follows: the fact that such a dilemma exists at all is an evidence of bad emotional education. If a child grows furious because he cannot draw in his father's books, this means that he has never been taught that the rights of others are facts as inevitable as the hardness of the wall. Very few boys will cry because they cannot walk through a wall. Few would cry because they cannot play with the electric light bulb if mothers were as wise as nature.

And this leads to another interesting question. How does nature manage to teach her lessons so well? How does it come about that the child accepts, as a matter of fact, physical impossibilities, while even in adult life he refuses to recognize what might be called social impossibilities, such as cheating or angering others without ultimate harm to himself?

The answer is twofold. Nature is inevitable. She never makes an exception. And secondly, and perhaps more important, nature hurts.

If running into a wall were sometimes followed by discomfort and sometimes not, then it is easy to see that a child would take a very long time to find out that bumping was harmful. If cutting the finger sometimes hurt and sometimes did not, and scraping the shin sometimes produced pain and sometimes not; if a fly in the eye were sometimes unpleasant and sometimes indifferent; then it is certain that the lesson of protection of the body, which *must* be learned, would be a much greater problem for parents than it is. But "that priceless danger-signal, pain," is invariably present in these cases, and is present on almost every occasion when actual harm is being done to the body. "If it hurts, don't do it," said the old doctor. The child doesn't, with exceptions already explained.

But the emotional education of a child is attended by no such certainty of punishment. True it is that we generally learn not to be angry with things, but the larger part of our emotional mistakes are made in connection with persons. And even when we do grow angry at, or because of, a thing, there is no immediate unpleasantness following, as when we bump into a wall. If the man who swears at the weather and grumbles at his porridge were immediately to receive some kind of an unpleasant bump on each occasion, such as he receives when he puts his hand through a pane of glass, then grumbling at the weather would be as rare as breaking windows with the bare hand. And if other emotional mistakes were likewise followed invariably by discomfort, then we would all be very much better balanced emotionally than we are now. On the whole, a child that associates with others at school or at home is apt to be more stable emotionally. That is because in a crowd of children misplaced emotion is very generally followed by unpleasant results, whether the emotion be anger or fear, or of any other kind.

And this leads to the last point that we shall make

this long section. It is often asked whether corporal punishment is justified. There is only one answer to this from the point of view of psychology. Nature's way of saying "hands off," is by discomfort. That is the only really effective way of drawing a ring about the otherwise attractive. Almost always, pain actually enters into this discomfort. Nature's way of teaching a child not to put his hand into too hot water is by causing pain. That is what the pain organ is for. Nature's way of teaching a puppy not to bite its own leg until damage is done is by causing pain. Right down the scale pain has the definite purpose of preventing damage.

Nature may seem at times to be hard, but she *teaches her lessons.* There seem to be occasions in the history of us all when the infliction of pain is necessary if an inhibition is to be securely established. No mother is doing her duty if she shirks her responsibility on these occasions. Of course, pain is a dangerous thing for the ignorant, the thoughtless and the uncontrolled to have at their disposal. But so is any other corrective, from five minutes in the corner to five years in prison.

Anger, fear, and other emotions, have, then, their definite place in emergency. They should not be called into play on ordinary occasions, but should be strictly reserved for the special situations which they were originally designed to meet. Repression of emotion is bad, but, with a firm and wise education, is, in a healthy individual, generally unnecessary. Often, in imparting this education it would seem that the proper thing is to imitate nature, who hurts.

And this seems to be the psychology of it!

Chapter X

MEASURING THE MIND

(a) THE STORY OF THE ARMY MENTAL TESTS

On April 6, 1917, America had declared war. The same day a group of psychologists met at Cambridge to consider how their science could best serve the country. History was made when the United States declared war on Germany. But an epoch was marked in the room in Emerson Hall, at Harvard, when the psychologists declared war on Germany.

Mind had come into its own!

Two thousand years ago, when Julius Cæsar was making his brilliant conquest of Gaul, the thought of organizing mind in a great war would have sounded absurd. To Cæsar, the idea of calling in for advice those whose business it was to understand mind, would have seemed madness. To Napoleon, men were pieces on the board, to be pushed here and there according to the ideas of those above them. The difference between them and chess pieces was that the soldiers provided their own motive power. And so he said that "An army moves on its stomach."

Today it might be said that an army moves on the cortex of the brain.

When the psychologists met to place at the disposal of the country their expert experience and knowledge they were proclaiming a new era in human progress.

The immediate result of the meeting was that a committee was formed which afterwards devised the famous Army

Mental Tests. Let us see what was the problem that these scientists found facing them. The country had declared war. This meant that the whole nation was to be organized to the highest point of fighting efficiency in the briefest possible time. Delay of a day would mean valuable lives lost. Delay of a week might mean a serious setback, only to be rectified by the loss of many lives and much treasure. Delay of six months might well have meant an irretrievable disaster. Hundreds of thousands of men had to be set doing the work for which their training and talents best fitted them. Those with the gift of command had to be given command, those with other special talents work accordingly. If a private with the makings of an officer was obliged to work his way up from the ranks, as had been the case in all previous wars, then the penalty for the intervening waste was to be paid in human blood.

No Shylock was ever so inexorable in demanding his pound of flesh as is the modern war in demanding the penalty for inefficiency and misplaced human material.

Eighteen months later, on November 11, 1918, one hundred and twenty officers and three hundred and fifty enlisted men were engaged in the psychological testing of recruits. Five hundred clerks were employed in tabulating and otherwise dealing with the results. One million and seven hundred thousand men had been examined, which is two and one-half times as many people as there were in Boston in 1920. Incalculable help had been afforded to commanding officers in giving a scientific estimate of the mental alertness of men and officers. Human waste had been very nearly eliminated.

The brains of the country had been organized for war! The task had been to pick good soldiers, and to pick out that kind of intelligence that makes good soldiers. As a British naval authority has said about candidates for officers' training, the shut-in, reserved, deliberate and introspective youth has his place in society, and perhaps this type of man represents the highest that is in human nature. But his place is not in command of a battleship, nor, we may add, of a battalion in the front line, where ability to think accurately and quickly is required. Consequently for the purposes of the United States army a set of tests was devised, which presented two hundred and twelve problems, elementary situations to meet, simple, each of them, in themselves, but hard to solve correctly at a high rate of speed. One who easily becomes "rattled" cannot do very well at the army tests. But neither should such a one be put in charge of the lives of a number of his fellow men.

Sample questions are as follows:

Test 1, number 7. The first sixteen letters of the alphabet are printed. The man is told to cross out the letter just after F, and also to draw a line under the second letter after I.

Simple, but only those who have corrected these papers can realize how many become confused, and underline G, or make some similar mistake. This series of questions, of which there were twelve was designed to test a man's ability to understand, remember, and carry out instructions, a most important thing in warfare.

In another series the man was asked to get the answers to twenty arithmetical sums, of this kind.

If an aeroplane goes three hundred yards in ten seconds, how many *feet* does it go in a fifth of a second?

Other tests called for the opposites of words, choice of common sense reasons, general information and so on.

Speed and accuracy in meeting concrete, everyday situations are required in the army, and to a remarkable degree these qualities were detected by the army tests. The best, and indeed the only test of the tests lay in the results. Judged by this standard the Army Mental Tests were completely successful. Despite a very natural conservatism, practically all of those in charge of selection and promotion of men were enthusiastic over the new method. The psychological examination would be given "as a matter of routine." The tests are "an absolute guide" to what may be expected of the men in the future. They give a "unique assistance." Such are some of the phrases used by the hard-headed men whose business was war.

Let us now examine some of the results of this psychological stocktaking of one and three-quarter millions of men. The highest five per cent, those who scored 135 and over, were rated as high "officer material," as far as their intelligence went. Such men can make a superior record in college or university. They are the men who can rapidly size up a practical situation, and quickly devise the right way of meeting it. Such, in general, are our successful business men.

At the other end of the scale come those who score 24 and less. Most of this class can just do military work, but some of them are actually feebleminded. The latter were labeled E, while those who could just be employed in the army were classed as D and D —. Between the two extremes came the C men, who scored from twenty-five to a hundred and four. This class contained sixty per cent of the whole, and made up the bulk of the army, including private, good private, and non-commissioned officer material. The average score of these men was from forty-five to seventy-four, which was thus the average score of the whole number of men examined.

And then came a paradox that has threatened to throw the whole of our political theory into the melting pot. When, for certain purposes, the army authorities selected a hundred thousand random men, and estimated their average mental age, they came to this astonishing conclusion.

The mental age of the army averaged something over thirteen years! Taking the army as an approximation to the whole country, we seem to be forced to the conclusion that the mental age of this country averages between thirteen and fourteen!

Now there has arisen a great deal of discussion about this extraordinary finding. In itself, it is extraordinary. It means that, intellectually, we are at the same average as a seventh grade in any grammar school. Expressed the other way round, it means that in the United States of America there is a great class of fifty million intellectual seventh graders in control of the destinies of the country, in so far as democratic control is real, and perhaps, as matters now stand, holding the casting vote in world politics.

A startling result, it seems, if it is true. And it appears to have the support of high scientific authority.

Let us examine the results a little closer. Perhaps they will not turn out to be so startling after all. First, it has been suggested that not all have justice done them by the tests. In fact, as has been already pointed out and as the army authorities themselves admit, there certainly are individuals whose intelligence they do not fairly estimate, and these cases, it is said, invalidate the general conclusion. It is doubtful whether the philosopher Kant would have scored very high. There is the authentic case of one of the best salesmen in New England, who could not pass the test at all. But such instances, it must be admitted, are rare, and for all practical purposes we may assume that most individuals were fairly dealt with by the tests. What has then been shown is that, in the ability to do such things as the army demanded, to cope with new situations of the practical type, situations where previous experience does not count, most men do not develop very much after they are thirteen years of age. Which means that the average boy scout of thirteen years or so is probably as good at devising means to meet simple practical situations as the average private of twenty.

That the average man does develop after thirteen is certain. But it seems to be equally certain that he does not develop in his ability to meet a novel situation. No modern psychologist has ever claimed that the ordinary man goes on developing intellectually after thirty, but it is quite certain that the average man of forty has something in his favor which he had not ten years ago. There are other things besides power to understand a concrete situation and to act upon it. Most of the judgments that we are called upon to make in everyday life do not tax us so much mentally as in a certain moral way, and in a certain way that appeals to our experience and life in the world.

The hard knocks and bitter experience of life which make us all so much more able to vote rightly at thirty than at twenty are not measured at all by the tests. The army tests measure only one, and that perhaps not the most important, aspect of a man. In pure intelligence we do not, as a nation, seem to advance very much after we are thirteen years old. But pure intelligence is not all, and we have to thank the army tests for removing a certain intellectual priggishness from our political thought. When the dust has died down, that will, I believe, be seen to stand as the great contribution of the tests to the science of sociology.

Another of the interesting results obtained was the comparison of the various trades and professions. Some startling figures came out, which may be seen in the fascinating book published about the tests, a reference to which will be found in the appendix. A list was given, showing the average position taken by some thirty trades and professions, and indicating how these stand in relation to each other.

Lowest, as might be expected, come laborers, who average C —. Miners, teamsters, and barbers are in the same group. A little higher up, averaging C, come twenty-one professions, including bricklayers, blacksmiths, plumbers, general mechanics, auto repairmen, and telephone operators in order of intelligence. In the C + class are listed photographers, clerks, nurses and bookkeepers. Then come the aristocrats of the occupations. Under B were rated:

Dental Officers
Mechanical Draughtsmen
Accountants
Civil Engineers
Medical Officers

Highest of all came engineer officers, who averaged A. That is to say, the average engineer officer is in the top five per cent of the population as regards intelligence.

What do these figures mean? Are we to believe that, as a general rule, a filing clerk is superior in intelligence to those geniuses who can take a Ford engine apart and put it together again so that it runs? This is not the opinion of the world at large, which pays the one man anything up to seventy dollars a week and the other not over thirty.

Now the tests have come into much undeserved criticism at the hands of those who do not understand what their makers claimed for them. None of these scientists who devised them ever maintained, for example, that filing clerks are really more intelligent than automobile repair men. Indeed, they took good care in their report to point out that the mechanics as a whole would not be fairly represented, because the best of them would have been kept out of the army to engage in war production of various kinds. Naturally, each factory would keep its best men back, because work could not go on without them. Many college men seem to have listed themselves under the head of clerk, having perhaps learned to use the typewriter at college. And in addition the tests seem to have been better adapted to those who were engaged in clerical pursuits than to those who spend their time doing practical work with machinery. Thus it is not fair to estimate the relative intelligence of the whole class of clerks and the whole class of mechanics by the army results, first, because the army tests were not made upon representative samples from each profession, secondly, because the tests probably favoured one class more than another.

However, as a rough guide to the professions the tests have a decided value, provided always that we recognize their limitations. For example, a high school senior interviews his head master as to his future profession. The boy wishes to be a doctor. The boys of his class have all been tested and this particular student's score is 95.

"Well, Fred," says the principal, "your score shows us one thing. If you succeed in qualifying as a doctor, which is doubtful, and which will mean very hard work, you will have to work a great deal harder than most other physicians to make a good living. The average doctor in the war scored a long way over a hundred in the test, while you made only ninety-five. If you like to go into a profession in which you will find the other men in general more capable and more intelligent than you are, go ahead." If, in spite of this plain statement, the young man persists, then at least we know that he understands the position. If he has strength of purpose enough to overcome the odds that are against him, then he will probably make a good physician.

But there are other ways in which the same tests may be used for vocational purposes. For example, a friend of mine wished to send out a man to do business abroad for him. The venture was something entirely new and a capital of about a hundred thousand dollars was involved. Being a little uncertain about the man he asked if I could help. The person in question had a fine record for integrity and faithful service, knew his business inside out, and had never been known to make a mistake. His specially strong point was accountancy, but he was supposed to have an unusually good knowledge of the whole field of his particular work. He scored a hundred on the army test, which is very considerably lower than the average for accountants in the

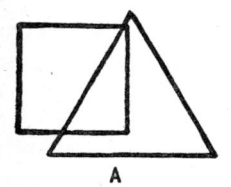

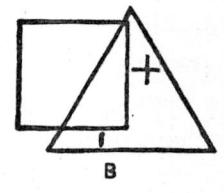

army. When asked to "make a figure 1 in the space which is in the square but not the triangle and also make a cross in the space in the square and in the triangle," he marked the simple form "A" as shown in "B."

This will seem incredible to those who have not actually seen it done. But it happened! Other direction tests were performed by the same man, some of them right and others wrong. In the set where the man was asked to solve twenty fairly simple arithmetical problems in five minutes, he actually did six, of which two were wrong. This was his worst performance, although his profession was to work with figures.

The report that I gave to my friend was something as follows:

This is a man who, you say, knows his trade. I cannot tell you about that, but I can show you what he did when I asked him to carry out a few simple directions. It seems to me that a man who cannot keep in his mind a couple of simple things like that is rather a poor business risk. When he is up against keen competition, it is my opinion that he will be outwitted every time by men who think more quickly and more accurately than he does. In general intelligence he is hardly up to the standard of the men who can make an average record in college. It may be that he has other qualities that will make him succeed in a position involving responsibility and initiative. But the chances seem to me against it. I certainly would not risk a hundred thousand of my own dollars, if I had them, upon this man."

To return to the army tests. Other tests were developed for ability in special trades. For example, there was a standard test for automobile drivers. This consisted in actually making a trial trip under standard conditions. Similarly, locomotive engineers were required to do certain things with a locomotive before they were actually classed as drivers.

Those who laid claim to any given ability or proficiency

in any skilled trade, were required to pass a standard test upon that trade. For example, "Machinists and Mechanics" were asked:

"What is a small file called?"

"What form of a die is used for removing the flash?" and rated accordingly to their answers. Other tests consisted in the recognition of certain tools of the trade. Thus a carpenter was shown pictures of various carpentering tools, among other technical details. He was also required to identify different kinds of wood. Enormous saving to the army and the nation was effected by these means. It was possible immediately to detect the man who had helped father shingle the roof and considered himself qualified to take the good money of the taxpayers as an expert carpenter. It also ruled out such applicants for skilled positions as those who applied to a Canadian house decorating concern, who had a rush order for a painting job. Eight so-called skilled painters were hired, and on the morning when they were to report all appeared, but no one seemed inclined to begin work. Finally, it appeared that each was waiting for the others to begin! None had ever painted a house before!

The end of the testing movement is not yet. Psychologists have only begun to standardize the activities of man, and to measure his abilities. The direction that future work will take is hard to prophesy. Already, in the home and in the school, in the workshop and in the counting house, tests of one kind and another are being used. Tests of intelligence are helping college authorities to place students; special tests are helping employers to save the enormous waste that comes from hiring a man, training him, and then having to let him go because he is unsuitable for the work. Tests are being devised to help employers choose and promote their employees, to help factory owners pick the right applicant for a position requiring a peculiar dexterity, to pick good salesmen, to choose a stenographer.

There is no reason why a test should not be devised that will bring about a material saving of money for any large employer of labor.

This is the era of psychology. A large part of practical psychology is destined to crystallize into a test of some kind or other. And the greatest, the most scientific, the most thorough experiment upon testing, the one most fraught with consequences for the future, the best balanced, and the sanest of all the attempts to measure the human mind, generally and in a hundred special ways, was the work undertaken by those who devised the Army Mental Tests.

(b) MENTAL TESTS AND THE CHILD

"That is an intelligent boy," said an old schoolmaster to me, as we watched one day a group of children play on the shore.

"How do you know?" I asked.

"Why, he is only eight years old, and yet he acts exactly as any ordinary boy of twelve. He has as much sense as any twelve-year-old."

This was while I was at college, and before we had begun to hear so much about mental tests. But the schoolmaster's remark was so much in keeping with the modern idea of mental testing that it might have been said by a psychologist of today.

We have spoken throughout this book of the human being as incessantly adapting to conditions without.

The person who, seeing a dark cloud, takes an umbrella out with him is adapting to that particular situation better than the one who goes umbrella-less and gets wet. The business man who, seeing that certain political changes are coming, forecasts the probable effect on his business and buys accordingly, is adapting better than the man in the next office who reads the same newspaper, practices the same business, but does not take account of political changes when he does his buying. The child who, seeing marmalade on the table, brings a chair to stand upon, and can thus reach the pot, is adapting better than the one who sees the jampot, wants the jam, cannot reach and does not think of the chair.

In each of these cases, the one that has adapted better would be called the more intelligent. In general, and with certain reservations, we say that intelligence is power of adaptation, which means that it is the power of doing things to meet situations of one sort or another. These may be as simple as the situation which arises when a baby's toy falls from the cradle on to the floor, or as complicated as the situation which faces a statesman when the country is passing through a crisis. The baby who looks over the cradle for a fallen toy is acting on the same principle as is the statesman who decides upon a policy after an exhaustive economic and political study. Each is acting to meet a situation, and each is able to do so by the aid of his own past experience, and of the nervous organization which he inherited. But the nervous organization of the one enables him to deal with a much more complex situation than the other, and to make the right response. The difference is one of degree, not of kind.

At about six months or earlier the child begins to meet the situation of a fallen toy by looking over to the floor. This might then be taken as a test of intelligence for that particular age. If a six-months baby can do this, then we might say that the child was of average intelligence for his age. If he could do things that could generally be done only by older children, we should say that he was above the average in intelligence. If he could not do things within the power of most children of his own age, then we should say that he was below the average. Thus intelligence would be measured by the things a child could do. And if we had a list of the things that an average child can do at ages one, two, three, and so on up to adulthood, we would have a scale by which it would be possible to measure the intelligence of an individual about whom we were doubtful.

Now this is exactly what has been done in the famous "Binet" and other scales for the testing of children's intelligence. Binet, the French psychologist, made experiments with hundreds of Parisian children, to find the situations that were within the power of children of various ages. According to his table, a child of ordinary intelligence should be able to do the following things at the ages stated. The list is a shortened one, given by Doctor Goddard.*

Mental Age Four Years.

1. Give sex of self.
2. Names familiar objects (key, knife and penny).
3. Repeats correctly three digits, e.g., "7-2-9."
4. Tells which of two lines is the longer (5cms. and 6 cms.).

Mental Age Five Years.

1. Correctly compares 3 and 12 grams and 6 and 15 grams.
2. Copies a square of 3 or 4 centimeters well enough to recognize it as a square.
3. Repeats 10 syllables, e.g., "His name is John. He is a very good boy."

*In "The Training School" for 1910, page 146.

4. Counts four pennies placed in a row.

5 Reforms a visiting card from the two pieces made by cutting one diagonally.

Mental Age Six Years.

1. Tells whether it is morning or afternoon.
2. Defines by "use" at least three of the following: fork, table, chair, horse, mama.
3. Executes three simple commissions given at once.
4. Indicates right hand and left ear.
5. Chooses the prettier of two heads, one pretty, the other very ugly, when they are shown in pairs.

Mental Age Seven Years.

1. Counts thirteen pennies placed in a row.
2. Tells what he sees in pictures. Describes instead of simply naming things.
3. Tells what is lacking when shown pictures of a head lacking an eye, a mouth or a nose, or of a head and body lacking arms.
4. Copies a diamond.
5. Names promptly four colors: red, blue, green and yellow.

Mental Age Eight Years.

1. Tells difference between a butterfly and a fly; between wood and glass; between paper and pasteboard.
2. Counts backwards from 20 to 1, in 20 seconds.
3. Names days of the week in 10 seconds.
4. Tells how much they are worth, when shown three one-cent and three two-cent stamps.
5. Repeats correctly five digits, e.g., "4-7-3-9-5."

Mental Age Nine Years.

1. Makes change—9 cents out of 25.

2. Gives definitions better than by use.

3. Names the day of the week, the month, the day of the month, and the year.

4. Recites the months of the year in 15 seconds.

5. Arranges in correct order a series of weights of 6, 9, 12, 15 and 18 grams.

Mental Age Ten Years.

1. Names nine different pieces of money.

2. Draws two simple geometrical designs from memory.

3. Repeats six digits.

4. Answers intelligently simple problem questions, e.g., "What ought one to do before undertaking something important?"

5. Uses three words, as New York, money and river, in one sentence.

Mental Age Eleven Years.

1. Detects the nonsense in absurd statements.

2. Uses three words in one sentence (given also at age ten).

3. Gives sixty words in three minutes.

4. Finds three words in one minute which rhyme with words like day, mill or spring.

5. Forms a sentence, in one minute, out of ten printed words, in disconnected order, as the following: started-the-for-an-early-hour-we-country-at-.

Mental Age Twelve Years.

1. Repeats correctly seven digits, once in three trials.

2. Defines charity, justice, goodness.

3. Repeats a sentence of twenty-six syllables.

4. Resists suggestion.

5. Solves problems of fact. (a) "A person who was

walking in the forest of Fontainebleau suddenly stopped much frightened and hastened to the nearest police and reported that he had seen hanging from the limb of a tree a-what?" (b) "My neighbor has been having strange visitors. He has received one after the other a physician, a lawyer, and a clergyman. What has happened at the house of my neighbor?"

A child who can do the tests listed under year six is said to have a mental age of six years, and so on. Such a child may actually be only five or four, or even three years of age, although this last is extremely rare. Sir Francis Galton, the famous English Scientist, seems at four years to have been able to meet the situations that are generally beyond the powers of children below eight years of age. Consequently, little Francis would have a mental age exactly double his age as usually reckoned. But there are not many Francis Galtons.

This then is roughly the great principle of the mental tests as applied to children. Find out what a child of a certain age ought to be able to do. If any given child can do this, he is mentally of that particular age. If he can do it and more, he is of higher mental age. If less, he is less intelligent. This seems a simple procedure, yet the Stanford Revision of Binet's tests alone took several years' work, on the part of a large staff of investigators and students. And it is an achievement of which American science can well be proud. As a direct result of this and other researches of the same kind, thousands of children are now receiving the treatment at school to which their intelligence entitles them. The backward child is being placed in a class where he can go his own pace, and not waste the time of the class and the teacher. The brilliant child is being given that special attention to which his talents entitle him. Probably this one movement will in the future result in a greater saving of man-power than has ever been brought about by any piece of scientific work. For misfits mean waste of human power, and the testing movement aims to do away with misfits in our school classes. Requiring a trained psychologist to administer them with exactness, yet capable of being roughly given by any country school mistress, the tests are the greatest help which science has yet given to those to whom we entrust the education of our children.

Finally there should be mentioned an interesting application that has been made of the tests by the eminent British authority Spearman, now at Columbia. By applying to various tests a complex mathematical analysis, not yet accepted by all psychologists, Spearman claims to have found a common intelligence factor which is contrasted with special factors such as the mechanical and musical ones. A person may be high in intelligence ("g") and low in any or all of the special abilities, which include, besides, "logical" and "psychological" as well as arithmetical abilities. Our non-musical friends, who "used to know two tunes but have forgotten one of them" will then probably console themselves by the belief that, in spite of this deficiency, they are dowered with an astonishingly high degree of "g"!

Chapter XI

UNBENDING THE BOW

(a) HOW MOST OF US WASTE OURSELVES

THIS is a chapter on relaxation.

The reader who is a constant traveller on the subways or the elevated railways of a big city will probably have noticed the large number of his fellow passengers who sit in their seats or stand and hold to their straps, the while wrinkling with their brows and setting their teeth. To watch them, one would imagine that they were pulling along the train by their eyebrows, or running the street car with the muscles of their jaws. These men are not pulling the car along with their eyebrows. They are holding on with them to their business.

I once saw a man who, by means of an apparatus fixed on his face, professed to lift a large weight by wrinkling his forehead. He performed this trick only twice every night, and four times, I think, every Wednesday and Saturday. The men in the street car carry as heavy a load, but they are doing their trick all the time. They are the men who never relax.

Emotion, it will be remembered, arises when our body is placed under martial law, mobilizing our resources so that we may be ready for the intense exertion which is to follow. The state of consciousness which arises at the time of this mobilization we call fear or rage, or whatever the case may be. Emotion is thus very intimately bound up with the action of the muscles, and it is indeed probable that, could one prevent one's muscles from contracting, fear and other emotion would be nearly impossible. This is not to deny that fear is dependent also upon internal changes. It simply means that, robbed of the muscular action which almost invariably accompanies emotion, the internal changes seem to be minimized. They lose their sting. And worry is an emotion, not powerful and acute, but chronic and long drawn out, and of insidiously low potential, as the electricians say.

Let me now recommend a simple experiment. The next time the reader is suffering from a mild degree of excitement or feels himself worrying, let him pay special attention to the muscles of his back, right between and on the shoulders. In nine cases out of ten, he will find that they are stiff and taut. Let him now relax them and he will feel immediate relief. The relaxation of the muscles has given the "stop" signal to the bodily changes, whatever they are, that go with excitement or worry.

Several persons have told me that, as far as they could tell, when they were over-excited their shoulder muscles were always tense. Several of them have said that they found it impossible to be excited when they let these muscles go.

Now it would be found that of the men in the street car, almost all whose brows were contracted were also tense in other parts of their body, even when the muscular tension was due to such a thing as eye trouble. If they could be induced to let the rest of their muscles relax, an extraordinary change of expression would come over their face. The hard, drawn look would disappear, the jaws would lose the look of the steel trap, the shoulders would droop. I have seen the transformation many times. Any reader may see it who either suffers himself from the too-early drawn brow or whose friend suffers.

Let me give another illustration. A man got up one morning, went down to his bank, drew out a fifty-dollar bill. Then he walked out of the bank, tore the bill in half and threw it into the gutter.

The man was a fool!

How many men in such a city as New York are equally foolish? To take our good nervous energy and use it to hold fast the eyebrows and to hold tight the shoulder muscles is far worse folly than to tear up a ten-dollar bill, for nervous energy is harder to replace than dollars. All of us, strong and weak, have a certain limited amount of energy at our disposal. The efficient man uses it to live. The inefficient man to make internal friction and stress. The man who has the habit of unnecessary muscular tension, or of worry, which is apt to go with unnecessary tension, is going every morning to his bank and taking nervous capital to throw into the gutter.

This is one of the things in which modern life has made us inefficient. A cat that is angered shows its wrath by an immediate arching up of the body and spitting, or perhaps by a swift scratch with the paw. After the occasion for the passion had passed, the animal will still lash its tail from side to side for a while. The digestive processes, we know, will be halted for a considerable time. But with the exception of the tail there seems to be no tightening of the muscles very long after the need for action has passed. The cat does not waste her energy, and in that she is wiser than many of us.

In the same way, a young child that is put to bed immediately relaxes all its muscles. If you take up such a child when it is sleeping its small limbs fall "all over the place." But many adults, when they sleep, may be seen to clench their hands and set their teeth. They look as though they were trying to hold up the pillow. If we wish to enter the kingdom of heaven, which is the land of happiness, we must do so as a little child.

Now there are many people who know all this and will say at once, that while other people may be able to relax, they themselves can never do so. Such people are generally rather proud of their supposed inability, as though it gave them a superiority over ordinary mortals. As a matter of fact, they have nothing to be proud of. They might as well, indeed, plume themselves upon being spendthrifts or on not brushing their teeth. Everyone can learn to relax, and perhaps one measure of a man's calibre is to be found in the completeness with which he is able to let everything drop after hours of stress.

The greatest of all men slept like a little child during the storm.

(b) RELIEVING SLEEPLESSNESS BY RELAXATION

One day there came to see me a man who had long suffered from insomnia and general worry. He had heard that psychology could help such cases as his, and, on talking the matter over with his physician, had decided to come and find out whether anything could be done for him. Ordinarily, professional duties make it impossible for one engaged in teaching to give the necessary time to a case like this. But sometimes exceptions may be made, and this seemed to be the time for an exception.

Had the reader been present, this is what he would have seen. A tall, powerful man, of about the average weight, with a look of authority about him that was accentuated by the well-cut clothes he was wearing. When he spoke, one felt that he had the habit of command. When he was not speaking, he was never still, but his hand continually played with his watch chain, or twisting up pieces of paper or tapped on the sides of the Morris chair on which he sat.

His story was that, before the war, he had been a marvel of strength. Nothing that was physically impossible to other men, and was within human power, seemed impossible to him. He would work up to twelve o'clock at night, go out for a walk for an hour, sleep till seven o'clock and be ready to start another day. This kind of life he had led for years, but the war brought an additional load upon him and he began, as he put it, "to notice the strain" of a burden that would have killed most men. He began to feel as though he would like another hour in bed in the morning. He began not to go to sleep until an hour or so after lying down, and to notice that he had a digestion, of which latter he had always been happily ignorant.

After the war ended, things went on for a time until one night, before going to bed, he had engaged in a heated argument, which kept him awake. The next night he had been in bed half an hour or so, when suddenly an awful thought flashed into his head.

"Suppose I do not go to sleep tonight. That will be terrible, and there is that important business tomorrow."

He did not go to sleep until something round three o'clock.

The next night things were as bad. All day he had been saying to himself that he felt miserable, and thinking that he would be unable to sleep. As night came nearer, a shadow seemed to rise up out of nothing and drop over him in terrifying proportions. After he had retired for the night, he lay rigid, eagerly watching for the least sign of sleep and listening with agony to the strokes of the neighbouring clock. As each hour struck he would grow still more rigid, until he finally stepped out of bed, put on his clothes and walked outside through the town for an hour. Then he came back nd went to bed again and lay with but a few moments' sleep at intervals until the whistles blew in the morning.

The next day he went to his doctor who sent him away to Florida. There he found things a little better, but did not receive the complete cure he had hoped for. Back he came after three weeks, started work again, and found his sleeping as bad as ever. Complete cure for him would, as he knew, have come with a rest of a year or more, and his doctor was constantly urging him to give up everything and go to Europe. The banker, however, felt that he could not, in fairness to his business and his clients, leave at such a critical time.

A depressing picture. For two months, this highly efficient, talented man of business, lives under the shadow of a daily fear that gathers as the sun crosses the sky. In the morning, fairly cheerful; as the day passes, little by little more consumed at heart with secret dread of the evening. At night, he lies tense on his bed, hearing the chimes of the clock like the strokes of a guillotine. For three weeks he heard every hour struck at night between ten o'clock and sunrise. And in spite of everything, he kept his bank going at a time when every other savings bank in the State was said to be really showing a deficit for the year, and when financial firms were daily failing in his city.

It was then that his physician suggested that, as the trouble seemed psychological rather than physical, it would be a good thing to see whether he could obtain help from a psychologist.

It was easy to see that, as his doctor had pointed out, he never relaxed. The lines of his face were set hard, he had a frown a quarter of an inch deep between the eyes, his hands, when he had finished gesturing with them, remained stiff, with the fist clenched. The first thing necessary was to show him this and explain how he wasted his valuable strength by useless muscular effort. He was placed in a Morris chair, told to make himself as comfortable as possible and try to let his muscles go. Then one of his hands was raised, and he was shown how he could not let the muscles of the arm relax, letting the arm fall when support was taken away, but held the arm there stiff in the air.

Both hands and arms were tested by holding them up and letting them fall, care being taken to catch the falling limb. The tired man was then told to lie back in the chair, as comfortably as possible, and to let his whole body relax in the same way as his arms now relaxed. Then he was spoken to something as follows:

"I want you now, please, to take a deep breath, through your nose and out of your mouth. Make it sound as though you were an actor on the stage, when the curtain goes up, who is trying to show to the audience that he has just passed successfully through a crisis. Sound as if all the cares of the world have just been lifted from your shoulders, and as though you are now perfectly happy and going to remain happy for the rest of your life."

Two or three attempts are almost always required before an easy sigh is produced. It is remarkable how difficult it is even to sound refreshed. Almost everybody who is in a nervous condition, such as this, forces out the breath as though he was trying to blow up a lung tester. It is indeed rare, at the first sitting, that one succeeds in inducing a real sigh of relief.

"Now let your shoulders relax, just as did your arms. Think of them as relaxed and then forget about them. Let your chest go, and the muscles of the stomach. Let your legs go, and feel them hanging loosely and limply from your hips. Feel the chair and the floor hold them up, feel the pressure of your legs on the chair and on the floor. Now let your arms go, and feel the arms of the Morris chair holding them up. Feel them hang loosely and limply from your shoulders. Relax the big muscles of the back, used so much during the daily work, and which hold the spine up straight. Relax your throat and neck, and face and forehead. Especially that little furrow between the eyebrows. Let it all go. Now let the jaw muscles relax. Don't let the teeth touch. Let everything go."

I wish that I could let the reader in to a scene like this, that he might see the astonishing effect of this simple procedure. The man is lying easily and quietly in the chair, looking fast asleep or even dead. His eyes have closed. There is on his face an expression of peace and quiet that has been absent for many a week. His shoulders have sunk into the cushions of the chair as though there was nothing to keep them up. He is breathing quietly as if his troubles were over. Wrinkles seem suddenly to have been ironed out, and instead of the tense, tight look about the face, there is an expression of normal weariness and fatigue, such as ought to be after the superhuman exertions of the man.

He is resting for the first time in months.

Sometimes it is good to speak of these changes. Accordingly I say:

"You are resting now, for the first time in months. Your face has an expression of peace that it has not shown for a long time. Your breathing is more regular, and I can see that your heartbeat is slower and less excited. You are resting now like a little child."

Sometimes, now, I go over the parts of the body again, to make sure that there is good relaxation in all of them. Thus I say:

"Now I am going over all the parts of the body again, and I wish you again to think of them as relaxed. Let your arms go, and your shoulders, your chest and stomach, your legs and back, your throat and neck, face and forehead and jaws. Do not let the teeth touch. Feel as though the chair was holding you up, sink into it, and give up control of all your limbs. . . . Rest now as long as you feel that it is a* rest for you to lie there."

There he lies, looking as though he were Prometheus, inventor of fire, tortured for ten thousand years by the gods for his boldness, and now given respite from his agony for half an hour. Nothing could be quieter or more profoundly like a picture of quiet after long labour. . . .

After ten minutes he opens his eyes and looks around him. I tell him to go home, to go to bed at his usual time that night, and to come again after two days.

The next time he comes, he looks rather foolish.

"How have you been?"

"A little better, I think."

"How did you sleep?"

"Very well the first night, not so well the second night."

"Why was that?"

"I went to New York, and did not get to bed until three.

*The printer of the first edition of this book printed this line twice, the only considerable mistake he made!

Then I had a conference at half past eight, so I had to get up at seven."

But out of the four hours that he was in bed he slept three and a half! And this after a hard day's work, lasting up to three in the morning! This is the man who heard all the night chimes for three weeks! And he has felt better the last two days than for some months. But there is a hesitancy about him. I recognize it, for I expect it.

He does not, at heart, believe that his improvement is due to the visit. He thinks it has come because of the change in the weather, or because he has been careful about what he has eaten, or because he has been to New York. He cannot believe that such a simple thing as sitting in a chair could do him so much good.

It *is* incredible, but so are many other simple things!

The only reason why he has come back is, he tells himself, because, after all, it is not fair to come only once and take up my time for nothing. But almost without exception, they do come back.

Then I suggest, after talking over his difficulties, that he shall relax himself again at my direction. With a smile of tolerance he obeys.

This time I go into things a little more thoroughly. Thus, after giving him the same directions, he lets the muscles of his body go. When I see that he seems to be fairly well relaxed in this way, I tell him:

"Now imagine that the chair is pushing you up; you can feel the pressure of the chair on your back and limbs, you can feel the pressure of the floor on your feet. Let the chair hold you up, and think of the floor as holding, pressing up the chair. The walls hold the floor, and the earth holds up the walls. The earth is a part of the great universe, it is floating round the sun, slowly and majestically, and you are resting on the earth. You are floating with it. You are part of the great universe, and I want you to think of yourself floating up and away from the earth and up to the stars. Millions of years the stars have been shining before you and I were born, and they will shine millions of years after we are gone. All our troubles shrink into insignificance if we weigh them by the standards of the great universe of which you are a part.

"Rest now, and relax, and lie there as long as you feel rested."

In ten minutes he opens his eyes, and I send him home to go to bed, with instructions to go through the relaxing night and morning in bed, and also once during the day.

The next time he is not so scornful. Everybody, including his wife, has been telling him how much better he looks. He begins to seem younger, his step has more elasticity. Little by little he obtains relief. After a month, he looks and feels so much better that he wishes everyone to come and take the same treatment! He is practically cured!

If the reader could have seen the banker after he had learned to relax, he would not believe that it was the same man. There is a difference in colour, "poise," voice. The former insomniac now sleeps eight hours a night, and even then does not want to get up in the morning. He attacks his work in an entirely different way. Instead of the feverish, jerky method, which marks the nervous man, there seems an easy-flowing, deliberate approach, with suggestions of an enormous reserve of power. This last, of course, is given largely by his wonderful physique and unusual mental vigour, and no amount of relaxation exercises could give quite the same thing to one without the natural advantage.

But before, he was wrongly using his natural gifts, squandering them, throwing them away like the spendthrift of the last chapter. Now, by constant practice, in his everyday life, of the principle of relaxation, he is economizing his nervous resources. He is little by little adding to his reserve of strength so that, when and if occasion arises, he may have wherewith to make a supreme effort. He is a biological capitalist, spending his bodily resources, and that means his mental resources also, where they will count, not squandering them on unessentials. His energies are devoted to the business of living, not to the useless overhead expenditure of fidgeting and unnecessary tension.

"We think with our muscles," says James. A physical overtension is almost always accompanied by mental disturbances of a more or less serious nature. Which first causes the other, it is hard to say, but together they form a vicious circle. By this method of relaxation it is possible to break into the circle with very great benefit to the state of both body and mind.

And in this possibility of mental relief lies the importance of muscular relaxation, in this, the Story of Man's Mind. It is nothing new. Psychologists have known of it for years, as of the other effects of relaxation to be described in the next few sections.

(c) THE MAN WHO FEARED A TREE

One of the remarkable things about the state of relaxation, as described in the last chapter, is that things said or thought while in this state have a vastly greater chance of being remembered. If I tell a man, in the ordinary way of things, that he will remember to take his medicine, the chances of his forgetting are very high. If, while he is in the state of relaxation, he is told the same thing, it is almost certain that he will remember.

Not only such a thing as taking medicine, but any form of command is far more effective when given to one who is thoroughly relaxed. It seems as though, by loosening up the muscles of the limbs, a large number of competing stimuli are thrown out of operation. Those stimuli which are left seem therefore to have far more effect, just as a business man is more successful when he has fewer competitors. To put the same thing in other words, when we are in a state of relaxation, there are fewer things to choose for attention.

In terms that have become popular, a person in the state of complete relaxation, such as has been described, is very suggestible. And this fact can be used, and is often used, in dealing with more complicated troubles of a psychological character.

Take the case of a young man who was very nervous, and who had formed the habit of biting his lower lip. When he came to the office, he had bitten "a great hole," to use his own description, and the place gave him considerable pain. Asked why he did so, he said he could not tell, but that he "just found himself" biting. This was now the third week that he had been biting his lip, and he felt that he simply could not stop the habit.

Now the whole principle of work by the method of relaxation is to learn to obtain results *without the usual kind of effort.* As Doctor Worcester has observed, it is the method of "Resist not Evil." The more of the usual kind of effort a man takes to rid himself of such a habit as this, the more firmly he often succeeds in driving the habit in. This is the principle that has been successfully emphasized by

Coué. Those pious but ineffectual advisers, who had been telling the young man to "Be a man and cut it out. Make up your mind, and you will get rid of it" had never been forced to face a similar difficulty. To tell a nervous person to "cut out" a bad habit, whether it be biting nails or biting the lip or blushing or anything else, is simply to increase his trouble in the very large number of cases.

When such a person comes and asks for help, his case is at first carefully talked over. Why does he bite his lip? He does not know. Is there anything that comes to his mind as he bites it? He thinks not.

There seems in this case no *meaning* to the habit, although, to be quite certain of this, many more visits are necessary.

"The harder I try not to bite it, the more I bite it."

"Then stop trying. If you want to bite your lip, go ahead and bite it. Bite it all you want to. It isn't harming you, anyway. You will drop the habit as you get better. Forget about it."

After talking over things in this way, we begin the relaxation practice. Exactly the same procedure is gone through. When the young man is thoroughly relaxed, lying quiet with his eyes closed, breathing regularly, then I say to him:

"You have been biting your lip. You are going to find that from this evening the desire for biting loses its force. Soon you will have lost the desire altogether."

Then he is sent home, to go to bed.

Later in the week I expect him back, and wait in the office at the appointed time. He does not come. I am rather angry at this, and decide that when, and if, he does turn up again, I shall say that I cannot be bothered with him.

Meeting him later in the street, I ask him about himself

and remind him of his appointment. He is very apologetic. He had forgotten to come.

"How is the lip-biting?"

"Disappeared."

Three months later I had another short conversation with him. Up to that time he had never bitten his lip again. He was cured.

Unfortunately, this is an unusual case. All such habits do not disappear so quickly. Generally, at least a month is necessary before any result at all is seen. But in a very large number of such cases that have come to me, the habit has disappeared ultimately. In no case has there failed to result some improvement.

One of the commoner kinds of trouble which it is possible to relieve in the same way is abnormal fear. This can take all imaginable forms, from the fear of mice to the fear of thunder, from the fear of being left alone to the fear of crossing a crowded street. It occurs in all degrees of intensity, from a slight feeling of anxiety to a terrible, gripping nightmare. Let me quote the account of a young man who had this trouble in a terrible form.

"I was studying for my doctor's degree. Work had begun in September, and up till Christmas everything had gone well. After Christmas I began to feel very low nervously, to start when there was a slight noise, to have attacks of indigestion, and to lose sleep. I went to my doctor, who told me I would have to 'go easy,' and that I ought to take three months right off, which was impossible at the time. Then the sleeplessness began to grow worse, and one evening as I was over my books the Fear came. Nothing can describe it. The feeling is as though one were suddenly taken by the throat and thrust into the jaws of hell.

Earth seemed to open, and all the obscenity of ten thousand devils would roll out in a dark flood and sweep over me. I stood gasping for breath. The Bad of all the world seemed concentrated in that one terror. Suddenly it lifted. The dark, evil Thing rolled away, and I stood there, helpless and grateful and exhausted.

The first occasion of the Fear was my examination. For some reason or other the idea had come over me that I would not pass. So I would work twice as hard to make certain, and that only made the Fear come back sooner. It used to come generally in the evening, at intervals of about a week. The night after, I expected, and generally had, a bad time."

This young man's physician sent him to a psychologist, under whose care he began to improve.

"After a while, I began to notice that the attacks were not so frequent, nor so intense. I could think of the examination with something like composure. But a curious thing I now began to observe is this. Before, the Fear had attached itself to the examination only. Now it seemed more free and unattached. For instance, one night after making a call on a college professor, it came upon me as I left the gate, in a much less ugly, less devastating form. The reason, I could not see, except perhaps a possible connection between my host's profession — he belonged to another University — and my work.

"On another occasion, I was wandering down by the river side in the evening, and stood still to watch a tree outline its form against the setting sun. Suddenly round the tree came the halo of the Fear, but merely a shadow of the old terror. I was able to stand and watch it, and jeer at it, so to speak. 'Ah,' I thought, 'you are losing your power over me. I shall soon be free from you altogether.' "

A similar treatment was used by the psychologist to whom this young man went as in the cases which I have described. First the matter would be talked over, then a thorough state of relaxation brought about. During this, the suggestion was made that the fear would gradually lose its gripping force, that it would slowly decrease in vitality, and that it would finally disappear altogether.

Three months later, the examinations were taken without a tremor, and, thanks to the student's additional work, they were passed very successfully. It is now some years since the occurrence of the above. There has been no fear since then.

Such cases are, of course, abnormal and rather unusual. But some kind of mild fear is very common among those who are nervously inclined. Sometimes it is someone who is afraid of thunder storms. At the least rumble of what might be mistaken for thunder, the whole house has to be put in a state of special preparations against the possible storm. Sometimes it is a public speaker who suddenly begins to fear his audiences. Sometimes a college student finds that he cannot cross the college campus without a sinking fear of evil impending. Or an athlete, an unusually good diver, has suddenly grown afraid of the water, and turns his head and so spoils his dive. An organist may weep, whenever he plays the organ, and find himself becoming totally unfitted to perform. An actor may suddenly be stricken with stage fright. A business man, and this is a very common case, may be certain that his business is going on the rocks.

All these are instances of emotion that goes off at the wrong stimulus, and cases of each of them I have known permanently cured, as far as I know up to date, by this method. Some such cases are due to more serious trouble, and this possibility must always be ruled out by the expert examination of a physician who is a specialist in these things. Indeed, it cannot be too strongly insisted that these fears or phobias, as they are called, sometimes mask very serious mental disease. But many of them belong to otherwise normal people. And such fears, that are primarily accidents, not symptoms, I have seen wiped permanently away by the method of relaxation.

(d) RELAXATION AS A LOVE CHARM

Anyone of a slightly nervous, rather irritable, "tense" type can by the same method entirely transform his outlook upon the world, and greatly increase his happiness and the happiness of those who live with him. By the same means minor faults of character can be straightened out, timidity often overcome, moods be made to vanish.

Let me recommend first an experiment. If the reader wishes to have an unusually happy (or for that matter, unhappy!) day tomorrow, let him sit in a morris chair, and carry out the method outlined two chapters ago. Take four or five very deep breaths, letting them out as though everything were to be successful for the future, and all troubles were passed. Now go over the muscles, as before described, or better still, have someone repeat the directions. Relax the shoulders, chest, stomach muscles, the legs and arms, the muscles of the back, the throat and neck, the face and forehead, and the jaw muscles. Let everything go; feel the chair holding up the weight of the body, feel the arms limp and loose from the shoulders. Then try to imagine the chair as holding the body up, the floor as holding the chair up, the walls as holding up the floors, the earth holding up the walls.

When a slight feeling of mental heaviness sets in, which should happen, and generally does happen, at about this stage, then is the time for the suggestion to be made. Thus one might say to oneself, "I am going to find that I feel very cheerful tomorrow." This is repeated eight or ten times, rather quickly and with full belief, as far as possible, that the result will actually follow. If it is insomnia that is giving the trouble, or waking too early in the morning, the proper thing to repeat to oneself is:

"I am going to find that my sleeping improves. Tomorrow morning I shall not wake so soon, but shall be so drowsy early in the morning that I cannot keep awake."

With such a thing as a happy mood, the result, barring special circumstances, almost always follows. With sleeplessness, two or three days may be required for very mild cases, and much longer for more pronounced cases.

In this way, an astonishing variety of different things may be treated. There is, for example, the case of the school teacher, who finds that his class is getting on his nerves. This state of things can be improved, provided that there is no more trouble than a purely nervous one. If a teacher has been preparing his work well and carefully, if he knows his subject, and there are no unusual circumstances, he can improve his own morale in the class room by exactly the same method. Let him place himself in the attitude of relaxation as already described. Then let him repeat to himself some such formula as this:

"Tomorrow I am going to find that I am not uneasy in the presence of the class. I am going to teach with a vigour and energy that will surprise them." If this is said over and over a few times, with as much intensity as possible, the teacher will surprise the class in a few days. The same thing is true of public speaking. Nervousness in the face of an audience, if it be of a mild nature, can be very much relieved.

The same method can be used to produce results that seem almost incredible, and the recital of which seems to savour almost of the charlatan. Thus if a speaker finds himself going "stale," he can suggest to himself that he will be unusually interesting, that he will find that he will speak well, and so on. This result seems to be unusually easy to attain.

One of the striking uses to which the method is being put is in the case of unhappy marriages. A married couple is happy for the first four or five years. Then little by little, as children and other things begin to prove a trouble, the wife finds that she no longer has the old affection for her husband. The glory seems to have departed out of life.

Or perhaps the wife is hard worked, and along comes some other woman who appeals better to the man. Little by little, against his will, he finds himself drifting away from his wife, towards the precipice.

There are of course those who say at once, "Let him pull himself together. A man has no business to drift away from his wife." But what is called love is so capricious that the finest people in the world often find they cannot control it.

What I would advise in such a case, is this. Let the falling partner first of all put before him (it seems generally to be him)-self the virtues of his wife. Let him tell himself that he married a wife because he was so and so, and she was so and so. Let him weigh the whole situation in his consciousness. Then let him recall the old happy days when the world was full of singing birds and the sun shone more brightly, and remember how he felt towards his wife.

Then let him relax the muscles of his body as described and say to himself something like this:

"I am going to find that, as the days go on, I grow more affectionate to my wife. I am going to get back from the past the old feeling of love for her. At the same time I shall become more and more indifferent to — " whoever it may be.

In most cases, it will not be long before this happy man will hear something like this:

"You *have* been nice to me lately!"

Of course, it is not meant to suggest that the love of Romeo for Juliet could have been thus whittled away. But most assuredly could the love of Romeo for Rosaline have been so disposed of.

And we are not all Romeos, nor are all the co-respondents in the divorce courts Juliets.

One such case I have heard of where exactly the case described had happened. The wife and husband had lived happily together for ten years. Then suddenly the husband began to fall in love with a dear friend of both, and whom, in the course of his business, he was obliged to meet often. All three were people of the highest character. The wife had decided not to stand in the way of her husband's happiness, although she herself was as fond of him as ever.

There seemed to be no escape from the precipice into which all three were slipping.

Fortunately, they came into the hands of a man who was able to use the proper methods against this moral disease. In six months the husband and the wife were on all the old terms of love and intimacy, and the last I heard of them was that they were making up a party, all three of them, to go to the theatre.

Married infidelity is, in very many cases, a disease, and it will be treated as such in the future. And *where the disease is not too fundamental,* where it depends on accidents such as overwork, some such method as this will be used. Where the disease is more serious, more deep-going methods will be necessary. Sometimes the disease like any other will be incurable.

Chapter XII

SICK MINDS AND WHAT WE LEARN FROM THEM

(*a*) AUTO-SUGGESTION

The inhabitants of a village in the South of England show the visitor a certain hole in the ground, some fifteen feet long and four feet deep. "That," they tell him, "is the track of a giant. See the mark of his heel, and there is the print of his toes! He lived in the time of the ancient Britons."

The visitor who is of a sceptical mind may perhaps protest.

"Impossible! How could there ever be a giant of that size? He would be something like thirty yards tall."

"How can it be impossible?" is the answer. *"There is the track of his foot."*

It is a very important thing in science to remember that while we may often accept a man's facts, we must in many cases reserve the right to differ from his explanation of them. And in the study of the sick mind, called by the learned psychopathology, we can often accept the fact that this or that method has resulted in a cure. But always we reserve the right to reject any theory of the mind which has been built up around the cure. Let this reflection serve as a preamble to the chapter.

For example, when we hear of the wonderful cures accomplished by autosuggestion, we may admit unhesitatingly that the cures have probably taken place. That, in any case, is for the medical men to decide. In fact, we know that the most astonishing things have been accomplished by this means. Warts have been driven away by suggestion. Blisters have been raised by applications of ice, supposed to be a red hot iron. A mother, in an authentic case, once received a purple weal on her neck when a window fell down and just escaped her son's head. In that wonderful book, "The Golden Bough," it is somewhere related that a certain primitive people feared to touch the person or clothes of their chief, for he was *tabu*. The belief was that he who touched would die. One day a man found a cloak by the wayside and carried it home. To his horror he was told that it belonged to the chief.

That man died the next day!

All these are instances of suggestion or autosuggestion. Let me now anticipate from the next part of this chapter. Autosuggestion and suggestion, as the words are popularly used today, are in precisely the same class of phenomena. In both cases a stimulus produces a reaction which would usually be prevented by various resistances in the body. A suggestible person will pick a pocket when another bids him. Most of us would resist the idea. If we are told we look sick, we generally try to resist the suggestion. It is possible for the suggestion to be so strong, as in the case of the savage, that it produces death. Normally there seems to be a bar between what are called the higher processes, connected with what is called consciousness, and almost all the changes and processes that take place in the body, such as the operation of the liver and the kidneys, the growth of the finger nails, the healing of a scar. Sometimes, however, in very rare cases the bar seems to be broken down, and stimuli can, by way of the cortex of the brain, affect parts usually unaccessible.

Then we have the "miracles of suggestion."

In thus providing a check, as in most other things, nature is wise. Imagine the day of a man who lacked these steadying resistances. A friend says "It looks like rain." At once the resistanceless man runs for his umbrella. Another remarks that it is a sleepy morning. At once he falls asleep. His employer tells him that his weekly check reads at twice the usual amount. At once he sees it so. When he walks in a dark room, he has all the time the actual pain of knocking his shins! For a practical joke his friends tell him he has the stars and stripes marked on his face, or that his heart is beating twice as fast as usual. At once it is so, for he has no means of resisting the suggestion.

Those who wish to see whither this would lead should read the last part of Bernard Shaw's "Back to Methuselah." In this play, the "Ancients," who live many centuries in the future, can suggest two heads, a multitude of arms, or fantastic shapes to their body. By taking thought they can increase their stature a cubit or diminish it at will.

Unlimited suggestibility might not, then, be a very desirable thing, as some would have us believe.

The general rules for suggestion are well laid down in other books than this. It may here, however, be emphasized, that the time of going to sleep is the time when suggestion has most effect, for then it is that many of the inhibitions of waking life seem to be lifted. The time during sleep is even better, but, except with children, it is difficult to talk to a sleeping person without waking him. This is a fact of the highest practical usefulness. Much has lately been made of it, and it is often thought that the fact has been but recently discovered. But psychologists have known of it for many years.

Let us see how we may apply it.

Suppose that we have a child who will not drink his milk. At night, just before he goes to bed, we go to him and say something like this.

"Tomorrow you are going to have such nice milk. The milk is going to taste so nice tomorrow that you will want some more." This is repeated several times, changing the form of expression. The next day, perhaps, no difference is noticed in the child. Then the same thing is repeated again at night, or in the morning, if the mother happens to be there exactly as the child awakes. On the third day results ought to appear. If not, the method should be tried for at least a week, and it is rare indeed that such a thing as a poor appetite cannot in a healthy child be very much improved.

Suppose, again, that the child has not been "good" for the last week or so, and that he is old enough to understand what being "good" means. Then, after he is in bed, we go to him and tell him a story about a little boy who was good, making the lot of the child in the story a desirable one. If this is done for two or three evenings, the results are often very striking.

An adult may do the same thing, by repeating to himself whatever it is he wishes to imprint. If at morning or in the evening, between sleep and waking, any one, man or woman, will make his resolutions, such as that he or she will be cheerful, feel better, or not worry, it will be found that the resolutions are much more apt to take effect than if made during the day. The effect can be made still stronger by putting one's body in a state of relaxation as described in a former chapter. In fact, the state of relaxation is one of the best means of making suggestion easy.

Suggestion, then, and autosuggestion are no mysterious force, no special faculty. Suggestion is simply inducing an action that is usually checked by resistance within the body. It implies, so to speak, the use of strategy in dealing with the resistances rather than a frontal attack upon them.

One thing, finally, as to the psychology of prayer. We are all of us, it has been seen, in a very suggestible state when we are going to sleep and when we are waking up. Now these are the times that a wise tradition has set aside for praying. It must have been the case that those of the older generation who diligently and faithfully said their prayers at rising and at bedtime thus exerted a very great influence on their characters. One who repeats such a simple and impressively wonderful prayer as the "Our Father" before he goes to sleep and after he wakes up in the morning must, by the fact of his suggestibility at these times, tend to attain that part of his prayer which concerns his own character. One who prays faithfully might well, in course of years, change his whole outlook upon life. The powers of prayer as a means of social control have, perhaps, never been realized. As an instrument to raise morale in times of crisis it holds astonishing possibilities. It seems to be psychologically certain that if, beginning with the year 1900, every inhabitant of Europe had, night and morning, faithfully said a prayer for peace, there could have been no great war.

Who will then dare not to insist that his children say their prayers? And may not the decay of the prayer habit be, in part at least, the cause of that decay of morals which many think they see around them today. Certainly, a world that said each night the "Our Father" would be, in spite of itself, a better world than this is.

(b) WHAT IS HYPNOTISM?

One of the picturesque characters of the Paris just before the days of the Revolution was Friederich Antony Mesmer. Born in 1733, and educated for medicine, this remarkable personality astonished the world by the cures which he claimed to bring about by a newly discovered force. This was said to be at the disposal of certain people, who could, by the proper process, apply it to the healing of disease. It was, he said, in many ways like the "electric fluid." It could be stored in jars and passed on from one conductor to another. Mesmer named it Animal Magnetism.

Now the astonishing thing about Mesmer's claims was not his theory, which was no more nor less fantastic than those brought forward by many a charlatan before and since, but the truly remarkable control which he actually seemed to exert over his patients, and the high proportion of genuine cures. So convincing was the evidence that the learned world of the time was almost startled into belief!

On admittance into the scene of the strange cures, one found himself in a large, dimly lighted hall, almost dark except for the rich coloring of the stained glass windows. In the middle could be distinguished a wooden, circular box, up from which came movable iron handles. Arranged in tiers round the circular box sat the patients, holding the free end of the handles, and fastened to each other by cords. From time to time, the sound of sweet music broke the silence, and sweet perfumes floated across the air. Every now and then a patient would break out into convulsions, and would be hurried by the attendant into a padded room. Mesmer, the presiding genius, is omnipotent. The slightest sign from him and all obey. So irresistible is the effect of the mysterious fluid.

Now to a modern reader the name of Mesmer will have suggested the source of this mysterious power. The so-called "Animal Magnetism" was what has later come to be known as Hypnotism, and was originally called Mesmerism after the famous doctor. In fact, a committee of eminent French scientists decided, in 1784, that it was "imagination," not magnetism, that produced convulsions and cures alike. In 1815 Mesmer died, after a career that had brought him into contact with all classes of society, from beggars to the crowned heads of France. It was even said that Marie Antoinette attended one of his sessions. So great was the curiosity aroused by his cures.

Let me give now an instance of the way in which the modern practitioner uses the power which Mesmer first brought into prominence. The examples are taken from the treatise of Dr. Moll, which will be found among the references at the end.

A young man of twenty is placed on a chair and given a button, at which he is told to look intently. In three minutes he closes his eyes and cannot go to sleep. He is told that he cannot open his eyes, and in spite of effort finds that this is true. He is told that his hands are stuck to his knees, but finds as a matter of fact that he can easily lift them. He is all the while perfectly conscious.

In another experiment, a woman of fifty is told that she cannot pronounce her own name, she is dumb. At the proper permission she can speak. Another patient, a man, is asked if he is asleep. "Yes, fast asleep," he answers. A piece of cloth is put into his hand, which he is told is a dog. This he believes on waking. He is then told he is in the zoölogical garden, and sees trees that are not there.

Other patients see the hypnotizer with horns on his

head; still others cannot see persons in a room. Others again see people not there at all. They may be made to see a face on a blank card, or to see as blank a card with a face upon it. They may be thrown into a state of extreme rigidity, in which astonishing things may be done to them without apparent harm. They may be made insensible to pain or to feeling in their limbs; sometimes they feel pain that does not exist. Minor surgical operations may be performed upon them, if the hypnotizer has merely suggested that these will be painless.

Small wonder that Mesmer thought he had discovered a universal force, for indeed the limits of the power of this strange thing seem not to exist!

A power that assumes so many forms has naturally been given many explanations. Charcot, the great French experimenter, who frightened people into hypnotic state by the use of gongs and other similar devices, claimed that it is due to an artificially induced nervous condition, of the same general nature as hysteria. True it is that a person in the hypnotic state looks very much like one with certain kinds of mental trouble. Charcot's great opponents were the professors at the Nancy Medical School, who maintained, on the contrary, that the hypnotic state was a perfectly normal one, and consisted in an unusual suggestibility. If that be so, then the hypnotic sleep is merely a suggested sleep, and is not a newly discovered state. A number of modern psychologists hold with Bernheim, of the Nancy School, that hypnotism is increased suggestibility, and the reason given for this is that, by one means or another the attention is narrowed down as it were into a small spotlight. Those things on which the spotlight can be focused, then, stand out clearer and more free from competition. The process is the same as that described before, when by relaxing away many of the competing and distracting sensations from the external muscles of the body, we make a person somewhat drowsy, and at the same time very suggestible. In fact, the state of relaxation described in a previous chapter is simply a very mild form of hypnosis, as it is called, but so mild that it is probably the same as the normal, nightly state of each of us as he goes to sleep. Pavlov claims that hypnosis is due to the physiological process of Inhibition.

Going back to Mesmer, it is easy to see that the conditions at his sittings were all exactly those which are most favorable to the hypnotic state. The silence, the atmosphere of mystery, the intent and prolonged attention on one thing, are all known by the modern practitioners to be a distinct help in producing hypnotic effects.

In conclusion, a few words are necessary with regard to the use of hypnotism in medicine. In spite of the opinions of certain very learned friends, I believe that hypnotism is a perfectly safe method of cure in qualified hands. Arsenic is a poison, and in unqualified hands it will kill. But in the hands of a trained physician, it becomes a very valuable remedy. In just the same way, hypnotism, in skilled hands, is a very valuable means of cure. Those who have practiced it extensively claim that it can accomplish results otherwise impossible. In case of dissociated personality, for instance, it is invaluable. In certain other nervous disorders it has its very distinct place. And, properly used, it does not "weaken the will," whatever that may mean, any more than does a tonic weaken the physical system. Misused, hypnotism and strychnine are both bad. Properly used, both are good, and both have their legitimate place as a means of cure.

Further, the fact that a person can be hypnotized does not argue a "weak will." What is absolutely essential, is the consent of the patient, at least on the first few occasions, and so it actually comes out that persons of weak mentality cannot be hypnotized. You cannot hypnotize a madman.

And lastly, it is impossible by hypnotic means to cause another to commit a crime. Many experiments have been made, but all with the same result. Any suggestion that is morally repugnant to the patient is not carried out. Real daggers given to a hypnotized person will not be used to commit murder, however strong the suggestion. Real poison will not be placed in a cup from which a real person is to drink. A real, serious theft will not be committed, though such an action as stealing from the hypnotist's office can readily be brought about. Which is all a pity for the feature writers in the Sunday magazines.

(c) TWO PERSONS IN ONE BODY

One day there came into the office of a famous Boston specialist, called Morton Prince, a young woman who had been suffering with nervous trouble. The lady was quite pale and nervous looking, and she had the curious symptoms that go with what is known as hysteria. She could not sleep, and her general health was wretched.

In order to relieve her of some of her trouble, Doctor Prince had recourse to hypnotism. And this brought remarkable results, results which, while they have been paralleled in other rare cases, are yet so astonishing that they take one's breath away. While in most cases patients wake from hypnotic treatment practically as they were before, in this case the hypnotic sleep seemed entirely to change the patient's character. In place of a quiet, reserved woman, with an infinite capacity for suffering, and the ideals and aspirations of a saint, there appeared a breezy, slangy, up-to-the-minute young lady, who might have stepped from the cover of one of the popular magazines.

The same body sat before Doctor Prince. But an entirely different person seemed to inhabit it.

The two personalities belonging to the one body differed not only in vivacity and facial expression, but in practically every other way that two human beings can differ. The second person was less intelligent, less mature, and more healthy than the first. She was of a relentless, heedlessly selfish turn of mind. She liked different books, different people.

She was less educated. The first Miss B, as we may call her, had been to college. The new Miss B could not read French. This fact later became of the greatest use, for Doctor Prince used to talk to his patient in that language when he wanted to be sure that the other personality in her could not understand!

Now these were strange happenings enough. But more was to follow. After a time, yet another personality appeared in the same body, and then another, until finally Doctor Prince has to speak of the individuals in the body of Miss B as "the family." There was the saintly, reserved woman, who had come to the office, the mischievous, elfish "Sally," as she christened herself, the strong, impetuous, rebellious B4, as she was called. Altogether, some six or seven personalities appeared, all distinguishable, yet many of them sharing the same memories, and all of them sharing the same body.

The jealousies and the difficulties caused by this extraordinary state of affairs are better described by Doctor Prince in his book, "The Dissociation of a Personality," than ever I could describe them. This book reads like a novel, and is twice as interesting as most novels. Some of the ludicrous and striking incidents may be mentioned. For example, Sally took upon herself to hate Miss B. Consequently she would annoy her in every way possible. Thus, Miss B would find herself with the taste of a cigarette in her mouth. She knew that Sally had been in "possession" and had been smoking. While Sally was in charge, as one might call it, of the common body, Miss B simply lost a day or a week. Consequently, she often found herself in the most embarrassing positions. There was a certain gentleman, whom Sally liked, but whom Miss B disliked. Sally would write him notes, and go on jaunts with him, and Miss B would wake up and discover this to her great chagrin. Sally could at times take possession and cheat Miss B out of such things as a theatre performance or a Christmas dinner. As an example of this last, Miss B was once at Christmas church service in the morning. After a while, she noticed that the choir was in a different place, which surprised her somewhat. Leaving the church, she found that it was not Christmas Day at all, but the day after. She had lost a whole day, beginning with the Christmas anthem and ending precisely twenty-four hours later at the same part of the service. Sally had cheated her of her Christmas dinner!

After a time there came to be a war between the various members of the family. One would write notes to another, insulting notes which would be answered in the same spirit. One would get hold of the family money, and put the other on an allowance of five cents a day. If one took a bath, and the personality happened to change immediately after, the bath would have to be repeated. The book is a true psychological Arabian Nights. Everything, including the apparently impossible, seemed to happen.

The culmination was reached when the "secondary personality," Sally, actually wrote her biography! After this, there seems to be nothing left that can ever surprise us again. A woman's personality splitting up into two people. Three, four and five individuals appearing in the same body, plaguing each other, and each desiring control of the common body. Finally, the split-off persons are recombined into one personality, for Doctor Prince was ultimately able to accomplish the cure, but not before one of the phantoms, one of the spirits raised up out of the woman's own consciousness, had written its autobiography, and one had achieved the supreme sacrifice of agreeing to annihilation for the common good!

How did it happen? Are we back in the Dark Ages, the days of demoniac possession?

The explanation has already been hinted. We saw in an earlier chapter that, at the beginning of life, each of us was not really a person in the fullest sense of the word. Various disturbances arise from all parts of the body, nerve messages that "mean" hunger, that mean a foreign body approaching the eye, or that mean the tinkle of the spoon in a cup. But at first only the nerve messages are there, not their meaning, for that can only be given by experience. The infant is scarcely a person. He is rather, as a great man has put it, like the Trojan Horse which was filled with a band of men. His experiences have hardly been combined into a whole, although, of course, his actions involve the combination of different parts of the nervous system, and most of them even involve the body as a whole. His mind is at best a pot-pourri of incompletely organized, relatively unconnected mental states.

After a time, however, we have seen that the child begins to organize his own individual experiences and his own individual actions. Instead of being a soft something in the cradle, that turns its eyes to follow a bright light across the room, and clasps its hands when some one puts something in them, he has now become a person who combines these two nature-given movements. He stretches out his hand, when the brightness approaches, with the purpose of clasping his fist and putting the spoon in his mouth. His own past experience has taught him that this particular visual experience means spoon, which is pleasant to suck. Of course, he does not "reason" this out, but the association is formed half consciously. And after a time these combinations themselves combine, and he "makes" space, time, the people round him, and so on. And little by little all his random, disconnected experiences begin to join themselves together in what we call memories. All his actions begin to be colored by the fact that they are the actions not of a strip of muscle, or a combination of muscles, but of muscles belonging to some one with experience rooted in the past, and with purposes for the future.

Let us now introduce ourselves to a new word which well describes what has happened. This mutual combination and correction of one's experience is called integration, which means to make a whole of parts, to make an orchestra out of fifty musical performers, to make a team out of eleven athletes. Integration of such things as muscular movements makes a body out of a collection of muscles and nerves. Integration of experience and actions makes a person.

Consider yourself, now, reader of this book, as a person who will act in certain ways, do certain things, feel certain other things. The reason is your natural equipment as a baby, which taught you much, plus all that your physical growth has given you, plus all that you have experienced, done, and felt in your ceaseless struggle with the world.

The product of all these things, integrated into a whole, scrambled more inextricably than ever egg was scrambled . . . that is You.

Your native endowment, individual experiences, education, upbringing, profession, by action and interaction within you, have integrated themselves into your personality, with a use of the word which is wider than that of the first chapter, where it was used to mean the general emotional and instinctive equipment of an individual.

Suppose now that, by some accident, the pattern is broken up. Perhaps some mischance rules that I forget the events of the last two years which have played an important part in my life. Such cases are known and are, indeed, not extremely uncommon. It may be that out of a unified whole, the wonderfully and completely interwoven fabric of my experience and my reactions begins to fall into two separate halves. Just why this should happen it is hard to say, but we know that it does occasionally come to pass.

In this case, we have two persons, each of them a little poorer than the real character, because each of them can draw on only a part of the experience, and sometimes on only part of the native endowment of the whole person. Each of them will remember certain things; none of them will know and do everything. Each half will be an integrated half, but neither of them will be fully integrated.

The egg will still be scrambled, but it will have fallen in pieces.

This is exactly what seems to have happened in the strange case we have described. Miss B's whole personality seems, for some reason or other, to have suddenly split up. The accumulation of experiences, instincts, feelings and capacities that formed the one young lady suddenly became two, three and more accumulations. Out of the dignified, normal lady there grew up a saint, an irresponsible child, and an energetic fighter. The child partook of the nature of both the others. When the first and the last were fused together to form the normal person, there was nothing left of the child. To use her own words, she was "squeezed out of existence." She had gone "to the place from which she came."

Such is the splitting which Doctor Prince summarizes by his title "The Dissociation of a Personality", and describes in his astonishing book.

The remarkable thing is, that it does not more often happen. Why should we be so consistent in our actions and our personalities? Why do not the perversities that lurk in all of us emerge, as they did in Miss B? Every reader of this book harbours within himself an infinity of characters, of more astonishing variety, of more diverse intention and morals, of more unbounded difference in word and thought than were ever called up by the most prolific literary imagination. By what power can we conjure these spirits to stay in the deeps? What is the word by which the Prospero, that is each one of us, confines these Ariels and these Calibans to the prison that is the healthy mind?

The puzzle in Psychology is not the abnormal, but the normal, not the fact that nature sometimes misses her mark, but that she ever hits it. The puzzle of our personality is not that these changes should sometimes occur, but that it is ever possible to preserve a unified, whole and healthily integrated mind.

"Life, like a dome of many coloured glass
Stains the white radiance of eternity."

One flick, and the infinitely mobile pattern may be changed, still keeping the same hues, the same scraps of glass.

(d) THE UNCONSCIOUS MIND? HAVE DREAMS A MEANING?

In 1885 a young Austrian named Freud was studying after a medical degree, under Charcot, the famous hypnotist who was drawing crowds to watch his work in Paris. Just before this time certain things had happened which were later to make this young man's name famous all over the world.

A certain Doctor Breuer was treating a girl for hysteria. The young lady showed a number of symptoms, such as disgust at food, trouble with her vision and so on, and in addition had the peculiarity that at certain times she lost her memory and ability to speak. At these times she repeated certain meaningless words.

Doctor Breuer, being a man of resource, wondered whether these words could be in any way connected with her illness. In order to find out, he hypnotised the young lady and repeated them to her.

And then the striking thing happened, a thing which has proved the starting point for a whole new psychology, a new theory of life, of art, religion and literature, as well as of treatment of nervous diseases, and has resulted in the most bitter controversies among psychologists.

The apparently random syllables had a perfectly definite meaning when the girl was hypnotised. Somehow, the hypnotic process seemed to reach down to a layer of the mind which was inaccessible at ordinary times.

When Freud, the young student of Paris, had returned to Vienna, he worked with Doctor Breuer, and soon after hit upon the great idea which had, indeed, been conceived by others, but had never been worked out with such wealth of speculative and observational detail as this remarkable young man gave it.*

If a hysterical patient, under hypnotic influence, reveals mental processes of which he or she has hitherto been unconscious, it is possible, said Freud, that there are in all of us whole regions and tracts of the mind of whose existence we have no inkling. In fact, there are many things that can be explained only on this assumption.

Thus was made the great hypothesis of the unconscious mind, which controls most of our thoughts and actions, and of which, simply because it is unconscious, we have in the past been ignorant. Taking into account this newly discovered, submerged element of our personality, we must revise our whole notion of life, consciousness, human motives, thought and actions. And we can almost never give a reason for anything we do. For the reason we give is generally only superficial, the real cause lying hidden in the subconscious.

To take an elementary instance, this unconscious mind, says Freud, is the explanation of many actions which seem to ourselves to be meaningless and "silly". For example. When we forget a name or an appointment, it is because our unconscious mind wants us to forget it. There is, for example, the case of a professor who forgot to go to his own wedding. One can safely say that the professor was not very much in love. No one ever heard of a very much

*He was influenced also by a visit to Bernheim (1889).

infatuated lover forgetting to go and see his lady. And if he gave as an excuse that it had "completely slipped his mind" she would be justified in breaking off the engagement. On the other hand, a friend of mine once told me that he bought a ring which was intended for a young woman of his acquaintance, and when the "psychological" moment came to slip it on, he found he lost it! Freud would say that he did not want to put on the ring. The fact remains that he did not marry the lady!

This leads us to another principle emphasized by Freud, namely what has been called the principle of "psychic determinism." It may be briefly explained thus. Just as every physical fact has an explanation, so every mental fact may be traced to its cause, generally in that part of our mind of which we are not conscious. Conscious processes are simply isolated parts, all joined together beneath, like the islands on a rocky coast, by the underground connections of the unconscious.

A patient complains of fainting in the street. She does not know what makes her faint, or whether anything makes her. According to the theory of psychic determinism, however, there is a reason hidden in the unconscious.

Investigations are set on foot, and it is discovered that the fainting spells occur only when a certain make of automobile is either seen or heard.

But this again must have its meaning. It is further found that that particular make of car has been connected with an unfortunate love affair. The whole problem is thus solved. A reason has been given for the apparently causeless action.

We have been a long time reaching the title of the section. But it is easy now to see what Freud will say about dreams. These, he says, like every other mental process, have their own meaning. They are not just accidents and sports, like the sounds made on the pianoforte by a kitten. In fact, it is through dreams that we are often best able to discover certain wishes of which we are unconscious.

There is, for example, the case of the English boarding school boy who dreamed that he went up to London to see the queen. What could this mean? Now a queen is some-one in the highest authority, or was, as these were the days of Queen Victoria. And the corresponding person in authority in that schoolboy's life was — his mother. Consequently the boy was saying to himself, as plainly as he could say it. "I want to see my mother."

Why did he not simply dream straight out that he was at home seeing his mother? Because, in English schools, this would be considered an unmanly thing, and he would not admit the existence of such a wish, even to himself. And so he had to disguise the thought by clothing it in strange garments. As a matter of actual fact, the dreamer was in a particularly nervous condition, and he had the same dream so many times that it began to worry him. Consequently, he told his family doctor, who knew little about Freud but much about boys. The boy was ordered home, and completely recovered.

Almost always, according to Freud, are dreams thus expressed in a roundabout way, or symbolically. And always, he says, does a dream express a wish of one kind or another, though this is often very hard to discern. The parents are represented by the king and the queen. Brothers and sisters appear as small animals, such as rabbits. Birth appears as water. Death as taking a journey or being in a railway train. Many dreams, he interprets as having a sexual meaning. The urge of sex we have seen, is very strongly repressed in ordinary life, and is therefore more likely to make itself felt in dreams.

Let us take another example. A young man, a student at a university, dreams that he is in a room, and is watching his soul, which is tacked to the ceiling with small nails. People are passing beneath through the room, and throwing things at his soul which hurt it very much.

What is this about?

Now the young man is rather older than the rest of the students, having been at the war for several years. He is living together with a number of youths, whose childish behaviour annoys him greatly. In particular, he resents the lack of privacy. Consequently, his dream is simply a symbolic expression of the fact that people are wounding his most delicate feelings and aspirations; people who are intimate enough with him to be able to spy on his most private life. Nothing can be more private than one's soul. If this dream had appeared as a poem in free verse or otherwise, no one would have questioned the imagery. It might have gone thus:

"They passed by me, and hurled things at me,
Sharp, jagged things that wounded my soul.
And my soul was white, as the colour of a dove,
And they wounded it."

These are nearly the exact words of the dreamer, as he related the dream to me.

Why do we dream? The answer, according to Freud, is very interesting. While we often dislike a dream, because we think it disturbs our night's rest, as a matter of fact it is the dream that really keeps us asleep. It happens in this way.

Suppose I lie not very deeply asleep in the morning and someone outside is running a lawn mower over the grass. If I hear the noise and realize that it is time to get up, then my sleep has to be interrupted. Obviously, then, if I wish to remain asleep, I cannot admit to myself that it is a lawn mower I hear. Equally obviously, however, the sound waves strike my ear, and the impulse is started in the auditory nerve, which is the hearing nerve. I can, then, only consistently go to sleep by hearing the noise as something else than the sound of the lawn mower in the next garden. This is what I actually dream.

"I am in the garden of my mother's home in the early morning, which was the time when a large playing field near by was often mowed. I am half asleep, and think, 'I shall be able to rest here quite a while yet.'"

In this actual dream, we see how the real facts are distorted, and a wish is tactfully insinuated by the dream process. So far from recognizing the sound as a signal to get up, I actually interpret it as a signal that I need not get up, yet. The details are all there. When I was at home, I was on holiday, which I should like to have been at the time of the dream. When I was on holiday, I did not get up till late in the morning. And most of us would like to be back in the old days, when we went to our mother's home for holidays.

Let me take one more example of a dream that can be interpreted according to Freudian principles.

A young married woman dreams that she was stuffing a cushion out of which flew a cuckoo. Immediately her mother-in-law, who was staying with her (in the dream only, not in fact) cried "Put it out. It will bring terrible unhappiness on the house." At once she put the bird out.

How is this interpreted? The central figure is the cuckoo. Now in a number of languages, this particular bird, which, of course, usurps a place in the nest, is used as a symbol in connection with married infidelity. The interpretation, is then, someone was making himself attractive to the lady, and that she was trying to avoid anything unbecoming her position as a wife. Naturally, her mother-in-law would be expected to uphold the husband's interests. When she was given this explanation she at once admitted that such a situation occurred. A friend had actually annoyed her with his attentions. Only the night before the dream, she had thought to herself that she must put a stop to this, as it might easily lead to unhappiness, and had actually said to herself. "All sorts of unhappiness begin that way."

Dreams, then according to Freud, have a definite meaning, which generally comes up out of the unconscious. They symbolically represent a wish. By interpreting a person's dreams, we can often tell him what is in his unconscious.

Can we believe everything in Freud's account of dreams? Well there are many psychologists who claim that he has exaggerated certain parts of his theory, when he states that all dreams express a wish. Some believe that he is not justified in saying that all mental processes have a definite mental cause. A large number do not believe in this theory of the unconscious. But all acknowledge the enormous debt we owe him for the study of dreams and the symbols they contain, and all admit that psychology will be different, and better, as a result of his stimulating speculations and observations.

Which is, after all, the highest praise that can be given to one who calls himself a psychologist.

(e) WHAT IS PSYCHOANALYSIS?

Very interesting is the method used in psychoanalytic treatment. When the cures were first begun, in 1892, the object of investigation was to discover the hidden meaning of the hysterical or other symptom. There is the famous case of the lady who continually experienced the odour of burnt pastry. Beyond this, she was entirely without the sensation of smell. In addition she was troubled by various other distressing symptoms.

The problem in this case was to find the meaning of the persistent odour. By Freud's hypotheses, it must have a meaning, for he believed that all mental events meant something. Consequently, the young lady was questioned about the smell.

At first she connected it with the arrival of a letter, and with the affection shown her by some children in her charge on a particular occasion, when she had smelled some burning pastry. Further questioning brought the fact that the head of the house had spoken to her about her charges, saying he counted on her to bring up his orphaned family. At the same time she began to fall in love with him, and later found that she had to repress her growing affection. The meaning of the strange sensation now becomes clear. The full memory of her affection had been checked. She could not allow herself to dwell on it; but that part of the scene which was connected with the odour of pastry was not forbidden. Consequently we find this odour forcing itself upon her; slipping past the barrier, so to speak.

This strange story ran through many changes, of which the incident related was only one. Each explanation was followed by some measure of relief. Relief followed confession, and this method of cure by talking was called the cathartic or cleansing method. By causing the patient to bring up into consciousness the little rebellious fragment of experience which caused the trouble, a fusion was made of the discordant mental elements, very much as in the case of dual personality already described.

At that time Freud supposed that the reason for the trouble was that the emotion that went with this particular experience had not been expressed. Consequently, every effort was made to bring up the original scene with all possible vividness, and to let the uprushing emotions have the fullest possible play. By working these off, the cure was supposed to be made. Hence the term cathartic, which implies an emotional purging. The tormenting memories that were at the root of the trouble, but of which the patient in normal life was unconscious, could always, said Doctor Breuer, be traced to some such experience where emotion had been suppressed.

Here, then, is the original method of Psychoanalysis. It aimed to bring up the past, to release the pent up expression properly belonging to the troublesome incidents, and thus to make the mind at one with itself. The process of giving rein to the suppressed emotions was called Abreaction, or "working off".

This simple theory soon had to be abandoned. It was found that a large number of these nervous cases could not be traced to such a single occurrence. So far from being caused by a single definite incident they had, on the contrary, grown up from imperceptible beginnings, such as arise in countless homes where a situation of tension comes about, but where it is impossible to put a finger on any definite event as a starting point. In addition, it has been found that in many cases actual harm is done by the terrific strain of working off the emotion.

Consequently, Freud has now revised the original rather crude theory. Instead, he and the other leading psychoanalysts adopt a much more difficult method. The history of the case is carefully considered from a historical standpoint. Childhood memories are brought up, where these exist, and they almost always exist. For it is only by studying the beginnings of a thing that we can really understand it. An endeavour is made to find out the reasons for the continued existence of the symptoms, in spite of the efforts of the personality to rid itself of them. Here is an individual that is a contradiction. Why, for example, cannot the girl mentioned rid herself of the unpleasant odour of burning pastry? Why cannot the lady stop herself fainting when no apparent physical reason can be found? How is it possible that the patient with the disagreeable symptom does not himself rid himself of it by recognising and removing the cause that lies in his own mental life?

The reason, says the psychoanalyst, is twofold. First, as we have seen, the patient is generally unconscious of the true state of affairs. Consequently, one task is to make him or her conscious of the reason for the trouble. Secondly, the little split-off piece of the personality causing the symptoms has surrounded itself with a barrier or resistance. As soon as the analyst begins to reach the sore spot the patient finds himself changing the subject, and if the analysis begins to be successful a definite resistance develops against him. The rebellious part is, so to speak, fighting for its existence, just as did the split off personality in Doctor Prince's case. And so we have Freud exclaiming that exactly the things which the patient tries to conceal are the most important, and that a struggle against the efforts towards cure is the invariable rule!

The chief aim, then, of the analysis of today is to break down these resistances that are really holding the personality apart. The process has been called by Freud one of after education. The individual is made to be at one with himself, just as the early saints found quiet in atonement with God. With the cancer-like growth of resistance removed, peace reigns instead of war, harmony succeeds tension, efficiency replaces internal friction.

(f) COWARDS OF US ALL

During the earlier years of psychoanalysis many people felt that it overstressed the sexual side of life. True it was that Freud carefully explained that by sex he did not mean what the man in the street meant but something much broader. Even so, it was difficult to see why these primary urges were repressed when the individual was brought up against the hard facts of life, against Reality. What principle in the human mind is it that thrusts into outer darkness the elemental desires? Why does the growing child submit itself to the restraints of civilized and moral life? There must be some cause why the ordinary person makes the voluntary act of self sacrifice that transforms him from a young barbarian to a respector of persons and of the moral code.

Freud has lately reached a novel answer to this question. It is contained in his doctrine of what he calls the Super-Ego.

A schoolboy friend of mine was once studying for his matriculation examination, which would admit him to the medical course. On the morning of the examination he unfortunately cut his thumb while shaving. Too bad! He had to wait for another six months, when the examination would be held again. The six months passed, and the day of the examination had come once more. The same thing happened, again, and again the test had to be postponed.

Those who have read what has been said about Freud will see that according to the principle of psychic determinism these misfortunes could not be due to accident. But why should a young man give himself a year's extra work and postpone the beginning of his professional life? Something in him had made him not want to take the examination; not the fear of failing, because there was little question of that. He is now a successful doctor, having passed through the course without any special difficulty. Let us then go back into his history, which will be disguised sufficiently to prevent recognition.

Thomas Black's father died when he was a child. His mother was a parlour-maid who worked for years in the house of a provincial doctor of rather aristocratic appearance and with a fine professional practice. The parlour-maid was a woman of unusual capacity who soon began to "run" the domestic affairs of the doctor's house. She was in fact what the ladies call a "treasure". Soon the physician and his wife began to recognize that the boy, who lived in the house, was of unusual promise, and sent him away to school with their own son. Here an interesting thing began to happen. Young Thomas did everything he could to dissociate himself from his friend the doctor's son. An elaborate tissue of falsehood was built up to show that the two boys did not know each other. They would be heard discussing their home town together as if they were acquaintances delighted to find each other again. They arrived and went home by different trains at the beginning of term, and so on.

Naturally, you will say! Of course the boy did not wish it to be known that his mother was a parlour-maid, and, as boys will, adopted this rather too circumstantial method to conceal it. But there were other things. Thomas was a burly boy, rather good at sports and intensely interested in the teams. In practice games he was in fact a star. But whenever selection was being made for a team his performance was ridiculous. If it were cricket, he would play brilliantly and miss the easy catch which would have decided the game. If it were football he would pass the ball directly to the opponent's best man. Once he was selected for a match. When play began it seemed as though he were paralyzed, and he finally distinguished himself by a stroke so absurd that his athletic career was at an end. A nervous boy? Not at all. One time he clambered along the eave trough of the big school to settle a bet as to how many swallows' nests there were under the eaves!

And his misfortune was not confined to the playing field. Away from the class room he was quite good at his work. Put him into class, however, and he would be sure to say something that would draw down on him the derision of the form master. "Black" said the headmaster to him one day, "there is no need to punish you. You seem to go about looking for ways to punish yourself."

Which was, as a matter of fact, exactly what he was doing. He was punishing himself for being at a school out of "that state of life into which it had pleased God to call him." Part of his personality was ambitious. Part disapproved of his ambition. The disapproving part is in what Freud now calls the super-ego.

As we grow up, says Freud, we gain our notion of right and wrong, social fitness, decency and propriety, from those in authority over us. There comes a time when we take these persons of authority into ourselves as part of our own personality. Instead of their disapproval, it is now our own disapproval that frowns on actions and thoughts outside the code. When we have offended, it is we who punish ourselves and we also, another part of us, that feel relief, as though we had now expiated the transgression. This self punishment is due to a feeling of guilt of which we may not be conscious; and in fact a very common stage in psychoanalysis as now practiced is the appearance of a feeling of guilt which seems to have been created by the analysis, but which has really been uncovered by the removal of resistances.

Thus the super-ego, according to Freud, is a somewhat broader name for what has, through the ages, been known as conscience. It forbids not only moral offences, but offences against the total code of social inhibitions into which we were brought up—social, political, sexual, artistic, professional. "In spite of the fact that Jones is an artist, he will always *remain* a puritan at heart" we say. So he will. We cannot get away from our upbringing, so we are "nervous" when the great opportunity comes to get away from it. Conscience doth make cowards of us all.

We have gone into the matter of Psychoanalytic cure at some length, because it seems to represent one of the most interesting of modern developments in the theory of psychology and of what is popularly called "nervousness."

A thorough account of the far reaching movement begun by Freud would have to include a much fuller discussion of his theory of dreams, a theory which we have only touched upon. It would have to deal with his theory of art, of religion, of humour, his ideas about the growth of the unconscious, of the place of sex, and much besides. All these are fascinating subjects, and have been dealt with competently in many books, both popular and technical. But the general theory of cure seems to be the most fundamental and the most typical. Like every other part of the theory, it has received much opposition from psychologists of the highest repute. And, like every other part of the theory, it has been misunderstood and misquoted by very many charlatans, who find in the Freudian psychology an easy way to make money out of pseudoscience.

For the rest, we must say about the value of the whole movement, *viderint posteri*, let posterity decide.

(g) THE FEELING OF INFERIORITY

A movement so far reaching and so enthusiastically accepted and rejected as that of Freud cannot stand still. It will be developed by others who do not agree with the original discoverer. One who aims to pull crashing down about him the whole structure of psychological thought must not be surprised if some of the fragments fly beyond his control. The man who attempts such wholesale wreckage is apt to find himself in the position of the boy who took a bicycle to pieces, and had a jam pot full of parts left over when he put it together again.

In fact, some of Freud's own followers have claimed that in his reconstruction he has not accounted for everything. Agreeing with him in general, they claim that he has overlooked certain important factors that must be considered in a proper account of a human mind, healthy or sick.

Of these dissenters, perhaps the most interesting is Alfred Adler. Adler's position is briefly this. Every neurotic person, that is, in general, every person who has what is called "nervous" trouble, is striving towards an imaginary goal and the goal is always the same, namely the "wish to be a complete man."

To explain; not long ago there came to me a young man who was troubled by a recurring dream. In it he was running a race, in which he led at first, but was soon passed by others in the field. The dream was accompanied by distinctly unpleasant feelings, and was vaguely felt to be important.

On questioning him, the fact came out that he was at present in college, that he had been one of the leaders at school, but that he felt that he was now being left behind by those whom he had formerly beaten. This young man was perfectly healthy from a nervous point of view, and indeed might be taken as a good example of the very finest type of American manhood. But he admitted having been uncomfortable over the fact that he was falling behind. He had given the thing considerable thought, and there seemed not much else to do than to accept the fact.

Here was a case where an unusually sturdy mentality prevented serious trouble. But suppose the trouble had begun much earlier. Suppose that the case had been that of an only child, brought up at home for the first seven or eight years of his life to believe that he was the cleverest boy there was. Perhaps he has been taught at home and has been led to despise others whose attainments are not equal to his own. Thereafter, he goes to school and finds to his amazement that there are other boys in the world equally clever with him, or, worst still, others who seem actually to surpass him. At once he begins to try to show himself that he really is superior, and there begins a tremendous conflict, which may well result in severe nervous trouble if not wisely handled.

Suppose, now, that instead of this "psychological" reason for his efforts, there is a physical cause. For some reason or other, perhaps certain organs in the body are underdeveloped, perhaps it is his heart that has a slight leak in one of the valves. Almost as soon as he begins to associate with other children, he notices that he cannot do quite what they do, that he tires more easily than others.

Thus he at once suspects that he is not quite the same as other children. And Adler claims to have shown when one organ is inferior, there is very apt to be inferiority in a number of other organs. So that we have a picture of a child who starts out in life by finding that the other children can do all things which he cannot; that they are in some unaccountable and mysterious way superior to him, in short, that he is an inferior person.

With this beginning, all his efforts and all his thoughts are centered about this one point, his inferiority. His most passionate desire is to be like others. Every child, Adler points out, has made a careful estimation of his own worth, and the ugly child, the spoiled child and so on are apt to find themselves wanting. Adler shows the tortures of those with failings such as stomach trouble, who have to be careful about their eating and are looked down upon by the other children, or of those with skin diseases, which make the individual an object of aversion to others. Little by little, such children become separated from others, misunderstood.

As a result, the individual imagines he is slighted by his parents or teachers, and, feeling inferior, he sets up certain rules of conduct which shall serve to protect him against the world. Grown up, he is often the man who prides himself upon his "principles," which have to stand, whatever else must go. He is the man who will drive his children out of doors rather than "compromise with evil" that they have committed, or accept their repentance and desire to overcome their weakness. The normal man, of course, also has his principles. But they are not of the unbending variety that is found in the neurotic. The normal man is the master of his rules of conduct. The neurotic is their slave.

In the intense desire to prove his superiority, such a man is afraid to meet the world on even terms. He has the sneaking suspicion that the way ought to be made easy for him; that, somehow or other, he should not be held fully accountable for his acts. So afraid is he of having his defect proved upon himself that he will take the most careful pains to prepare himself for any contest where he actually does meet others in competition. Quite different is this from the normal man's conduct, who has formed his own opinion of himself, and who may not care much one way or another how any particular contest may turn out. And in the same way, the neurotic is perpetually trying to discount the future in the present. He cannot enjoy the present advantage, for fear that it will be taken from him the day after tomorrow. He is tormented for fear that he will lose his fortune or his job or his standing in the community. He is afraid of life, for he feels that he is not equipped for it.

Most interesting is his attempt to disguise his true feelings by assuming the opposite trait. Thus, one of this type often covers his diffidence under a show of bluster. He puts on the breastplate of truculence to cover his timidity. He engages feverishly in the pursuits of everyday people to prove that he is not "different." If he is of a retiring disposition, he tortures himself with a hail-fellow-well-met enthusiasm. If he despises flirtation, he immediately thinks this shows his "queerness" and starts an affair with one of the other sex, from which he is lucky to escape on the safe side of marriage.

Prometheus chained to the rock while a vulture tore at his heart as a punishment for the impious invention of fire shows a picture of the agonies these men endure. For often they are men of the highest parts, and even genius, but always gnaws at their heart the sickening pang that they are not as others are, and the desperate resolve to clutch at normality. And just as in the fable the wounds of Prometheus were allowed to heal, so that he might be ready for fresh torture, so from time to time the neurotic forces his pain from him, only to have it start up again after the wound is made whole.

Thus a defect is compensated by an endeavor in the opposite direction. The famous example is Demosthenes, the stutterer. To compensate for his failing he practiced so hard and so assiduously that he became the most famous orator of his day, and perhaps the greatest in the world. But underneath his apparent fluency and mastery of the spoken word lurked, even to his hearers, a taint of something unnatural and strained. Aeschines, his rival, taunted him with the cry that his speeches "smelt of the lamp." His was an artificial fluency, gained by much preparation, not dowered by nature.

Often the feeling of inferiority has its roots in social considerations. Take the case of a girl, daughter of a small shopkeeper who lived in a little English town where social prestige was all important, where an unusual number of residents belonged to the wealthy classes, where the only social stock-in-trade was the profession of one's father. Starting perhaps with some such actual organic inferiority as that described by Adler, her inferiority-feeling was increased by her social status. In addition, her father was of an overbearing, strict, ambitious disposition, and she had the suspicion that nothing she did ever quite measured up to his standard. The history of such a person could almost be prophesied. A story of failure at school, because she insisted on competing with those intellectually above her. A history of several positions undertaken beyond her physical and mental powers, because she would not consent to take her place "in that state of life to which God had pleased to call her." A continuous see-saw between the attempt to "order herself lowly and reverently towards her betters," and at the same time to prove to herself that she was the equal of those socially and mentally above her. The whole pathetic failure was excused in her mind and to other people as due to the "overweening ambition" of her father, while she lost sight all the time of the fact that the ambition was really hers. Finally came removal from the neighborhood to take up work in a "good house," and, when the war came, work as a nurse, which in England carries a high social prestige, because girls of the "best families" enter this profession.

It may be said that in many small English towns there is one large "inferiority complex" on the order of the House that Jack built. The daughters of the domestic servants feel themselves inferior, and behave as though they were inferior, to the daughters of the small storekeepers; these again have the same feeling towards the semi-professional class, such as the auctioneers and the larger merchants, who have the same feeling towards the retired army and navy officers, if there be such, and so on up the social scale. Finally, all are inferior to the local landed proprietor, who in his turn feels himself in a class below any nobility that happens to live in the neighbourhood. In the United States of America inferiority of social position does not seem to have taken upon itself such a definitely psychological tinge as in older civilizations. Social superiority, indeed, there is, but this does not, to use an Irishism, imply a corresponding inferiority.

When we come to understand the psychology of such events as the French Revolution and the Russian disaster, as well as of the history of England in the last fifty years, we shall find that the inferiority complex has had a far larger part in causing unrest than has ever been imagined by most historians. Revolutions are often psychological, with an economic motive to set them off. America may well congratulate herself that she has for the most part been able to keep this particular kind of psychology across the Atlantic Ocean.

Chapter XIII

CONCLUSION

This then is the picture which with broad strokes we have tried to sketch. A human being, receiving messages from the world without through the organs that nature has provided for the purpose, interprets and selects the messages this way or that, being helped in the task by the stores of experience which all of us carry. Some of these messages result in action; some of them, past experience or inheritance has declared, do not call for action. We are all the products of ourselves and of those who have handed down our bodies to us.

What is it, then, to live in the world and to know the world? To be conscious or aware of things without us? What is the difference between feeling one's own toothache and watching the decayed tooth of another to see how the pain makes him behave? That is one of the riddles of the Sphinx, and it is a riddle that can never be answered. For many of our scientists have said, "What is consciousness or knowing or mental picture, except behaving in this way or that way in the world? Tell me, what is your mind except behaviour?"

And that is the eternal dilemma. For if the question is answered, then at once it is said, "You are speaking or writing. That is behaviour." And the man who knows what it is to feel the toothache, is dumbfounded. He cannot answer without action of some sort, and if he acts, at once he will be told that his consciousness of the world, his being aware of things outside him, is nothing but behaviour.

And some will say that even without outward expression to be conscious is simply to behave. For there are, they say, tiny movements of the body, of the glands and the muscles, that take place when we think, that are really our thoughts. But never has it been proved in experiment that there are such slight motions which can really explain our thoughts. And even if this were not so, then the changes in the body would not *be* the thoughts. They would be the bodily accompaniments of the thoughts.

The consciousness, the inner world, of each of us is like a secret that cannot be told. When a secret is told, it is no longer a secret. When a fact of consciousness is told it is no longer consciousness but behaviour. It is an inner shrine into which we ourselves may enter, but into which we can take no one. For if we try, the doors swing upon the visitor, and we find ourselves within, while he stands gazing at the door. And so he says that what we think a shrine is simply a doorway with ever swinging doors. For whenever we have tried to take him in, he has seen the doors swinging. When the doors are quiet, he is always away.

The inner self can never be shown to another. For when we try to show it, it seems to suffer a change into something which it is not.

And with this riddle we leave the tale that we have tried to tell. Briefly, inadequately, it has been told, yet always with a humble reverence for the labours of the many who have made it possible. Many pages have been left unwritten, and many, perhaps, that should not have been written, have been written, because the story teller liked those chapters. For, as in dealing with people one is guided by one's friendships, so it is in writing a story.

In conclusion, to my fellow psychologists. If there be

any of this company who has read so far, I would wish to acknowledge what he knows too well already, namely that many of the descriptions used in this book lack that accuracy which strictly technical terms alone can bring, and that many inconsistencies are therefore patent to the critical eye. It is because the language of ordinary human intercourse is not adequate to express the distinctions of exact thought that the physicist and the mathematician, equally with the psychologist, have devised their own language. Yet the author is willing to assume the function of a scapegoat, if only by this means more people may become interested in the most noble of all studies, the science of human mind and behaviour.

APPENDIX

FIFTY-FOUR INTERESTING BOOKS ON PSYCHOLOGY

The following list is given for the convenience of any who may wish to take up in greater detail the subjects treated in the book. It must be remembered that the real "Story of Man's Mind" is not written in this volume, nor even in the books recommended, but in a large and growing technical literature, scattered among monographs, books, and magazines of many languages.

The eight books marked with a star are specially recommended as providing a layman's introduction to the professional psychologist's point of view on certain points.

The Principles of Psychology. William James. Henry Holt & Co. Two volumes.
    The great psychological classic.

Psychology. R. S. Woodworth. Henry Holt & Co.
    One of the latest textbooks for the beginner. Written simply and colloquially by the well-known Columbia psychologist.

Essentials of Psychology.* W. B. Pillsbury. Macmillan.
    A wonderfully inexpensive textbook, covering the whole ground in a simple way. The author has found this book of great value in presenting the outlines of the science to beginners.

Textbook of Psychology. E. B. Titchener. Macmillan.
    A masterpiece of scholarly writing suited for the advanced student and the man who wishes to take time to think.

The Foundations of Experimental Psychology. Ed. Murchison. Clark University.
    A fascinating but difficult work.

CHAPTER 2.

The Investigation of Mind in Animals. E. B. Smith. Cambridge University Press.
    An easy introduction.

Evolution of Animal Intelligence. S. J. Holmes. Henry Holt.

The Animal Mind. Margaret Floy Washburn, New York. Macmillan.
    A difficult, but astonishingly able book.

CHAPTER 3.

The Psychology of Childhood. Norsworthy and Whitley. Macmillan.

*Brightness and Dullness in Children.** Herbert Woodrow. Lippincott.
    This latter is an unusually readable and stimulating account of the growing intelligence of a child.

Educational Psychology. Briefer course. Edward L. Thorndike. Teachers College, Columbia University.
    The standard short book dealing with the psychology that underlies educational problems.

Handbook of Child Psychology. Ed. Murchison. Clark University.

    A very interesting account of language with reference to the child is to be found in

Language. By O. Jesperson. Henry Holt.
    This book is written from a non-psychological point of view.

CHAPTER 4.

General Psychology in Terms of Behavior. S. Smith and E. R. Guthrie. Appleton.

Psychology from the Standpoint of a Behaviorist. J. B. Watson. Lippincott.
    Each of these explains psychology in terms of stimulus and response without reference to the "thoughts" of the person who is acting. The first book is the easier. Professor Watson is the originator of the "Behaviorist" movement.

Behaviorism. J. B. Watson. People's Institute Publishing Co. Extension courses.

CHAPTER 5.

The Psychology of Advertising. W. D. Scott. Small, Maynard & Co.

The Theory and Practice of Advertising. Same author and publisher.

*Advertising and Selling.** Harry L. Hollingsworth. D. Appleton & Co.
    "Published for the Advertising Men's League of New York."

Advertising: Its Principles, Practice and Technique. D. Starch. Scott, Foresman & Co.

CHAPTER 6.

*The Training and Economy of Memory.** Henry T. Watt. Longmans, Green & Co.

Psychology of Learning. W. H. Pyle. Warwick & York.
    This book will be found rather hard to read, but it brings together most of the facts.

Adult Learning. E. L. Thorndike. Macmillan.

The Mentality of Apes. W. Köhler. Kegan Paul.

Gestalt Psychology. W. Köhler. Liveright.

Inquiry into Human Faculty. Francis Galton. In Everyman Series.
>Perhaps the most stimulating book ever written on psychological and kindred subjects.

On Telepathy.
>Sir Oliver Lodge has an article on the whole subject of Psychic Science in Thompson's "Outline of Science," Vol. 3 (Publishers, J. P. Putnam).

Phantasms of the Living. E. Gurney and F. W. H. Myers and F. Podmore. London, Trübner & Co.
>This latter book is an astonishingly circumstantial and able statement of the argument for Telepathy and other psychic phenomena.

Telepathy and Clairvoyance. R. Tischner. Kegan Paul.
>The case for and against Psychical Research. Ed. Murchison, Clark University Press.

CHAPTER 7.

*How We Think.** John Dewey. Heath & Co.

CHAPTER 8.

*An Introduction to Social Psychology.** W. McDougall. Luce.
>One of the most widely read books on psychology during the last twenty years. It forms the starting point for all discussion of the instincts.

The Wild Boy of Aveyron. Itard. The Century Co.

Social Psychology. F. H. Allport. Houghton, Mifflin.

The Language and Thought of the Child. Piaget. Kegan Paul.

Psychology of Clothes. J. Flugel. International Psychoanalytic Publishing Co.
>A psychoanalytic study.

CHAPTER 9.

Increasing Human Efficiency in Business. W. D. Scott. Macmillan.

Bodily Changes in Pain, Hunger, Fear, and Rage. W. B. Cannon. Appleton.

International Symposium on Feelings and Emotions. Clark University.
>By a number of authors, and reflects the current uncertainty.

CHAPTER 10.

Army Mental Tests.* Yerkes and Yoakum. Holt.
> Explaining simply the nature, purpose, and results of the tests.

The Intelligence of School Children. L. Terman. Houghton, Mifflin.
> Professor Terman's adaptation of the Binet tests is very widely used. He here gives various results of testing children and shows how it is possible to train oneself to use the tests.

Trade Tests. J. C. Chapman. Henry Holt.
> Describes the army tests for skill in various trades.

Mental Growth of the Pre-School Child. A. Gesell. Macmillan.
> Contains beautiful photographs.

Applied Psychology. A. Poffenberger. Appleton.

CHAPTER 11.

Religion and Medicine. Elwood Worcester, etc. Moffat, Yard & Co.

Power Through Repose. Annie Payson Call. Little, Brown & Co.
> These two books describe the method given in the text.

Progressive Relaxation. Jacobsen. Chicago University.
> Enters exhaustively and scientifically into the technique.

CHAPTER 12.

Suggestion and Autosuggestion. C. Baudouin. London, George Allen & Unwin.

Hypnotism. A. Moll. Scribner's.
> The standard work on this subject.

The Dissociation of a Personality. Morton Prince. Longmans, Green & Co.
> A most amazing study of a "family" of persons who lived in the body of one young woman.

The Psychology of Insanity.* Bernard Hart. Cambridge, University Press.
> A small, masterly, and cheap book by an eminent British authority. Its simple explanation of abnormal mental phenomena upon Freudian lines has made it a classic.

Literature about Freud and his school.
> A little Freud is a most dangerous thing. Perhaps the best introduction for the non-professional reader is:

The New Psychology. A. G. Tansley. Dodd, Mead & Co.

Introduction to Psychoanalysis. S. Freud. Boni & Liveright.
> Is an authoritative statement by the founder of the movement.

The Neurotic Constitution. A. Adler. Moffat, Yard & Co.

INDEX

A

Abelard, 158 *seq.*
Abreaction, 287
Acquisition, instinct of, 177
Actions, learned, 176
Adler, 293 *seq.*
Advertisement, 87 *seq.*
Advertisement, topical, 92 *seq.*
Affect, 202
Amoeba, 6 *seq.*
Ants, 10 *seq.*
Aristotle, 157 *seq.*
Attention, 83 *seq.*
Attention, attitude and, 90
   conditions of, 87
   education and, 94 *seq.*
   experience and, 90
   movement and, 88
   selection in, 88
   size and, 88
Attitude, 90
Auto-suggestion, 263

B

Baby, 22 *seq.*
Bernheim, 270
Blind spot, 59
Blood, alkalinity of, 187
Breuer, 279 *seq.*

C

Cannon, 187, 212 *seq.*
Carthasis, 287
Cats, 17 *seq.*
Charcot, 269, 279
Cleopatra, 152
Clothing, instinct of, 187 *seq.*
Cockroach, 13
Concept, 152 *seq.*
Conditioned Reflex, 29 *seq.*

Conscience, 289 *seq.*
Cortex, cerebral, 50 *seq.*

D

Dark, fear of, 192
Determinism, psychic, 281
Diminishing returns in learning, 126
Dissociation, 272
Dodge, 72, 73
Dog, 15 *seq.*
Doughty, 161
Dreams, 283 *seq.*

E

Emotion, 206 *seq.*
Emotion and muscular tension, 242

F

Falling in love, 184
Fear, experimentally induced, 219
Fighting, instinct of, 187 *seq.*
Forgetting, 135 *seq.*
Forgetting, curve of, 134, 135 *seq.*
Freud, 217 *seq.*, 279 *seq.*

G

Galileo, 101
Galton, 130, 192, 239
Gestalt, 19, 26, 27, 103, 106, 165
Golden Bough, 264

H

Habit, 106 *seq.*
   value of, 107 *seq.*
Hannibal, 152
Hearing, 60
Herodotus, 34
Hoarding, instinct of, 178
Horse, calculating, 141 *seq.*
Hunger, 77
Hunting, instinct, 177 *seq.*
Hypnosis, 268 *seq.*

I

Illusions, 104 *seq.*
Images, memory, 129 *seq.*
Inferiority, feeling of, 293 *seq.*
Inhibitions, 180 *seq.*
Insight, 165
Insomnia and relaxation, 244
Instinct, 172 *seq.*
Integration of personality, 276
Itard, 166 *seq.*

J

James, 78, 108 *seq.*, 206 *seq.*, 252
John of Salisbury, 160
Julius Caesar, 100

K

Keats, 86
Kinaesthetic sense, 75
Koffka, 19
Köhler, 19, 36
Krasnogorsky, 31

L

Lange, 201
Language, 34
Lea, 204
Letters, follow up, 134

M

Macaulay, 119
Marriage, 180
Medusa, 9, 10
Memory, 3
  rules for, 116
  systems, 112, 119 *seq.*
Mendel, 2
Mental age, 239
Mental age, average, 227
Mental tests, 223 *seq.*
Mesmer, 269 *seq.*
Mind, unconscious, 280 *seq.*
Moll, 269

N

Nerves, function of, 44 *seq.*

P

Pain, 201
Pain spots, 67
Paradoxical cold sensation, 68

Pavlov, 30 *seq.*, 38, 185 *seq.*, 197, 202, 271
Perception, 102 *seq.*
Phobia, 252 *seq.*, 209
Plato, 107, 156 *seq.*, 194
Pleasure, 195
Podmore, 146 *seq.*
Prince, Morton, 272 *seq.*
Protagoras, 1, 2, 3

R

Reason, 161 *seq.*
Reflex, 23 *seq.*, 50, 173
Relaxation, 241 *seq.*
  and suggestion, 258
Repetition, effect of, 107
Repression, 217 *seq.*
Resistance, psychic, 288 *seq.*
Revolution, psychology of, 299
Richter, 188
Romulus, 179

S

Sandford, 141 *seq.*
Semicircular canals, 69 *seq.*
Shaw, Bernard, 265
Sherrington 185, 203, 210 *seq.*
Smell, 63
Snakes, fear of, 192
Social sense, 39 *seq.*
Spearman, 240
Super-ego, 289 *seq.*
Synapsis, 107, 173

T

Taste, 63
Telepathy, 141 *seq.*
Tennyson, 119, 140
Thorndike, 17, 128, 129
Troland, 148

V

Vision, 55 *seq.*

W

Wandering, Instinct of, 177
Warm spots, 66
Watson, 76, 219
Weber's law, 81
Wild Boy, 166 *seq.*
Worcester, 253
Wordsworth, 133